## NE능률 영어교과서

대한민국 고등학생 **10명 중 4.7명이 보는 교과서**

영어 고등 교과서 점유율 1위

(7차, 2007 개정, 2009 개정, 2015 개정)

KB124529

## 리딩튜터

그동안 판매된
리딩튜터 1,900만 부
차곡차곡 쌓으면 19만 미터

**에베레스트 21 배 높이**

190,000m

READING TUTOR

에베레스트 8,848m

## 능률보카

그동안 판매된
능률VOCA 1,100만 부

대한민국 박스오피스
**천만명을 넘은 영화 단 28개**

VO CA

## 그래머존

그동안 판매된 450만 부의 그래머존을 바닥에 쭉 ~ 깔면

**1000km 서울 - 부산 왕복가능**

서울

부산

# READING
# Inside

## LEVEL 2

| | |
|---|---|
| **지은이** | NE능률 영어교육연구소 |
| **선임연구원** | 조은영 |
| **연구원** | 이지영, 이희진 |
| **영문교열** | Curtis Thompson, Angela Lan, Olk Bryce Barrett |
| **디자인** | 김연주 |
| **내지 일러스트** | 최주석, 한상엽, 김동현 |
| **맥편집** | 김선희 |

# NE능률이
# 미래를
# 창조합니다.

건강한 배움의 고객가치를 제공하겠다는 꿈을 실현하기 위해
40년이 넘는 시간 동안 열심히 달려왔습니다.

앞으로도 끊임없는 연구와 노력을 통해
당연한 것을 멈추지 않고

고객, 기업, 직원 모두가 함께 성장하는 NE능률이 되겠습니다.

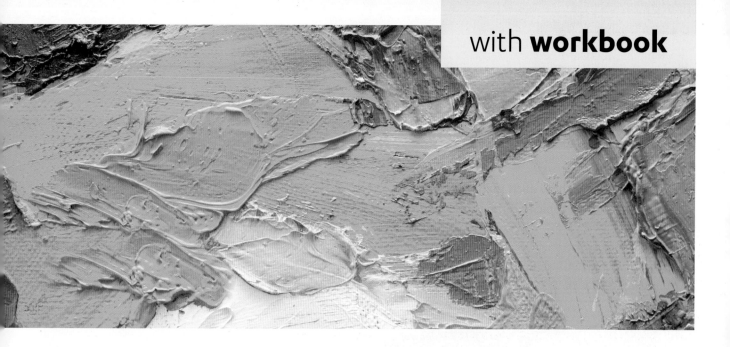

# READING
# Inside

with **workbook**

# LEVEL 2

# STRUCTURES

● This shows how each reading passage is related to the topic and the school subject.

## ● Reading Comprehension

The students' understanding of the passage is checked through a series of multiple-choice and descriptive questions. This also helps to strengthen students' reading accuracy.

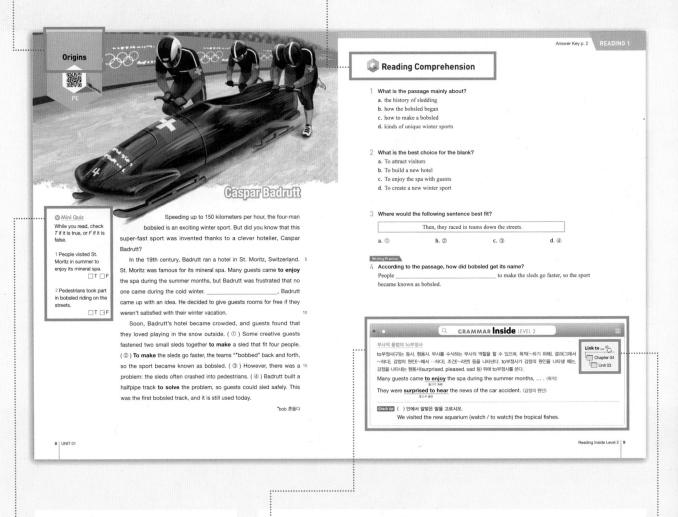

### ● Mini Quiz

While learners are reading the passage, they are asked to do some simple tasks. Through these simple activities, students can understand the information in the passage more easily and get ready to answer the Reading Comprehension questions.

### ● GRAMMAR Inside

This helps learners grasp the key structures of sentences and strengthens their understanding of the passage. It is also related to the best-selling grammar series *Grammar Inside*.

📁 From the **Link to...** ,

learners can see which chapter and unit of the *Grammar Inside* series are directly related to this section.

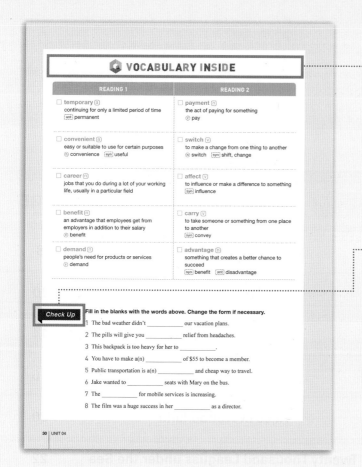

## VOCABULARY INSIDE

This presents come content words in context and provides synonyms, antonyms, related parts of speech, and idioms to improve students' vocabulary. Learners should check if they know the words first before proceeding with the further learning.

**Through** Check Up ,

students can better understand the practical usage of words by filling in the blanks with words from the chart.

**Workbook**

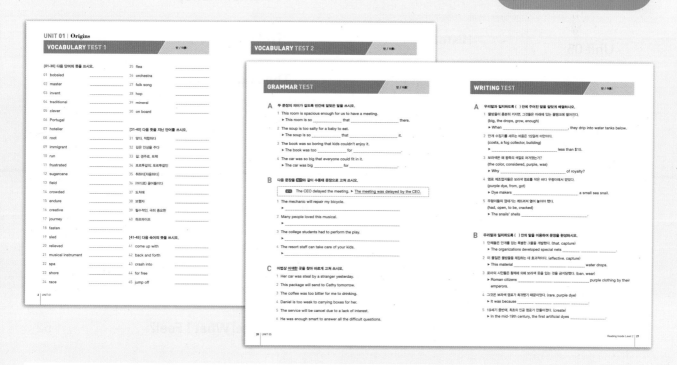

The workbook, which is composed of four pages of vocabulary tests, grammar tests, and writing tests, helps reinforce what students have learned in the main text.

#  CONTENTS

# Link to GRAMMAR Inside

# UNIT
# 01 | Origins

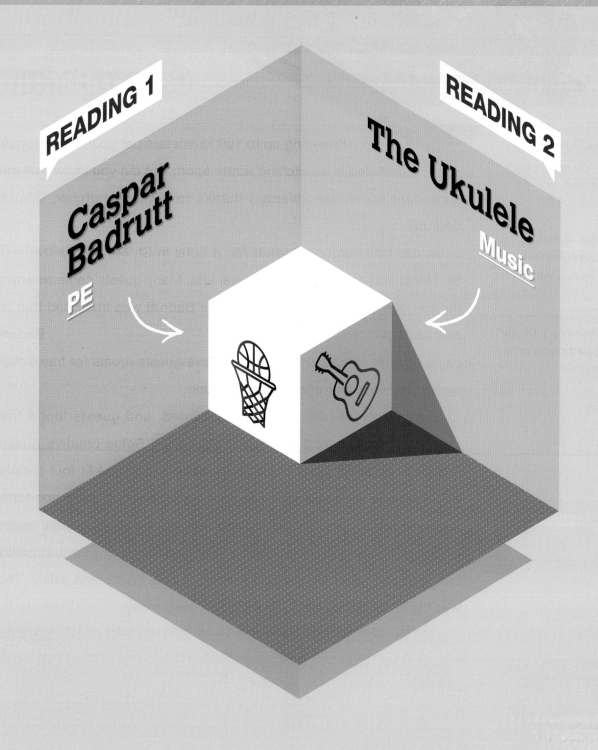

READING 1

Caspar
Badrutt

PE

READING 2

The Ukulele

Music

PE

185 words

## Caspar Badrutt

**◆ Mini Quiz**

While you read, check *T* if it is true, or *F* if it is false.

1 People visited St. Moritz in summer to enjoy its mineral spa.
☐ T ☐ F

2 Pedestrians took part in bobsled riding on the streets.
☐ T ☐ F

Speeding up to 150 kilometers per hour, the four-man bobsled is an exciting winter sport. But did you know that this super-fast sport was invented thanks to a clever hotelier, Caspar Badrutt?

In the 19th century, Badrutt ran a hotel in St. Moritz, Switzerland. 5 St. Moritz was famous for its mineral spa. Many guests came **to enjoy** the spa during the summer months, but Badrutt was frustrated that no one came during the cold winter. _____, Badrutt came up with an idea. He decided to give guests rooms for free if they weren't satisfied with their winter vacation. 10

Soon, Badrutt's hotel became crowded, and guests found that they loved playing in the snow outside. ( ① ) Some creative guests fastened two small sleds together **to make** a sled that fit four people. ( ② ) **To make** the sleds go faster, the teams "*bobbed" back and forth, so the sport became known as bobsled. ( ③ ) However, there was a 15 problem: the sleds often crashed into pedestrians. ( ④ ) Badrutt built a halfpipe track **to solve** the problem, so guests could sled safely. This was the first bobsled track, and it is still used today.

*bob 흔들다

**Reading Comprehension**

1  **What is the passage mainly about?**
   a. the history of sledding
   b. how the bobsled began
   c. how to make a bobsled
   d. kinds of unique winter sports


2  **What is the best choice for the blank?**
   a. To attract visitors
   b. To build a new hotel
   c. To enjoy the spa with guests
   d. To create a new winter sport


3  **Where would the following sentence best fit?**

   | Then, they raced in teams down the streets. |
   |---|

   a. ①          b. ②          c. ③          d. ④

**Writing Practice**

4  **According to the passage, how did bobsled get its name?**
   People _____ to make the sleds go faster, so the sport
   became known as bobsled.

---

● ● ●     🔍   GRAMMAR **Inside** LEVEL 2                            ☰

**부사적 용법의 to부정사**

to부정사(구)는 동사, 형용사, 부사를 수식하는 부사의 역할을 할 수 있으며, 목적(~하기 위해), 결과(그래서 ~하다), 감정의 원인(~해서 …하다), 조건(~라면) 등을 나타낸다. to부정사가 감정의 원인을 나타낼 때는, 감정을 나타내는 형용사(surprised, pleased, sad 등) 뒤에 to부정사를 쓴다.

 **Link to ...**
📁 Chapter 04
📁 Unit 03

Many guests came **to enjoy** the spa during the summer months, … . 〈목적〉
            즐기기 위해
They were **surprised to hear** the news of the car accident. 〈감정의 원인〉
            듣고서 놀란

- - - - - - - - - - - - - - - -

**Check Up**  ( ) 안에서 알맞은 말을 고르시오.
     We visited the new aquarium (watch / to watch) the tropical fishes.

# The Ukulele

For more than 130 years, Hawaiians—from artists to Waikiki beach boys—have learned to master their traditional musical instrument, the ukulele. Although the ukulele is the most popular instrument in Hawaii, it actually has Portuguese roots.

In 1879, a ship named the *Ravenscrag* arrived in Honolulu, Hawaii. 5 There were 400 Portuguese on board. They were immigrants **who** came to work in the sugarcane fields. They had endured four months at sea to get to Honolulu from Portugal. After the difficult 15,000-mile journey, the Portuguese were excited and relieved to finally arrive. When they got to shore, a man named João Fernandes jumped off the ship. He 10 started playing folk songs on a *machete, a traditional Portuguese instrument.

Fernandes's playing impressed the Hawaiians **who** were listening on the beach. They thought his fingers hopped like fleas across the instrument. Therefore, they called the instrument a "ukulele," the 15 Hawaiian word for "jumping fleas," and adopted it into Hawaiian culture.

Today, the instrument is still popular. There are ukulele festivals and schools throughout Hawaii. There is even a full orchestra of children **who** play ukuleles! Although the instrument came from Portugal, it is 20 now an essential part of Hawaiian culture.

*machete 마체테(포르투갈의 전통 4현 악기)

## V Mini Quiz

Find the answers from the passage and write them.

Paragraph 1

1 Where did the ukulele come from?

→ _____

Paragraph 2

2 Who played a machete in front of Hawaiian people?

→ _____

**Reading Comprehension**

1 **What is the best title for the passage?**
   a. The History of Hawaiian Culture
   b. Who Created the Hawaiian Ukulele?
   c. A Famous Ukulele Player in Portugal
   d. The Hawaiian Instrument with Portuguese Roots

2 **How did the feelings of the Portuguese change in the 2nd paragraph?**
   a. exhausted → happy          b. amazed → nervous
   c. satisfied → embarrassed    d. disappointed → joyful

3 **Which CANNOT be answered based on the passage?**
   a. How did the ukulele get its design?
   b. When did the *Ravenscrag* arrive in Hawaii?
   c. Why did the Portuguese come to Hawaii?
   d. Where do Hawaiians play ukuleles now?

> Writing Practice

4 **According to the passage, why did the Hawaiians call the ukulele "jumping fleas?"**
   because they thought Fernandes's fingers _____ across
   the instrument

---

🔍 **GRAMMAR Inside** LEVEL 2    ≡

**주격 관계대명사**

관계대명사는 문장 내에서 「접속사 + 대명사」 역할을 하고, 관계대명사가 이끄는 절은 앞의 명사(선행사)를 수식한다. 관계사절 내에서 주어 역할을 하는 관계대명사를 주격 관계대명사라고 하며, 선행사가 사람일 때는 who나 that, 사물일 때는 which나 that을 쓴다.

**Link to ...**
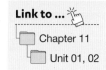
📁 Chapter 11
📁 Unit 01, 02

They were *immigrants* [**who**(**that**) came to work in the sugarcane fields]. 〈선행사가 사람〉
← They were *immigrants*. + *They* came to work in the sugarcane fields.

I often visit *the flower market* [**which**(**that**) is near the subway station]. 〈선행사가 사물〉
← I often visit *the flower market*. + *It* is near the subway station.

# ⬡ VOCABULARY INSIDE

| READING 1 | READING 2 |
|---|---|
| ☐ **invent** ⓥ <br> to make or think of something for the first time <br> ⓝ invention ⸤syn⸥ make | ☐ **instrument** ⓝ <br> a device used to play music |
| ☐ **mineral** ⓝ <br> a natural, nonliving substance in the earth such as salt or coal | ☐ **immigrant** ⓝ <br> someone who comes to another country to live <br> ⓥ immigrate |
| ☐ **frustrated** ⓐ <br> feeling very annoyed and discouraged because of failing to do something <br> ⓐ frustrating ⓥ frustrate <br> ⸤syn⸥ disappointed | ☐ **impress** ⓥ <br> to make someone feel respect or admiration <br> ⓝ impression ⓐ impressive |
| ☐ **creative** ⓐ <br> having a lot of new ideas and imagination <br> ⓥ create ⓝ creativity <br> ⸤syn⸥ imaginative | ☐ **adopt** ⓥ <br> to choose to use a particular idea, plan, or object <br> ⓝ adoption |
| ☐ **fasten** ⓥ <br> to close something tight by using a tie, a button, or a zip <br> ⸤ant⸥ unfasten | ☐ **essential** ⓐ <br> completely necessary or important <br> ⓝ essence ⸤syn⸥ crucial |

**Check Up**  **Fill in the blanks with the words above. Change the form if necessary.**

1 E-sports will be _____ as an Olympic event.

2 Millions of _____ came to the US in the 19th century.

3 Business leaders should have a(n) _____ mind.

4 _____ your seat belt for safety.

5 Sean was _____ by your bright idea.

6 Vitamins are _____ for our body.

7 How did you _____ these special shoes for patients?

8 The ukulele was my favorite musical _____.

# UNIT
# 02 | Numbers

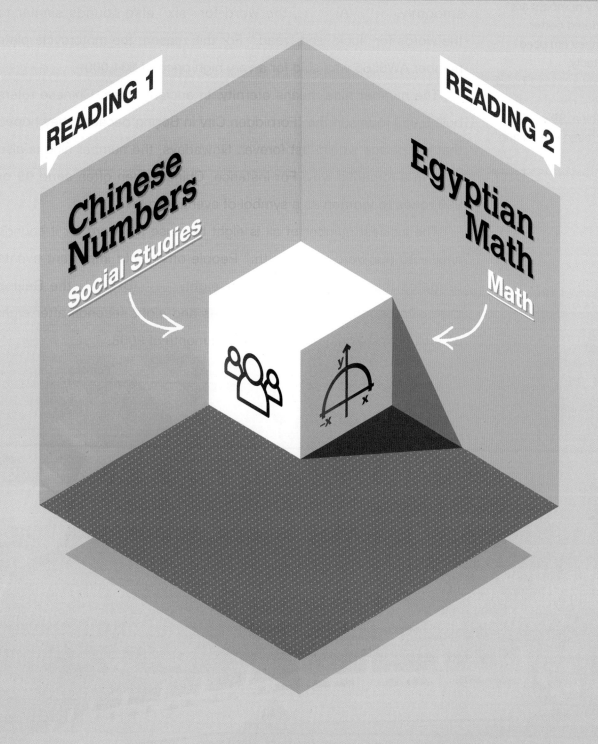

READING 1

## Chinese Numbers
### Social Studies

READING 2

## Egyptian Math
### Math

# Chinese Numbers

In Chinese culture, every number has its own meaning. Some numbers are especially lucky and have good meanings. Moreover, the Chinese think using these numbers repeatedly brings more luck. So what are the numbers?

First, the Chinese believe that the number six **brings you a** 5
**comfortable life**. In Chinese, the word for "six" sounds like the word for "flow," so people say the number six makes everything flow smoothly. _____(A)_____, the word for "six" also sounds similar to the words for "luck" and "road." For this reason, the motorcycle plate number AW6666 was sold for a very high price of $34,000. 10

The number nine means eternity. In ancient times, Chinese rulers built 9,999 rooms in the *Forbidden City in Beijing because they hoped that the palace would last forever. Nowadays, the number nine is also used in a romantic way. For instance, Chinese men often **send 99 or 999 roses to women** as a symbol of everlasting love. 15

The luckiest number of all is eight because the word for it sounds similar to the word for "wealth." People often hold important events on dates that include the number eight. _____(B)_____, the Beijing Olympics began exactly eight minutes and eight seconds after eight o'clock on the eighth day of the eighth month of 2008. 20

*Forbidden City 자금성

V Mini Quiz

While you read, check *T* if it is true, or *F* if it is false.

1 Lucky numbers are considered better when they are used repeatedly.
☐ T ☐ F

2 In China, 99 or 999 roses mean everlasting love.
☐ T ☐ F

**Reading Comprehension**

1  **What is the passage mainly about?**
   a. the Chinese method of counting
   b. the history of lucky numbers in China
   c. lucky numbers and their meanings in China
   d. why numbers are important in Chinese culture

2  **What is the best pair for blanks (A) and (B)?**

|        (A)        |        (B)        |        (A)        |        (B)        |
|-------------------|-------------------|-------------------|-------------------|
| a. In short       | – Instead         | b. For example    | – However         |
| c. As a result    | – Moreover        | d. In addition    | – For example     |

3  **Write the correct number next to each of the Chinese descriptions.**
   (1) It makes things flow smoothly.          _____
   (2) It indicates something that lasts forever.   _____
   (3) It brings good fortune and riches.        _____

4  **Which CANNOT be answered based on the passage?**
   a. What number sounds like the word "flow"?
   b. Why does "nine" mean eternity?
   c. Why is "eight" the luckiest number?
   d. What number is considered important for events?

---

Q    **GRAMMAR Inside** LEVEL 1    ☰

「수여동사 + 간접목적어 + 직접목적어」

Link to ...
📁 Chapter 05
📁 Unit 02

• 수여동사는 '~에게 …을 (해)주다'의 의미로, '~에게(간접목적어)'와 '…을(직접목적어)'에 해당하는 두 개의 목적어를 가진다.

　… the number six *brings* **you a comfortable life.**
　　　　　　　가져다 준다  당신에게  　　편한 삶을

• 「수여동사 + 간접목적어 + 직접목적어」는 「수여동사 + 직접목적어 + to[for/of] + 간접목적어」의 형태로 바꿔 쓸 수 있다.

(1) 간접목적어 앞에 전치사 to를 쓰는 동사: give, send, show, tell, teach, lend, write, bring 등
　Chinese men often **send** *women 99 or 999 roses* … .
　→ Chinese men often **send** *99 or 999 roses* **to** *women* … .

(2) 간접목적어 앞에 전치사 for를 쓰는 동사: make, buy, get 등
　Steve **made** *me cookies*. → Steve **made** *cookies* **for** *me*.

# Egyptian Math

From about 6,000 BC, early Egyptians started settling in the rich Nile valley. To build an organized society, they used math for practical purposes. They used it to record the changes of the moon's shape for farming and to construct their grand pyramids. They did these tasks by using a multiplication method called "doubling." This method **involves** 5 only **doubling** and **adding** numbers. Here's an example:

Let's solve the problem 24×25. First, make a chart like the one below. Next, pick one of the two numbers. Suppose you choose 24. In the left column, start from 1 and **keep doubling** this number. ( ① ) **Stop doubling** before the next doubled number is greater than 24. ( ② ) 10 Next, find the numbers in the left column that add up to 24. ( ③ ) These numbers are 8 and 16. ( ④ ) In the right column, start from 25 and **keep doubling** this number. Then, add the numbers in the right column that are across from 8 and 16—they are 200 and 400. Finally, you'll get 600, which is the answer to 25×24! Aren't you surprised that ancient 15 Egyptians had such a deep understanding of mathematics?

**Mini Quiz**

Read and underline the answers in the passage.

**Paragraph 1**

1 What does "these tasks" refer to in the passage?

**Paragraph 1**

2 What are we doing when we use the "doubling" method?

| 24 × 25 = ? | |
| --- | --- |
| 1 | 25 |
| 2 | 50 |
| 4 | 100 |
| 8 ✔ | 200 ✔ |
| 16 ✔ | 400 ✔ |
| 8+16 = 24 | 200+400 = 600 |

#  Reading Comprehension

**1** What is the best title for the passage?
  a. The History of Traditional Doubling
  b. The Practical Ideas of Ancient Egyptians
  c. The World's Oldest Multiplication Method
  d. The Principles of Ancient Egyptian Multiplication

**2** Where would the following sentence best fit?

> So, you need to stop at 16 because 32 is greater than 24.

  a. ①　　　　　b. ②　　　　　c. ③　　　　　d. ④

**3** What are true about ancient Egyptians? (Choose two.)
  a. They settled in the Nile valley.
  b. They were good at modern math.
  c. They used math to create an organized society.
  d. They recorded the changes of the moon to build pyramids.

**4** Fill in the blanks following the Egyptians' doubling method.

| $12 \times 36 = ?$ | |
|---|---|
| 1 | 36 |
| 2 | 72 |
| 4 | 144 |
| 8 | 288 |
| (1) _____ + 8 = _____ | (2) _____ + _____ = 432 |

---

◯ ◯ ●　　　　🔍 **GRAMMAR Inside** LEVEL 2　　　　☰

동명사나 to부정사를 목적어로 취하는 동사

• 동명사를 목적어로 취하는 동사: enjoy, avoid, mind, finish, keep, give up, quit, stop 등
  …, start from 1 and **keep doubling** this number.
  　　　　　　　　계속해서 두 배로 만들어라
• to부정사를 목적어로 취하는 동사: need, want, expect, wish, plan, promise, agree, decide 등
  So, you **need to stop** at 16 because 32 is greater than 24.
  　　　　　　멈춰야 한다

**Link to ...** 👆
Chapter 05
Unit 02

| READING 1 | READING 2 |
|---|---|
| ☐ **meaning** (n)<br>the idea that a sign, symbol, or word represents<br>(v) mean | ☐ **settle** (v)<br>to start to live in a particular place<br>(n) settlement, settler<br>[syn] inhabit |
| ☐ **comfortable** (a)<br>relaxed and pleasant; not having physical or mental pain, worries, or difficulties<br>(ad) comfortably<br>[syn] easy  [ant] uncomfortable | ☐ **practical** (a)<br>connected with real situations and events<br>[syn] realistic |
| ☐ **eternity** (n)<br>the whole of time<br>(a) eternal | ☐ **record** (v)<br>to write information down to be looked at in the future<br>(n) record  [syn] note |
| ☐ **ancient** (a)<br>having existed for a long time | ☐ **construct** (v)<br>to build something such as a building or a house<br>(n) construction  [syn] build |
| ☐ **everlasting** (a)<br>continuing to exist forever<br>[syn] eternal | ☐ **involve** (v)<br>to have something as a part of an activity, event, or situation<br>(n) involvement  [syn] include |

**Check Up**

**Fill in the blanks with the words above. Change the form if necessary.**

1 The entire bridge was _____ in 42 hours.

2 The professor had a(n) _____ knowledge of Spanish.

3 He promised to love me for _____.

4 This plan should be canceled because it _____ a lot of risk.

5 The first immigrants had a hard time _____ down.

6 What is the exact _____ of this word in Korean?

7 The _____ tree is the tallest in the forest.

8 She is satisfied with her _____ life.

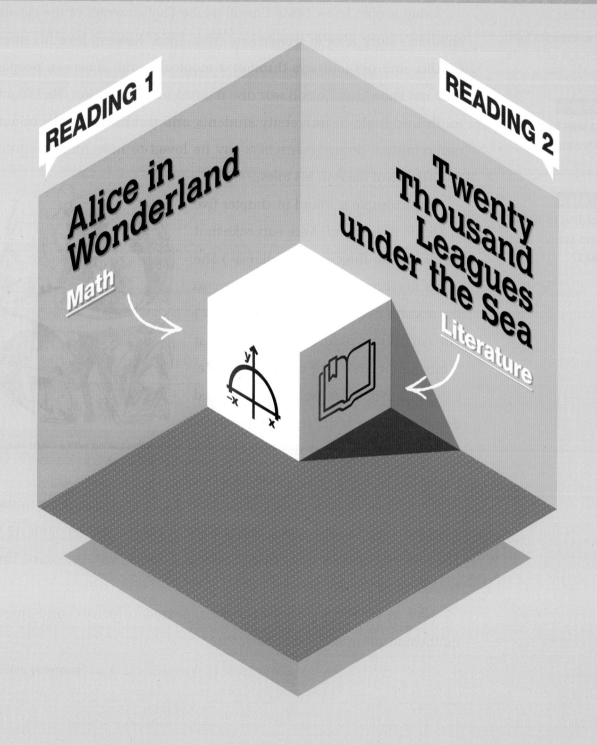

READING 1

Alice in Wonderland

Math

READING 2

Twenty Thousand Leagues under the Sea

Literature

# Alice in Wonderland

**✔ Mini Quiz**

Find the answers from the passage and write them.

**Paragraph 1**

**1** What was Lewis Carroll's other job?

→ _____

**Paragraph 3**

**2** According to "Rule 42," who cannot be in the court?

→ _____

Many people know Lewis Carroll as the English writer of the classic children's story *Alice in Wonderland* from 1865. Readers love his tales of Alice and her journeys through a magical world. However, people may not know that Carroll was also a gifted mathematician. He taught 5 math and logic to university students and published books about mathematics. <u>Some researchers say he loved to hide numbers and mathematical ideas in his tales.</u>

One example is found in chapter five of *Alice in Wonderland*. Alice eats cake that shrinks her to three inches tall. ( ① ) She 10 wants to return herself to normal size, so she asks for help from a caterpillar. ( ② ) The caterpillar suggests she should eat a mushroom that can change her size. ( ③ ) It means Alice **must** eat balanced amounts to reach the right proportions. 15 ( ④ ) Carroll borrowed the ideas in this chapter from traditional rules of *geometry.

▲ Alice talking with a caterpillar

Carroll also seemed to like the number 42, so it often appears in the story. For example, the queen orders Alice to leave based on "Rule 42." 20 The rule states people more than a mile high **must** leave the court. The book even has 42 pictures.

*Alice in Wonderland* is full of unexpected surprises, and these mathematical mysteries add more fun!

*geometry 기하학

**Reading Comprehension**

**1** What is the best title for the passage?
   a. The Lessons in *Alice in Wonderland*
   b. The Popularity of *Alice in Wonderland*
   c. Math Secrets Hidden by a Novel Writer
   d. The Importance of Mathematics in Literature

**2** What is NOT an example of the idea mentioned in the underlined sentence?
   a. The caterpillar appears in chapter five.
   b. There is a way to reach the right proportions.
   c. The queen makes orders following Rule 42.
   d. The book includes 42 pictures.

**3** Where would the following sentence best fit?

> He says one side of it will make her bigger, but the other will make her smaller.

   a. ①          b. ②          c. ③          d. ④

**Writing Practice**

**4** According to the passage, what should Alice do to return to her normal size?
   She must _____ of a certain mushroom.

---

● ● ●          🔍 **GRAMMAR Inside** LEVEL 1          ☰

**의무를 나타내는 조동사**
조동사 must가 〈의무〉를 나타낼 때는 '~해야 한다'는 의미로, have to로 바꿔 쓸 수 있다. 하지만 must의
부정형 must not은 '~해서는 안 된다'는 〈금지〉를, have to의 부정형 don't have to는 '~할 필요가 없다'
는 〈불필요〉의 뜻을 나타낸다.

Link to ... 👆
   📁 Chapter 03
   📁 Unit 02

... people more than a mile high **must(= have to)** leave the court. 〈의무〉
                                                        법정을 떠나야 한다
You **must not** make noise here. 〈금지〉
          소음을 내서는 안 된다
I **don't have to** wake up early tomorrow. 〈불필요〉
      일찍 일어날 필요가 없다

**Check Up** 우리말과 일치하도록 (   ) 안의 말을 이용하여 문장을 완성하시오.
   너는 저녁을 준비할 필요가 없었다. (prepare)
   → You didn't _____ _____ _____ dinner.

# Fiction

196 words

Literature

# Twenty Thousand Leagues under the Sea

## Written by Jules Verne

### Mini Quiz

While you read, check *T* if it is true, or *F* if it is false.

1 An expedition was sent to destroy a sea monster.
☐ T ☐ F

2 Captain Nemo did not survive the whirlpool near Norway.
☐ T ☐ F

In 1866, a strange sea monster is attacking ships around the world. So the US government sends an expedition to hunt the monster. The expedition includes a scientist named Pierre Aronnax, ① his servant Conseil, and a hunter called Ned Land.

(A) One day, the Nautilus gets sucked into a *whirlpool near Norway. It seems like the Nautilus will be destroyed. Fortunately, the three men escape on a boat. They are saved by local people, but they never find out if Captain Nemo and ② his amazing submarine survived.

(B) After several months, the expedition finds the fierce creature **that** they have been searching for. However, the monster that has been attacking ships is actually a submarine called the Nautilus. After a brief battle, Aronnax, Conseil, and Ned get captured. The men are guided into the submarine. And they meet the submarine's commander, Captain Nemo.

(C) Nemo lets the captives explore the Nautilus, though ③ he makes it clear that they can never leave. Then ④ he takes them on many adventures. They hunt sharks, fight off a giant squid, and even visit Atlantis, a land of fantasy. The men enjoy these expeditions, but they still want to escape and return to their own lives.

*whirlpool 소용돌이

**Reading Comprehension**

1  What is the passage mainly about?
   a. an evil captain and his crew
   b. three men's adventures at sea
   c. the discovery of a new submarine
   d. a pirate who enjoys hunting sea creatures

2  What is the right order of the paragraphs (A)~(C)?
   a. (A) – (C) – (B)          b. (B) – (A) – (C)
   c. (B) – (C) – (A)          d. (C) – (A) – (B)

3  Among ①~④, which refers to a different character?
   a. ①             b. ②             c. ③             d. ④

**Writing Practice**

4  According to the passage, what is the monster making trouble for many ships?
   It turns out that the sea creature is _____.

---

🔍 **GRAMMAR Inside** LEVEL 2          ☰

**목적격 관계대명사**
선행사가 관계사절 안에서 목적어 역할을 할 때, 선행사 뒤에 목적격 관계대명사 who(m), which, that을 쓸
수 있다. 선행사가 사람일 때는 who(m)를, 사물일 때는 which를 사용하고, that은 선행사의 종류에 상관없이
쓸 수 있다. 목적격 관계대명사는 생략 가능하다.

**Link to ...**
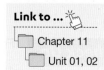

Christina called *the man* [**who(that/whom)** she hired to paint her fence]. 〈선행사가 사람〉
← Christina called *the man*. + She hired *him* to paint her fence.
..., the expedition finds *the fierce creature* [**that(which)** they have been searching for]. 〈선행사가 사물〉
← ..., the expedition finds *the fierce creature*. + They have been searching for *it*.

**Check Up** 우리말과 일치하도록 ( ) 안에 주어진 단어를 바르게 배열하시오.
   **1** 나는 마이클이 좋아하는 그 선생님을 본 적이 없다. (whom, Michael, the teacher, likes)
      → I haven't seen _____.
   **2** 딘은 그의 친구가 쓴 기사를 읽고 있다. (the article, wrote, that, his friend)
      → Dean is reading _____.

# 🔷 VOCABULARY INSIDE

| READING 1 | READING 2 |
|---|---|
| ☐ **journey** ⓝ <br> a trip from one place to another <br> [syn] trip, tour | ☐ **attack** ⓥ <br> to act violently in order to harm a person, animal, or place <br> ⓝ attack |
| ☐ **publish** ⓥ <br> to make something that someone has written available to the public <br> [syn] print | ☐ **expedition** ⓝ <br> a long trip for a particular purpose, especially to a dangerous or extreme place <br> [syn] voyage |
| ☐ **shrink** ⓥ <br> to become smaller or make something smaller in size or amount <br> [syn] reduce | ☐ **include** ⓥ <br> to contain something or have it as part of a whole <br> [syn] involve, contain　[ant] exclude |
| ☐ **suggest** ⓥ <br> to recommend something to someone <br> ⓝ suggestion　[syn] offer, propose | ☐ **search** ⓥ <br> to look for something or someone carefully <br> ⓝ search　[syn] seek |
| ☐ **unexpected** ⓐ <br> surprising and not expected <br> ⓐⓓ unexpectedly <br> [syn] sudden　[ant] expected | ☐ **capture** ⓥ <br> to catch someone or something, especially by force <br> [syn] catch, arrest　[ant] release |

**Check Up**

**Fill in the blanks with the words above. Change the form if necessary.**

1 The police planned to _____ for clues in the victim's house.

2 Cotton balls _____ when they get wet.

3 I _____ that we call the manager right now.

4 The photographer was injured by a wild animal that _____ him.

5 The price seems to _____ a bed and breakfast.

6 The actor wants to _____ his autobiography.

7 He looked nervous when he heard the _____ news.

8 The animal keepers were able to _____ the bear safely.

# UNIT
# 04 | Business

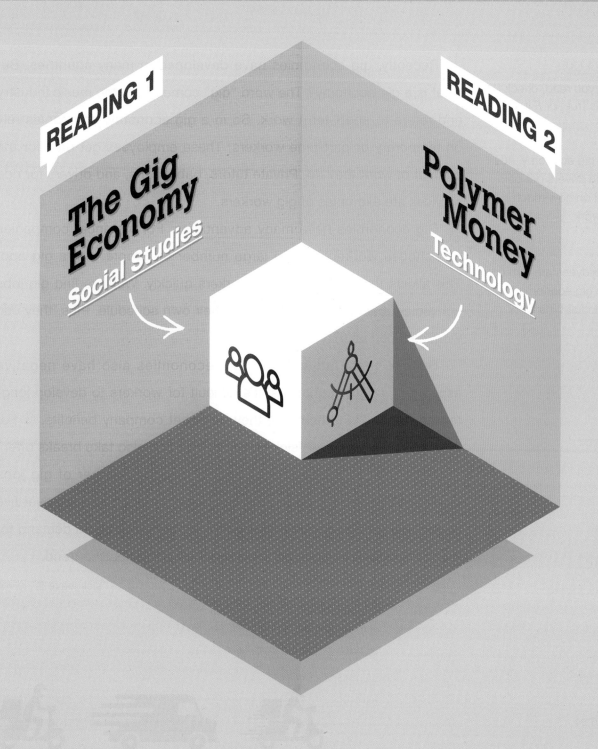

READING 1

The Gig Economy

Social Studies

READING 2

Polymer Money

Technology

# The Gig Economy

Recently, gig economies have developed in many countries. But what is a gig economy? The word "gig" comes from the music industry and refers to short-term work. So in a gig economy, companies rely on temporary or part-time workers. These employees get paid for the amount of work they do. Private tutors, babysitters, and drivers for ride 5 services are examples of gig workers.

Gig economies have <u>many advantages</u>. For instance, companies can choose workers from a large number of people with a gig app. This allows them to find skilled workers quickly. Workers find gig jobs convenient because they can make their own schedule. Plus, they can 10 work as much as they want to.

Despite these advantages, gig economies also have negative aspects. ① In gig economies, it's difficult for workers to develop long-term careers. ② Furthermore, they don't get company benefits. ③ For example, they don't get *sick leave. ④ They can also take breaks often. 15

Nevertheless, research has shown that the number of gig jobs increased significantly during the pandemic. In fact, there are over five million ride service drivers in the world, so there **must** be a demand for them. It's clear that gig economies **can't** be just a passing trend.

*sick leave 병가(病暇)

# Reading Comprehension

**1** **What is the best title for the passage?**
a. How Gig Economies Have Changed Businesses and Jobs
b. A New Law for the Rights of Temporary Workers
c. Gig Economies: Why They Should Be Avoided
d. The Advantages of Part-Time Employment

**2** **What is NOT included in the underlined part?**
a. Companies can find good workers easily.
b. Employees can plan their work schedule freely.
c. Companies can employ workers for long hours.
d. Workers can decide on the amount of work they do.

**3** **Which sentence is NOT needed in the passage?**
a. ①          b. ②          c. ③          d. ④

**Writing Practice**

**4** **Fill in the blank with words from the passage.**
It's true that gig economies have become more common during _____,
but they are more than just a trend.

---

**Q** **GRAMMAR Inside LEVEL 2**  ☰

추측을 나타내는 조동사

• 강한 추측을 나타낼 때는 조동사 must를 사용하며, '~임에 틀림없다'라는 의미이다.
..., so there **must** be a demand for them.
　　　　　수요가 있음에 틀림없다
The woman **must** be a musician. She plays the drums very well.
　　　　　음악가가 틀림없다
• 강한 추측을 의미할 때의 must의 부정은 can't[cannot]으로 나타내며 '~일 리가 없다'라는 의미이다.
It's clear that gig economies **can't** be just a passing trend.
　　　　　　　　그저 지나가는 추세일 리가 없다
They **can't** be at home now. I just saw them here a few minutes ago.
　　　　집에 있을 리가 없다

**Link to ...** 👆
📁 Chapter 03
📄 Unit 02

**Check Up** 우리말과 일치하도록 ( ) 안의 말을 이용하여 문장을 완성하시오.
너는 그 경기장을 못 보고 지나칠 리가 없어. 그것은 매우 거대해! (miss)
→ You _____ _____ the stadium. It is huge!

## Polymer Money

**✔ Mini Quiz**

Find the answers from the passage and write them.

**Paragraph 1**

1 Find the word in the passage that has the given meaning.

> one of the types or kinds of a particular thing

→ _____

**Paragraph 1**

2 What does "These" refer to in the passage?

→ _____

Although the world is shifting to paperless payments, many people still favor having paper cash on hand. However, increasingly, money is no longer made of paper at all. It is changing form as banks around the world switch to money made of high-tech plastic polymers. For example, Australia has used polymer money for decades, and England has recently switched all of their notes to polymer as well. New Zealand, Romania, and Canada have also started using polymer notes.

Polymer money is made from a thin, clear plastic film. It has added security features like *holograms and transparent windows. <u>These</u> make it extremely difficult to produce fake money.

_____, polymer banknotes are tougher than old-fashioned paper ones. They are less affected by rips and tears, so they last at least **2.5 times as long as** paper currency. Polymer banknotes are also cleaner than paper money, which can carry bacteria and viruses for days.

Because of their many advantages, many banks see polymers as the future of money. One day, you could see polymer banknotes everywhere, including Korea!

*hologram 홀로그램(입체 사진술에 의한 입체 화상)

**Reading Comprehension**

1 What is the best title for the passage?
a. Paper Cash: A Worldwide Form of Money
b. Why the World Prefers Paperless Payments
c. The Advantages and Disadvantages of Polymer Money
d. Goodbye, Paper: Why Polymers Are the Future of Money

2 What is NOT true about polymer money?
a. Australia has used it for more than 10 years.
b. It is made from a plastic film.
c. It is less affected by rips and tears.
d. It carries bacteria and viruses for days.

3 What is the best choice for the blank?
a. However        b. In addition        c. Nevertheless        d. Instead

**Writing Practice**

4 What are the two security features of polymer money mentioned in the passage?

_____

---

**Q  GRAMMAR Inside LEVEL 2**  ☰

비교 구문을 이용한 표현

- 배수사 + as + 원급 + as: ~의 몇 배로 …한[하게] (= 배수사 + 비교급 + than)
  …, so they last at least **2.5 times as long as** paper currency.
  종이 화폐보다 2.5배로 더 오래
  = …, so they last at least **2.5 times longer than** paper currency.

- one of the + 최상급 + 복수 명사: 가장 ~한 … 중의 하나
  Victoria Falls is **one of the biggest waterfalls** in the world.
  가장 큰 폭포들 중의 하나

- the + 비교급 ~, the + 비교급 …: ~하면 할수록 더 …하다
  **The sooner** you go to bed, **the earlier** you'll wake up in the morning.
  너는 빨리 자러 갈수록                   더 일찍 일어날 것이다

**Link to … 👆**
📁 Chapter 09
📁 Unit 02

**Check Up** 우리말과 일치하도록 ( ) 안의 말을 이용하여 문장을 완성하시오.
내 짐은 네 것보다 두 배 더 무겁다. (heavy)
→ My luggage is _____ _____ _____ _____ _____ yours.

# VOCABULARY INSIDE

| READING 1 | READING 2 |
|---|---|
| ☐ **temporary** ⓐ <br> continuing for only a limited period of time <br> [ant] permanent | ☐ **payment** ⓝ <br> the act of paying for something <br> ⓥ pay |
| ☐ **convenient** ⓐ <br> easy or suitable to use for certain purposes <br> ⓝ convenience  [syn] useful | ☐ **switch** ⓥ <br> to make a change from one thing to another <br> ⓝ switch  [syn] shift, change |
| ☐ **career** ⓝ <br> jobs that you do during a lot of your working life, usually in a particular field | ☐ **affect** ⓥ <br> to influence or make a difference to something <br> [syn] influence |
| ☐ **benefit** ⓝ <br> an advantage that employees get from employers in addition to their salary <br> ⓥ benefit | ☐ **carry** ⓥ <br> to take someone or something from one place to another <br> [syn] convey |
| ☐ **demand** ⓝ <br> people's need for products or services <br> ⓥ demand | ☐ **advantage** ⓝ <br> something that creates a better chance to succeed <br> [syn] benefit  [ant] disadvantage |

**Check Up** | **Fill in the blanks with the words above. Change the form if necessary.**

1 The bad weather didn't _____ our vacation plans.

2 The pills will give you _____ relief from headaches.

3 This backpack is too heavy for her to _____.

4 You have to make a(n) _____ of $55 to become a member.

5 Public transportation is a(n) _____ and cheap way to travel.

6 Jake wanted to _____ seats with Mary on the bus.

7 The _____ for mobile services is increasing.

8 The film was a huge success in her _____ as a director.

# UNIT
## 05 | Society

READING 1

The Color Purple

History

READING 2

The Fog Collectors

Science & Geography

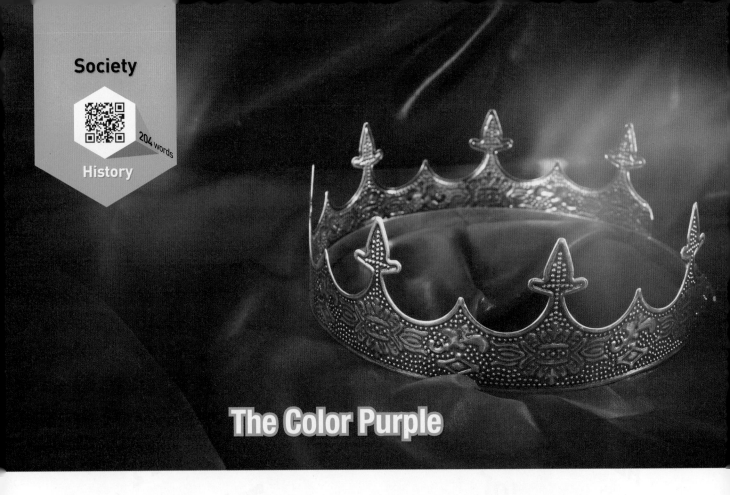

# The Color Purple

**ⓥ Mini Quiz**

Read and underline the answers in the passage.

**Paragraph 2**

1 Why were purple clothes associated with royalty?

**Paragraph 2**

2 How much was one pound of purple wool worth?

Have you ever noticed that kings and queens are often wearing purple in portraits? The connection between purple and royalty dates back to ancient times. In the Byzantine Empire, rulers wore fancy purple robes. _____(A)_____, people said that the children of royalty were "born in the purple." Roman citizens were even banned from 5 wearing purple clothing by their emperors.

So why was purple considered the color of royalty? It was because purple *dye was rare. For centuries, purple dye came from the Phoenician city of Tyre. Dye makers got it from a small sea snail that **can** only **be found** in the Mediterranean Sea near Tyre. The process of 10 making the dye was also very difficult. First, the snails' shells **had to be cracked** open and **put** in the sunlight for an exact amount of time. It took as many as 9,000 sea snails to make one gram of purple dye. _____(B)_____, this made the dye so expensive that only royalty could afford purple fabric. At one time, one pound of purple wool was worth 15 much more than the monthly salary of an ordinary person. In the mid-19th century, however, the first artificial dyes were created. This caused the color purple **to be used** more widely.

*dye 염료, 염색제

**Reading Comprehension**

1  **What is the passage mainly about?**
   a. the history of royal family portraits
   b. modern developments in purple dyes
   c. why purple was considered a valuable color
   d. the tradition of royalty to wear purple clothing

2  **What is the best pair for blanks (A) and (B)?**

|  | (A) | (B) |  | (A) | (B) |
|---|---|---|---|---|---|
| a. | For this reason | – Therefore | b. | In other words | – Instead |
| c. | As a result | – Otherwise | d. | For example | – However |

3  **Which are NOT mentioned about purple dye? (Choose two.)**
   a. where it came from before the mid-19th century
   b. how long it took to get the dye
   c. how many sea snails were needed to get one gram of it
   d. how valuable it was compared to gold

**Writing Practice**

4  **Fill in the blank with words from the passage.**
   The color purple became widely available after _____
   were created in the mid-19th century.

---

🔍 **GRAMMAR Inside** LEVEL 2                                    ≡

**to부정사와 조동사의 수동태**

수동태는 「be v-ed」의 형태로 주어가 동사의 영향을 받거나 동작을 당하는 것을 나타낼 때 쓴다.
조동사의 수동태는 「조동사 + be v-ed」로, to부정사의 수동태는 「to be v-ed」의 형태로 쓴다.

Roman citizens **were** even **banned** from wearing purple clothing … . 〈수동태〉
              └── 금지 당했다 ──┘

… a small sea snail that **can** only **be found** in the Mediterranean Sea … . 〈조동사의 수동태〉
                          └── 발견될 수 있다 ──┘

This caused the color purple **to be used** more widely. 〈to부정사의 수동태〉
                              └─ 이용되도록 ─┘

**Link to …** 👆
📁 Chapter 07
  📁 Unit 02

Geography & Science

# The Fog Collectors

## ⓥ Mini Quiz

While you read, check *T* if it is true, or *F* if it is false.

**1** The special nets are used to collect water drops from the fog.
☐ T ☐ F

**2** Each day, one net can collect enough water for seven families.
☐ T ☐ F

Water is rare in Manakhah, a mountain village in Yemen. During the dry season, villagers travel long distances to gather water from *reservoirs. This water is not clean, but the people are desperate. Although there is very little rainfall in the village, there is always a lot of fog. And fog is actually made up of water—it is a cloud of tiny water 5 drops. For this reason, some organizations began trying to "harvest" the moisture from the fog to solve Manakhah's water shortage.

The organizations developed special nets that capture fog and turn it into water. (A) This material is effective in capturing water drops. (B) The nets look like volleyball nets and are made from fine nylon. 10 (C) When fog passes through the nets, the tiny drops of water cling to them and gather together. When the drops grow big enough, they drip into water tanks below.

Building a fog collector costs less than $15. This is **cheap enough** for the people of Manakhah **to set** up hundreds. Each net can collect 15 more than 40 liters of water a day, which is enough for a family of seven to drink. With this technology, the people of Manakhah are able to harvest fresh water from fog.

*reservoir 저수지

# Reading Comprehension

1   **What is the best title for the passage?**
   a. A Creative Solution to a Lack of Water
   b. Special Nets to Clean Water in Reservoirs
   c. Many Problems Caused by Too Much Fog
   d. A Powerful Tool for Controlling Water Drops

2   **What is the right order of the sentences (A)~(C)?**
   a. (A) – (C) – (B)                   b. (B) – (A) – (C)
   c. (B) – (C) – (A)                   d. (C) – (A) – (B)

3   **What is NOT mentioned in the passage?**
   a. where Manakhah is located
   b. why rain is rare in Manakhah
   c. what material is used for the nets
   d. how much it costs to build a collector

Writing Practice

4   **Fill in the blank with words from the passage.**

   Q: How much water can a single net capture?
   A: It can capture more than _____ each day.

---

Q    GRAMMAR **Inside** LEVEL 2

<u>to부정사를 이용한 구문</u>

• 형용사[부사] + enough + to-v: ~할 만큼 충분히 …하다
  (= so + 형용사[부사] + that + 주어 + can + 동사원형)
  This is **cheap enough** for the people of Manakhah **to set** up hundreds.
  (= This is **so cheap that** the people of Manakhah **can set** up hundreds.)

• too + 형용사[부사] + to-v: 너무 ~해서 …할 수 없다
  (= so + 형용사[부사] + that + 주어 + can't + 동사원형)
  The house is **too small** for me **to live** in.
  (= The house is **so small that** I **can't live** in it.)

**Link to ...**

Chapter 04
Unit 04

# 🔷 VOCABULARY INSIDE

| READING 1 | READING 2 |
|---|---|
| ☐ **connection** ⓝ <br> logical relation between two things <br> ⓥ connect | ☐ **desperate** ⓐ <br> very worried and willing to do anything to change the situation |
| ☐ **royalty** ⓝ <br> people in a king and queen's family <br> ⓐ royal | ☐ **organization** ⓝ <br> a group of people who have a particular shared purpose or interest <br> ⓥ organize  ⓐ organized |
| ☐ **rare** ⓐ <br> not commonly found or happening very often <br> ⓓ rarely <br> syn uncommon, unusual  ant common | ☐ **harvest** ⓥ <br> to collect something that can be eaten or used <br> ⓝ harvest  syn gather, collect |
| ☐ **afford** ⓥ <br> to have enough money to pay for or do something <br> ⓐ affordable | ☐ **shortage** ⓝ <br> a lack of something that you need or want <br> ⓐ short <br> syn lack  ant abundance |
| ☐ **worth** ⓐ <br> having a certain value in money | ☐ **gather** ⓥ <br> to come together in one place <br> syn collect  ant separate |

**Check Up**  **Fill in the blanks with the words above. Change the form if necessary.**

1 The teacher told everyone to _____ together at the front of the classroom.

2 Some hospitals are experiencing a(n) _____ of doctors.

3 There is no money left, so we're _____.

4 We couldn't _____ to buy a new house.

5 Rick found a(n) _____ coin in his attic.

6 Members of British _____ attended the parade.

7 The brand is _____ billions of dollars.

8 Mr. Colbert is the leader of an international _____.

# UNIT
# 06 | Animals

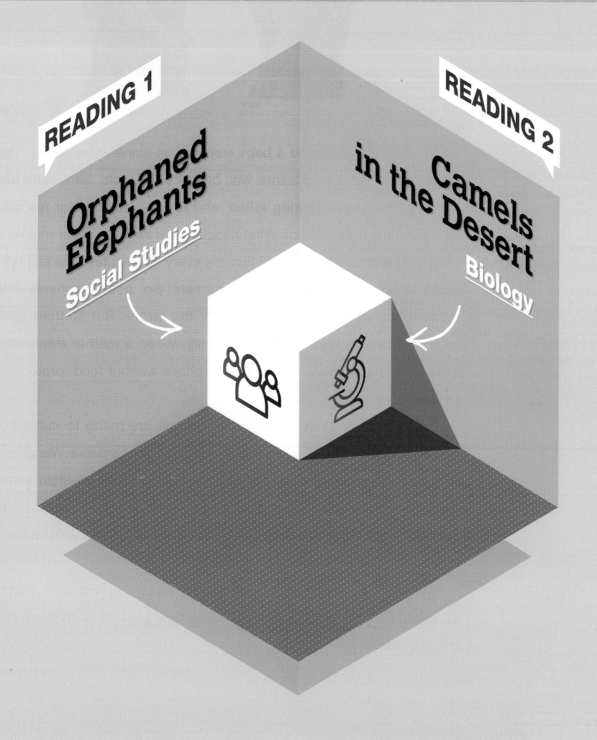

READING 1

Orphaned Elephants
Social Studies

READING 2

Camels in the Desert
Biology

# Orphaned Elephants

In 2002, people found a baby elephant all alone in the forest. This stressed and exhausted animal was only one week old. Sadly, she **had** just **seen** her mother **being killed**, and it was traumatic for her. She was given the name Wendi. What happened to Wendi and her mother?

A wild elephant is killed by hunters every 15 minutes. The elephant 5 *ivory is taken and sold in illegal markets. So, adult elephants with massive amounts of ivory are usually the target. But hunting adult elephants affects their whole community. When a mother elephant is killed, her young children are left as orphans without food, protection, or care. 10

Fortunately, animal conservation groups are trying to make this serious situation better. They rescue elephant orphans like Wendi and take them to an elephant orphanage in Tanzania. The elephants stay there for 9 to 14 years. The young, weak elephants receive around-the-clock care. As they grow older, they form their own social units and are 15 eventually released into protected areas.

Although the orphanage does great work, baby elephants should be raised by their mothers. Unless the horrible practice is stopped, this tragic situation will continue.

*ivory 상아

**Reading Comprehension**

1    **What is the passage mainly about?**
a. the life of Wendi, a rescued elephant
b. the reasons for hunting young elephants
c. methods of teaching young elephants to survive
d. a tragic situation faced by the elephant community

2    **Why does the writer tell Wendi's story?**
a. to describe how Wendi was rescued
b. to give an example of an elephant orphan
c. to explain how Wendi's mother was killed
d. to emphasize how serious Wendi's injury was

3    **What is NOT mentioned in the passage?**
a. how old Wendi was
b. why adult elephants are killed
c. where the elephant orphanage is located
d. how orphaned elephants get around-the-clock care

**Writing Practice**

4    **According to the passage, what does the underlined part refer to?**
It refers to killing _____ for their _____.

---

Q    **GRAMMAR Inside** LEVEL 2    ≡

**목적격 보어의 여러 형태 1**

hear, see, feel, smell 등 감각 기관을 통해 느끼는 것을 표현하는 동사를 지각동사라고 한다. 지각동사의 목적격 보어로는 동사원형을 쓰지만, 동작이 진행 중임을 강조할 때는 현재분사(v-ing)를 쓰기도 한다.

I **heard** someone **call** the police. 〈동사원형〉
누군가가 경찰을 부르는 것을 들었다
→ 목적어와 목적격 보어의 관계가 능동이므로, 동사원형이 쓰였다.

Sadly, she **had** just **seen** her mother **being killed**, and ... . 〈현재분사〉
그녀의 엄마가 죽임을 당하는 것을 보았다
→ 목적어와 목적격 보어의 관계가 수동이고, 진행 중임을 강조하여 「being v-ed」의 형태로 쓰였다.

Link to ...

Chapter 01
Unit 02

# Camels in the Desert

Camels have been known to go for months without water. Many people assume that the humps of a camel **are filled with** water, but it's not true. Camels store fat in their humps, not water. Their humps **are made of** fatty *tissue, which is stored as a source of energy. When a camel goes without food in the desert, one of its humps begins to shrink. Camels' humps also help with _____. In the daytime, the fat in their humps helps to keep the daytime heat out. It prevents them from overheating and sweating. Conversely, it keeps camels warm at night.

▲ a Bactrian camel

Although the humps do not store water, camels are still efficient in their use of water. This is due to the unique features of their blood cells. The blood cells are **oval. The oval-shaped blood cells make it possible for camels to consume as much as 30 gallons of water at a time. The cells are flexible and can change their shape easily. They allow blood to flow more easily when water levels in the body drop. It is true that camels could not survive in the desert without their humps. But it's still the oval-shaped blood cells that help them store so much water, not the humps.

*tissue (생물의) 조직
**oval 타원형의

## Reading Comprehension

**1**　What is the best title for the passage?

   **a.** How Camels Locate Food Sources in the Desert

   **b.** Why Camels Don't Feel Hot in the Desert

   **c.** What Helps Camels Survive in the Desert

   **d.** Why Camels Need Such Big Humps

**2**　What is the best choice for the blank?

   **a.** protecting the body from disease

   **b.** reinforcing the strength of their muscles

   **c.** adapting to changes in their body

   **d.** maintaining their body temperature

**3**　Which CANNOT be answered based on the passage?

   **a.** What is inside a camel's hump?

   **b.** How much water do camels need every day?

   **c.** Which body part helps control a camel's body temperature?

   **d.** What is unique about a camel's blood?

**Writing Practice**

**4**　According to the passage, what allows camels to carry so much water?

   The _____ allow camels to carry a lot of water.

---

### 🔍 GRAMMAR **Inside** LEVEL 2　≡

**by 이외의 전치사를 사용하는 수동태**

수동태(be v-ed)는 보통 by를 사용하여 행위자를 나타내지만, 다른 전치사가 사용되는 경우도 있다.

- be covered with: ~으로 덮여 있다
- be satisfied with: ~에 만족하다
- be made of[from]: ~으로 만들어지다
- be pleased with: ~으로 기뻐하다
- be interested in: ~에 흥미가 있다
- be filled with: ~으로 가득 차다 (= be full of)
- be known to: ~에게 알려지다

**Link to ... 👆**

  📁 Chapter 07

   📁 Unit 03

  Many people assume that the humps of a camel **are filled with** water, … .
              물로 가득 차 있다

  Their humps **are made of** fatty tissue, which is stored as a source of energy.
      지방 조직으로 만들어진다

# 🔷 VOCABULARY INSIDE

| READING 1 | READING 2 |
|---|---|
| ☐ **illegal** Ⓐ<br>against the law<br>ad illegally　ant legal, lawful | ☐ **assume** Ⓥ<br>to believe that something is true without proof<br>ⓝ assumption　syn believe |
| ☐ **community** ⓝ<br>the people or animals who live in an area<br>syn neighborhood | ☐ **store** Ⓥ<br>to keep something in a particular place<br>ⓝ storage　syn accumulate, save |
| ☐ **protection** ⓝ<br>something that keeps people or things<br>safe from damage<br>Ⓥ protect | ☐ **conversely** ad<br>in a contrary or opposite way<br>syn on the other hand　ant similarly |
| ☐ **conservation** ⓝ<br>the management of resources in ways that<br>prevent them from being damaged<br>Ⓥ conserve　syn maintenance, protection | ☐ **efficient** Ⓐ<br>performing or functioning with the least waste<br>of time and effort<br>syn economical |
| ☐ **release** Ⓥ<br>to let a person or animal leave a place<br>syn set free | ☐ **flexible** Ⓐ<br>able to change to suit new conditions or<br>situations<br>ⓝ flexibility<br>syn adaptable　ant fixed, inflexible |

**Check Up** | **Fill in the blanks with the words above. Change the form if necessary.**

1　The bazaar made it necessary for the local _____ to get together.

2　It is _____ to download that file on the internet.

3　My grandma usually _____ her jewels in the closet.

4　The police provided _____ to the witnesses.

5　The most _____ way to behave is not to delay.

6　Our schedule is very _____, so please contact us if you want to make a change.

7　I want you to _____ the fish back into the pond.

8　Add the milk to the powder, or, _____, the powder to the milk.

# UNIT 07 | Social Media

READING 1

The Effects of Social Media

Social Studies

READING 2

Cause Marketing

Social Studies

# The Effects of Social Media

### Mini Quiz

While you read, check *T* if it is true, or *F* if it is false.

**1** Social media offers information on social issues and channels for communication.
☐ T ☐ F

**2** A social media detox involves staying away from using social media.
☐ T ☐ F

**Host:** Recently, it seems like people spend hours every day online. But is this healthy? Today, we **have invited** psychologist Rebecca Stanford to the show. Dr. Stanford, let's talk about the effects of social media. The social media trend **hasn't slowed** down, has it?

**Dr. Stanford:** No, it **hasn't**. People **have made** it an important    5
part of their daily life. It provides access to news and information. Also, it's a great way to communicate with family, friends, and even celebrities. But social media also has another side to it.

**Host:** _____

**Dr. Stanford:** Studies **have found** that social media can cause    10
emotional problems. People worry about the *likes on their posts. And they constantly check social media because they are scared of missing something. Moreover, they keep comparing themselves with others on social media. This can lead to loneliness and even depression. When this happens, a social media detox is needed.    15

*like (소셜 미디어 상에서) 타인의 글에 공감을 표시하는 행위

**Host:** What is a social media detox?

**Dr. Stanford:** A social media **detoxification is a time when you take a break from using social media. ① First, pay attention to the time you are active online and set limits for yourself. ② Also, connect with your real life again. ③ Go to places you enjoy and    20
visit people. ④ More and more places have free internet service these days. Focus more on the real world and less on social media!

**detoxification 해독

**Reading Comprehension**

1 **What is the best title for the passage?**
   a. Understanding Social Media Trends
   b. Interviewing People with Depression
   c. The Importance of a Social Media Detox
   d. How Social Media Harms Your Social Life

2 **What is the best choice for the blank?**
   a. How can social media negatively affect us?
   b. What are some ways to avoid these effects?
   c. How do people overcome mental problems?
   d. Why do social media users often feel depressed?

3 **Which sentence is NOT needed in the passage?**
   a. ①          b. ②          c. ③          d. ④

Writing Practice

4 **Fill in the blanks with words from the passage.**
   Social media can cause _____, so a _____ is
   needed to help free yourself from these problems.

---

🔍 **GRAMMAR Inside** LEVEL 2    ≡

**현재완료**

현재완료는 「have v-ed」의 형태로, 완료(막 ~했다), 경험(~한 적이 있다), 계속(지금까지 계속 ~해 왔다),
결과(~해 버렸다) 등의 의미로 쓰인다. 부정문은 「have not v-ed」, 의문문은 「Have + 주어 + v-ed ~?」
이다.

**Link to ...** 👆
📁 Chapter 02
📁 Unit 02

Today, we **have invited** psychologist Rebecca Stanford to the show. 〈완료〉
I **haven't been** to Disneyland before.                              〈경험〉
The social media trend **hasn't slowed** down.                        〈계속〉
I **have hurt** my leg. So, I cannot walk freely now.                 〈결과〉

---

**Check Up** 우리말과 일치하도록 (  ) 안의 말을 이용하여 문장을 완성하시오.

나는 새로 산 스마트폰을 잃어버렸다. (lose)
→ I _____ _____ my new smartphone.

**⌄ Mini Quiz**

Read and underline the answers in the passage.

**Paragraph 1**

1 Find the word in the passage that has the given meaning.

> a group of people who have a particular shared purpose or interest

**Paragraph 2**

2 How does social media benefit companies?

# Cause Marketing

How would you feel if you could help the world by buying a product? You'd probably feel good and would consider buying the product again. This is the idea **on which** cause marketing is based. When customers make a purchase, the company makes a donation to a nonprofit organization. In this way, customers can help nonprofit organizations and companies can increase their profits.   5

Nowadays, social media makes cause marketing even more effective. Customers can have companies make donations just by sharing information on social networking sites. This also benefits the companies. They can reach millions of customers in a matter of hours, and it requires less money and effort.   10

The idea of cause marketing was first introduced by American Express in 1983. At that time, they launched a new campaign **in which** they asked customers for money. The money was raised to restore the Statue of Liberty. Every time a customer used an American Express charge card, one cent was donated to the restoration. This _____ between American Express and its customers raised $1.7 million. Furthermore, the company saw a 28% increase in card usage.   15   20

**Reading Comprehension**

1   What is the passage mainly about?
   a. why cause marketing is popular with customers
   b. the negative effects of cause marketing on society
   c. how cause marketing benefits everyone involved
   d. how companies have increased their profits online

2   What is the best choice for the blank?
   a. invitation          b. cooperation          c. difference          d. competition

3   Which CANNOT be answered based on the passage?
   a. What is the basic concept of cause marketing?
   b. How can people donate by purchasing a product?
   c. What was the purpose of the first cause marketing campaign?
   d. How much profit did American Express gain from social media?

**Writing Practice**

4   Fill in the blanks with words from the passage.

| The Benefits of Cause Marketing |
| --- |
| (1) _____ receive donations. |
| (2) _____ can help the world. |
| (3) _____ can increase their profits. |

---

🔍 **GRAMMAR Inside** LEVEL 3      ☰

「전치사 + 관계대명사」

• 관계대명사가 전치사의 목적어로 쓰일 때, 전치사는 관계대명사 앞이나 관계사절 끝에 올 수 있다. 전치사가 관계대명사 앞에 쓰인 경우에는 목적격 관계대명사 중 whom, which만 사용 가능하며, 관계대명사를 생략할 수 없다.
   ..., they launched a new campaign **in which** they asked customers for money.
   ..., they launched a new campaign *in that* they asked customers for money. (X)
   ..., they launched a new campaign *in (which)* they asked customers for money. (X)

• 전치사가 관계사절 끝에 오는 경우에는 whom(who), which, that 모두 쓸 수 있고 관계대명사를 생략할 수도 있다.
   David told me about a friend (**who[that]**) he went to school **with**.

Link to ... 👆

Chapter 09

Unit 03

# 🔷 VOCABULARY INSIDE

| READING 1 | READING 2 |
|---|---|
| ☐ **effect** (n)<br>a change resulting from someone or something else<br>(v) effect  [syn] outcome, result | ☐ **consider** (v)<br>to think carefully about something before making a decision<br>(n) consideration  [syn] think |
| ☐ **access** (n)<br>a way that lets you use or get something<br>(v) access | ☐ **customer** (n)<br>someone who pays for a product or service |
| ☐ **communicate** (v)<br>to express feelings or thoughts to another person with language<br>(n) communication | ☐ **donation** (n)<br>money or food that you give to help a person or organization<br>(v) donate |
| ☐ **emotional** (a)<br>relating to someone's mind and feelings<br>(n) emotion  [syn] psychological, mental | ☐ **profit** (n)<br>the money gained from a business's activities<br>(v) profit |
| ☐ **compare** (v)<br>to think about the similarities between two different things or among several things<br>(n) comparison  [ant] contrast | ☐ **require** (v)<br>to need something<br>(n) requirement  [syn] demand |

**Check Up**

**Fill in the blanks with the words above. Change the form if necessary.**

1 It is interesting to _____ the two musicians.

2 All workers are _____ to wear proper equipment to work.

3 Oil spills have several terrible _____ on sea creatures.

4 He made a large _____ to the charity.

5 Most _____ complained about the service at the store.

6 The internet gives us _____ to infinite information.

7 The prisoner isn't allowed to _____ with other prisoners.

8 She is _____ buying a new tablet PC.

# UNIT
# 08 | Psychology

READING 1

Stendhal Syndrome

Arts

READING 2

Do You Feel What I Feel?

Biology

# Stendhal Syndrome

**Amy:** Doctor, something strange happened last week when I was on vacation in Florence. I was wandering around a gallery to see Michelangelo's works. I never imagined anything so beautiful could exist. Just then, all of a sudden, I had trouble breathing. I became dizzy and sweaty. I didn't know **what to do**. What happened to me? 5

**Dr. Robert:** Well, you don't have to worry about your symptoms. They're not serious. They suggest you experienced Stendhal syndrome. Its other symptoms include a fast heartbeat and fainting. People may react this way when they 10 experience amazingly beautiful art.

The syndrome got its name from French writer Marie-Henri Beyle. ① His *pen name was Stendhal. ② He had other pen names apart from Stendhal. ③ In the 1800s, Stendhal was extremely amazed by the beauty of Florence's Basilica of Santa Croce. ④ The 15 feeling was so strong that he thought he was having psychological problems. This condition was named Stendhal syndrome after more than 100 similar cases had been reported. It can happen to extremely sensitive people. Jet lag can also worsen the situation. However, the symptoms don't last long. You should be back to 20 normal after a few days of rest.

*pen name 필명

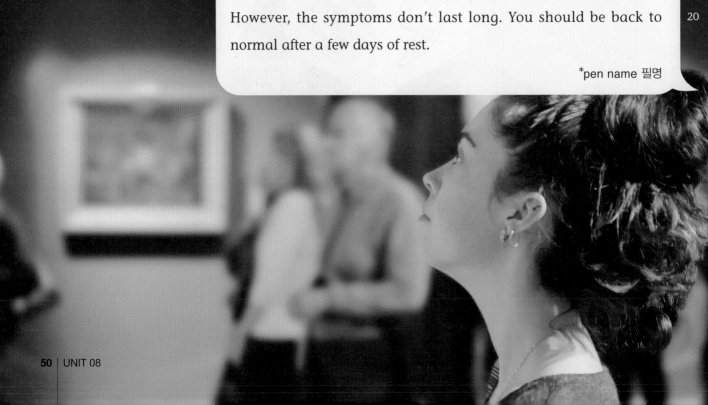

**Reading Comprehension**

1  What is the best title for the passage?

   a. Discover the Artwork of Stendhal

   b. A Writer Who Suffers from Stendhal Syndrome

   c. The Symptoms and History of Stendhal Syndrome

   d. Why Stendhal Syndrome Happens to Sensitive People

2  Which sentence is NOT needed in the passage?

   a. ①            b. ②            c. ③            d. ④

3  What is NOT mentioned in the passage?

   a. where Amy experienced Stendhal syndrome

   b. how the human body reacts to the syndrome

   c. who named Stendhal syndrome

   d. what makes the symptoms worse

**Writing Practice**

4  According to the passage, what type of people can experience the syndrome?

   _____ can experience it.

---

**GRAMMAR Inside LEVEL 2**

「의문사 + to-v」

「의문사 + to-v」는 문장에서 주어, 목적어, 보어의 역할을 하며, 의문사에 따라 그 의미가 달라진다.
또한, 「의문사 + to-v」는 「의문사 + 주어 + should + 동사원형」으로 바꿔 쓸 수 있다.

• what to-v: 무엇을 ~할지                • how to-v: 어떻게 ~할지

• who(m) to-v: 누구를[누구에게] ~할지       • when to-v: 언제 ~할지

• where to-v: 어디서[어디로] ~할지

   I didn't know **what to do**. (= I didn't know **what I should do**.)
          무엇을 할지

   I'm not sure **when to start** the party. (= I'm not sure **when I should start** the party.)
              언제 시작할지

Link to ...

📁 Chapter 04
   📁 Unit 01

**Check Up** 두 문장의 의미가 같도록 빈칸에 알맞은 말을 쓰시오.

   We haven't decided where we should go for summer vacation.

   → We haven't decided _____ _____ _____ for summer vacation.

**Psychology**

**Biology**

175 words

# Do You Feel What I Feel?

**ⓥ Mini Quiz**

Read and underline the answers in the passage.

**Paragraph 1**

1 Find the word in the passage that has the given meaning.

> a measurement of how hot or cold someone or something is

**Paragraph 2**

2 What happened to the volunteers' temperatures in the experiment?

One day, Dr. Neil Harrison felt cold **while** he was watching a film. It happened during one scene in particular. In the scene, a naked man was running through the frozen Arctic. Dr. Harrison wondered whether watching someone feeling cold had actually lowered his own body temperature. 5

Dr. Harrison and other researchers decided to test <u>this</u>. For their study, they found 36 volunteers and attached small thermometers to ① <u>their</u> hands. They then showed the group videos. In the videos, people were dipping ② <u>their</u> hands into icy water. The volunteers' temperature changes were measured at the same time. Surprisingly, 10 the temperature of ③ <u>their</u> hands dropped by an average of 0.2°C **while** ④ <u>they</u> were watching the video. This is a small but significant amount.

The researchers suggest that this change of body temperature is due to empathy. Empathy allows us to understand and share others' emotions. But the study shows that empathy can lead to _____ 15 _____. **When** we see someone experiencing cold or warm temperatures, our body temperature may actually change, which lets us experience how they feel.

**Reading Comprehension**

1 **What is the passage mainly about?**
  a. ways to maintain body temperature in cold weather
  b. how to understand others' emotions and react to them
  c. body temperature changes caused by watching others
  d. the relationship between emotions and body temperature

**Writing Practice**

2 **What does the underlined part refer to?**
  Dr. Harrison's curiosity about whether _____ can lower
  body temperature.

3 **Among ①~④, which refers to a different thing?**
  a. ①                    b. ②                    c. ③                    d. ④

4 **What is the best choice for the blank?**
  a. influencing emotional changes in others
  b. severe emotional and physical problems
  c. physical changes as well as emotional ones
  d. protection of one's body from outside danger

---

🔍 **GRAMMAR Inside** LEVEL 2                                    ☰

시간을 나타내는 접속사

when, as는 '~할 때,' while은 '~하는 동안'이라는 의미의 시간을 나타내는 접속사이다.
이 외에도 after(~한 후에), before(~하기 전에), until[till](~할 때까지) 등이 있다.

**When** we see someone experiencing cold or warm temperatures, … .
        우리가 누군가가 차갑거나 따뜻한 온도를 경험하는 것을 볼 때

One day, Dr. Neil Harrison felt cold **while** he was watching a film.
                                    그가 영화를 보는 동안

I will wait here **until** he comes back.
                 그가 돌아올 때까지

**Link to …** 👆
⌐⌐⌐⌐⌐⌐⌐⌐⌐⌐⌐⌐
📁 Chapter 10
  📁 Unit 01

**Check Up** ( ) 안에서 알맞은 말을 고르시오.
        **1** Clean the table (while, after) you have your meal.
        **2** Do not tell him the truth (as, until) I say you can.

# VOCABULARY INSIDE

| READING 1 | READING 2 |
|---|---|
| ☐ **imagine** (v)<br>to think of something in the mind as if it were real<br>(n) imagination | ☐ **wonder** (v)<br>to have a desire to know something |
| ☐ **exist** (v)<br>to be present in the real world<br>(n) existence   [syn] be present | ☐ **volunteer** (n)<br>someone who does something without being ordered or pressured to do it<br>(v) volunteer |
| ☐ **symptom** (n)<br>a sign that someone has an illness<br>[syn] sign | ☐ **attach** (v)<br>to join one thing to another<br>(a) attached   (n) attachment<br>[ant] detach |
| ☐ **react** (v)<br>to respond to something that happens<br>(n) reaction   [syn] respond | ☐ **measure** (v)<br>to find the size, amount, or degree of something<br>(n) measurement |
| ☐ **normal** (a)<br>ordinary, not unusual; generally free from mental or physical problems<br>[syn] usual, ordinary   [ant] abnormal, unusual | ☐ **significant** (a)<br>very large and easily noticed<br>(ad) significantly   [syn] noticeable |

**Check Up**

**Fill in the blanks with the words above. Change the form if necessary.**

1 Flu _____ tend to last for a week.

2 I _____ if the movie is based on a real story.

3 You can use a ruler to _____ the length of the pencil.

4 He didn't _____ when I called his name.

5 I don't believe that ghosts _____.

6 She _____ a name tag to her shirt and showed it to me.

7 I can't _____ anyone climbing that mountain. It's too high!

8 We need a lot of _____ to test the new medicine.

# UNIT
# 09 | Winter

**READING 1**

Christmas Trees

*History*

**READING 2**

The Reindeer: An Arctic Survivor

*Biology*

# Christmas Trees

## ⓥ Mini Quiz

While you read, check *T* if it is true, or *F* if it is false.

**1** It was Martin Luther that started the custom of hanging Christmas lights.

☐ T ☐ F

**2** Most Christmas traditions began during religious wars.

☐ T ☐ F

Among the various Christmas traditions, none is more popular than putting up a Christmas tree. How did this tradition begin? Historians believe the first Christmas tree originated in Germany. In 723, an English missionary traveled to Germany for religious reasons. Having arrived, he watched some natives gathering at an oak tree to pray 5 to their god, Thor. The missionary chopped down the tree. Then he **convinced** the people **to *worship** a nearby **evergreen as their holy tree instead.

During the Middle Ages, people in Germany began to display the trees in their homes on December 24. ① Later, they added apples and other decorations representing the Garden of Eden. ② In the 16th century, Martin Luther hung candles on a tree. ③ This was the first appearance of Christmas lights. ④ However, this tradition began to have a negative impact on European forests.

▲ Martin Luther
(1483-1546)

10

15

▲ Queen Victoria
(1819-1901)

As Germans migrated to England, they took their customs with them. The German wife of King George III **had** trees **decorated** at Windsor 20 Castle. Later, Queen Victoria and Prince Albert **made** Christmas trees **an official part of their holiday celebrations**. The royal family was even featured with their tree in newspapers and magazines. The influence of media publications 25 **has kept** the tradition **alive** ever since.

*worship 숭배하다
**evergreen 상록수

**Reading Comprehension**

1 **What is the passage mainly about?**
   a. the meaning of Christmas decorations
   b. how the tradition of Christmas trees began
   c. why Christmas is the most beloved holiday in the world
   d. different Christmas customs in European countries

2 **Which sentence is NOT needed in the passage?**
   a. ①          b. ②          c. ③          d. ④

3 **List the following Christmas tree traditions in chronological order.**
   (1) worshipping evergreen trees
   (2) hanging lights on the tree
   (3) displaying a tree at home in December
   (4) decorating the tree with apples and other ornaments
   _____ → _____ → _____ → _____

**Writing Practice**

4 **According to the passage, how did decorating trees become a Christmas tradition?**
   _____ was shown with trees in newspapers and magazines.
   _____ made decorating trees into a Christmas tradition.

---

Q **GRAMMAR Inside** LEVEL 2          ☰

목적격 보어의 여러 형태 2
목적격 보어는 목적어의 성질이나 상태를 보충 설명하는 말로, 동사에 따라 to부정사, 동사원형, 형용사 등을 쓸 수 있다.

**Link to ...**
📁 Chapter 01
📁 Unit 02

• 동사(want, ask, tell, allow 등) + 목적어 + to부정사
  Then he **convinced** the people **to worship** a nearby evergreen as their holy tree instead.
  그 사람들이 숭배하도록 설득했다

• 사역동사(make, let, have) + 목적어 + 동사원형
  Mr. Han **had** us **finish** the project.
  우리가 끝마치도록 했다

• 동사(make, keep, find, think 등) + 목적어 + 형용사
  The influence of media publications **has kept** the tradition **alive** ever since.
  그 전통이 살아있게 해 왔다

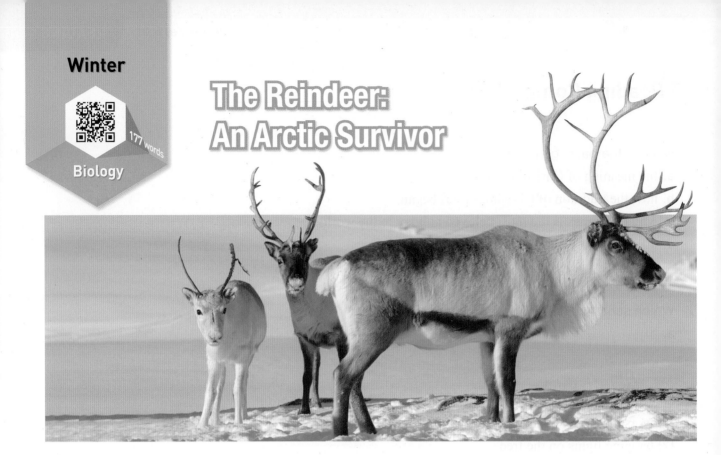

# The Reindeer: An Arctic Survivor

**❤ Mini Quiz**

Read and underline the answers in the passage.

**Paragraph 1**

**1** What does "two interesting adaptations" refer to in the passage? (Find two sentences.)

**Paragraph 3**

**2** What does "This" refer to in the passage?

Reindeer live in **the toughest** environment on the planet, the Arctic. The temperatures there are **as low as** -40℃, and night can last for months in winter. To cope with these conditions, reindeer have evolved two interesting adaptations.

First, scientists have recently found that reindeer's eyes change 5 color from gold to blue in winter. In summer, their eyes reflect most light through the *retina and appear gold. ___(A)___, in winter, their eyes change to reflect only a little light, turning blue. This makes the reindeer's eyes **more sensitive** to light and helps them see **better**. As a result, they can find food and notice enemies in the dark Arctic winter. 10

The second adaptation is reindeer's hooves. They have spongy pads on the bottom. The pads help reindeer get **traction on the soft, wet ground in summer. In other words, reindeer can run without slipping and move around quickly and easily. ___(B)___, in winter, these pads shrink to expose the sharp edges of the hoof. This allows 15 reindeer to run on the snow and get a grip on the ice.

*retina (눈의) 망막
**traction 마찰력

**Reading Comprehension**

1  **What is the best title for the passage?**
   a. Different Regions, Different Reindeer
   b. The Seasonal Adaptations of Reindeer
   c. Reindeer: Endangered by Climate Change
   d. Reindeer's Survival Skills in Warm Weather

2  **What is the best choice for blanks (A) and (B)?**
   a. For example      b. Therefore      c. However      d. Nevertheless

3  **What are true according to the passage? (Choose two.)**
   a. Night in the Arctic lasts all year around.
   b. Reindeer's eyes reflect more light in summer than in winter.
   c. Reindeer have evolved to hide in the dark.
   d. Pads on reindeer's hooves help them move around quickly.

**Writing Practice**

4  **Fill in the blanks with words from the passage.**

|  | **Summer → Winter** | **Benefits** |
|---|---|---|
| **Reindeer's Eyes** | Their color changes from gold to (1) _____ . | Reindeer can find food and notice (2) _____ . |
| **Reindeer's Hooves** | Their pads shrink to expose the (3) _____ _____ . | Reindeer can run on the snow and get a grip (4) _____ _____ _____ . |

---

🔍 **GRAMMAR Inside** LEVEL 2    ≡

원급, 비교급, 최상급
형용사나 부사에 -er, -est 또는 more, most를 붙여 대상의 성질, 상태, 수량의 정도를 비교할 수 있다.
원급은 「as + 형용사(부사)의 원급 + as」 (~만큼 …한[하게]), 비교급은 「비교급 + than」 (~보다 더 …한
[하게]), 최상급은 「the + 최상급」 (가장 ~한[하게])으로 나타낼 수 있다.

**Link to ...**

The temperatures there are **as low as** -40°C, … . 〈원급〉
　　　　　　섭씨 영하 40도만큼 낮은
This makes the reindeer's eyes **more sensitive** to light (**than** in summer) and … . 〈비교급〉
　　　　　　　　　　　　(여름보다) 빛에 더 민감한
Reindeer live in **the toughest** environment on the planet, the Arctic. 〈최상급〉
　　　　　　　가장 척박한 환경

# VOCABULARY INSIDE

| READING 1 | READING 2 |
|---|---|
| ☐ **religious** (a)<br>relating to the belief in the existence of a god or gods<br>(n) religion | ☐ **condition** (n)<br>the physical state of something<br>[syn] state |
| ☐ **convince** (v)<br>to make someone do something by persuading them<br>(n) conviction   [syn] persuade | ☐ **evolve** (v)<br>to develop new features over generations<br>(n) evolution   [syn] develop |
| ☐ **display** (v)<br>to put something where people can see it<br>[syn] exhibit | ☐ **reflect** (v)<br>to block the passage of something and make it change direction<br>(n) reflection   [syn] mirror |
| ☐ **represent** (v)<br>to serve as a sign or symbol of something<br>(n) representation   [syn] express | ☐ **sensitive** (a)<br>extremely responsive to small changes |
| ☐ **custom** (n)<br>something that people do that is traditional or usual<br>[syn] tradition, practice | ☐ **expose** (v)<br>to reveal something that was hidden or covered<br>[syn] reveal, uncover   [ant] cover |

**Check Up**

**Fill in the blanks with the words above. Change the form if necessary.**

1  The paintings by the students will be _____ in the classroom.

2  Charles Darwin said that species _____.

3  White doves are often used to _____ peace.

4  I saw the river _____ the night sky and the moon.

5  The secondhand piano was in good _____.

6  Some animals are very _____ to temperature changes.

7  My parents are _____, so they go to church every Sunday.

8  Last year, the drought _____ the bottom of the river.

# UNIT
# 10 | People

READING 1

Jackie Robinson

History

READING 2

Antonín Dvořák

Music

SPORT NEWS

Jackie Robinson

**⊘ Mini Quiz**

Read and underline the answers in the passage.

Paragraph 2

1 When did Robinson first win the World Series?

Paragraph 3

2 What did Robinson do after his retirement?

In the early 20th century, African-American baseball players were not welcome to play in Major League Baseball (MLB). On April 15, 1947, however, Jackie Robinson broke the baseball color barrier by joining the Brooklyn Dodgers.

Robinson was a brilliantly talented athlete. In his first year in the 5 major leagues, he hit 12 home runs and helped the Dodgers win the National League Championship. In 1949, he was named the National League's Most Valuable Player (MVP). He also led his team to their first World Series victory in 1955. His popularity even inspired the song "Did You See Jackie Robinson Hit That Ball?". 10

**Although** Robinson was a great player, some of his teammates didn't want to play with him. ① He was often insulted and received hate mail and death threats—simply because he was African American. ② However, he never got angry or fought back. ③ His behavior impressed whites as well as blacks and influenced the nonviolent 15 *Civil Rights Movement. ④ The movement continued throughout the 1960s. After he retired in 1957, he tried to fight for the rights of African Americans. On the 50th anniversary of his Major League debut, MLB retired his number, 42, and announced that no other player could wear it except on April 15, which is Jackie Robinson Day. 20

*Civil Rights Movement 미국 흑인 평등권 운동

**Reading Comprehension**

1　What is the passage mainly about?
　　a. how the Civil Rights Movement affected baseball
　　b. why people threatened African-American athletes
　　c. the first African American in Major League Baseball
　　d. a talented athlete who was stopped by the color barrier

**Writing Practice**

2　According to the passage, what does the underlined part mean?
　　In the early 1900s, African-American baseball players ＿＿＿＿＿＿＿＿＿＿＿＿＿＿＿＿＿
　　in Major League Baseball.

3　Which sentence is NOT needed in the passage?
　　a. ①　　　　　b. ②　　　　　c. ③　　　　　d. ④

4　What can be answered based on the passage?
　　a. How many home runs did Jackie hit in 1949?
　　b. Who sang "Did You See Jackie Robinson Hit That Ball?"?
　　c. Why did Robinson help the Civil Rights Movement?
　　d. When are MLB players allowed to wear number 42?

---

🔍 **GRAMMAR Inside** LEVEL 2 　　　☰

양보를 나타내는 접속사

though, although, even though는 양보를 나타내는 접속사로, '~에도 불구하고, 비록 ~이지만'이라는
의미이다. 비슷한 의미로 even if(만약 ~할지라도)를 쓸 수 있다.

**Although** Robinson was a great player, some of his teammates … .
　　　　　　로빈슨이 뛰어난 선수임에도 불구하고
**Though** it snowed heavily, they went camping.
　　　　비록 눈이 많이 왔지만

**Link to …** 👆
　　Chapter 10
　　　Unit 02

**Check Up**　다음 문장을 우리말로 해석하시오.

　　1　Though the information was not true, everyone believed it.
　　　→ ＿＿＿＿＿＿＿＿＿＿＿＿＿＿＿＿＿＿＿＿＿＿＿

　　2　Even though she left home early, Jane was late for school.
　　　→ ＿＿＿＿＿＿＿＿＿＿＿＿＿＿＿＿＿＿＿＿＿＿＿

# Antonín Dvořák

Even if you don't like classical music, you may have heard "From the New World." It is a world-famous symphony by Antonín Dvořák, a 19th-century Czech composer. Dvořák is famous for his beautiful symphonies, but interestingly, he had another passion: trains.

When he was nine years old, a new railway line was built right 5 through his hometown. One spring day, a mighty steam train rushed past him, making an overwhelming sound. That day, little Dvořák fell in love with trains. Dvořák's love for trains lasted throughout his lifetime. Whenever he traveled by train, he spent hours studying train schedules. And each time he changed trains at the station, he **used to chat** with 10 the engineers about trains.

His love for trains also _____. For example, his Symphony No. 7 was born at a railway station. When he was standing in a railway station in Prague, a melody came into his mind. This became one of his greatest works. Dvořák also admired the 15 complex design and technical achievements of trains. Like the many parts of a train, Dvořák's symphonies use many instruments working together to produce a dramatic effect.

**V Mini Quiz**

While you read, check *T* if it is true, or *F* if it is false.

1 When Dvořák was young, a new railway line was built in his town.
☐ T ☐ F

2 Symphony No.7 was played at a station in Prague.
☐ T ☐ F

**Reading Comprehension**

**1** What is the best title for the passage?

   **a.** A Composer Who Loved Trains

   **b.** A Symphony Performed on a Train

   **c.** Using the Sounds of Trains in Music

   **d.** Antonín Dvořák: A Musician and an Engineer

**2** What is NOT included in the underlined part?

   **a.** He studied train schedules for hours.

   **b.** He collected many kinds of toy trains.

   **c.** He chatted with engineers at stations.

   **d.** He admired the technical achievements of trains.

**3** What is the best choice for the blank?

   **a.** led to his success                **b.** motivated him to travel

   **c.** inspired his music                 **d.** made him want to study trains

**Writing Practice**

**4** According to the passage, what is the similarity between trains and Dvořák's music?

His music uses _____ to make a dramatic effect like

the many parts of a train do.

---

**GRAMMAR Inside** LEVEL 2

여러 가지 조동사

can, may, must 등의 조동사 이외에도 본동사 앞에 쓰여 다양한 의미를 더하는 조동사들이 있다.

…, he **used to chat** with the engineers about trains. 〈used to + 동사원형: ~하곤 했다〉
    이야기를 나누곤 했다

I **used to be** an interior designer. 〈used to + 동사원형: ~이었다 (과거의 상태)〉
  (과거에) 인테리어 디자이너였다

The workers **would like to take** a break. 〈would like to + 동사원형: ~하고 싶다〉
          휴식을 취하고 싶다

You **had better eat** healthier food. 〈had better + 동사원형: ~하는 것이 낫다〉
  먹는 것이 낫다

**Link to …** 🖐
📁 Chapter 03
📁 Unit 03

········································

**Check Up** 다음 문장을 우리말로 해석하시오.

   This news is a sensitive issue. We had better keep quiet about it.

   → _____

# VOCABULARY INSIDE

| READING 1 | READING 2 |
|---|---|
| ☐ **talented** ⓐ<br>having a special ability to do something<br>ⓝ talent  [syn] brilliant, gifted | ☐ **passion** ⓝ<br>a very strong feeling about something<br>ⓐ passionate  [syn] enthusiasm |
| ☐ **popularity** ⓝ<br>the state of being liked by a lot of people<br>ⓐ popular | ☐ **rush** ⓥ<br>to move very quickly in a certain direction<br>ⓝ rush  [syn] run |
| ☐ **inspire** ⓥ<br>to give someone the motivation to do or create something<br>ⓝ inspiration  [syn] motivate, encourage | ☐ **last** ⓥ<br>to continue existing or happening in time<br>ⓐ lasting |
| ☐ **insult** ⓥ<br>to say or do something offensive and aggressive<br>ⓝ insult | ☐ **admire** ⓥ<br>to respect someone or something<br>[syn] honor, respect |
| ☐ **movement** ⓝ<br>a series of organized actions taken by people to work toward an objective<br>[syn] campaign | ☐ **dramatic** ⓐ<br>exciting and impressive<br>ⓐⓓ dramatically |

**Check Up**

**Fill in the blanks with the words above. Change the form if necessary.**

1 The _____ of skateboarding is increasing.

2 The man has had a _____ for music for a long time.

3 When I was young, a dinosaur movie _____ me to change my life.

4 He is a _____ drummer, so he joined a band.

5 The final match of the World Cup was _____.

6 The movie *Titanic* _____ for three hours and 15 minutes.

7 I have always _____ my father for his courage and strength.

8 When the fire alarm rang, a group of people _____ to the door to get out.

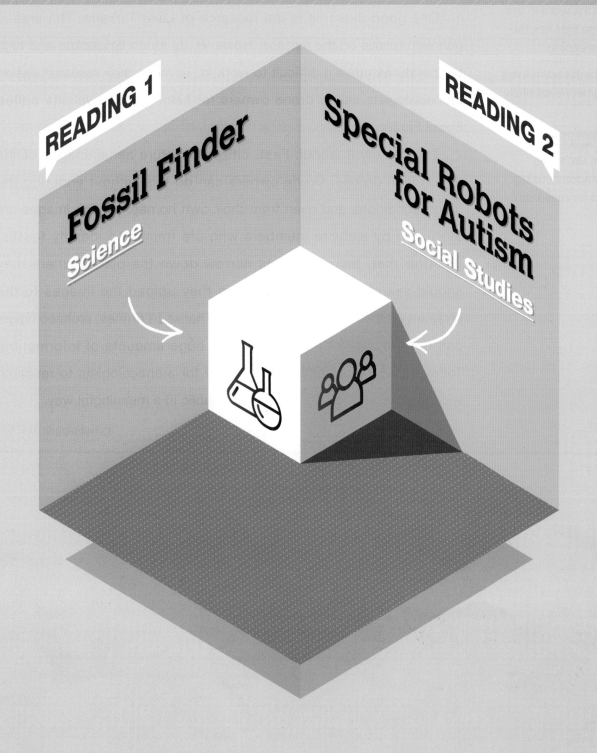

# UNIT
# 11 | Machines

**READING 1**

## Fossil Finder
_Science_

**READING 2**

## Special Robots
## for Autism
_Social Studies_

# Fossil Finder

**⊙ Mini Quiz**

Read and underline the answers in the passage.

**Paragraph 3**

1 Find the word in the passage that has the given meaning.

| to look for something or someone carefully |
| --- |

**Paragraph 3**

2 What are some advantages of using drones for research?

Drones are more than toy airplanes. These **flying** robots can soar above buildings and treetops and capture pictures or videos from hard-to-reach angles. While most people just enjoy flying drones as a hobby, *archaeologists are now able to take advantage of them for research.

One good example is the research of Lake Turkana. The area is rich with fossils on the surface. However, its rough landscape and high temperatures make it difficult to work in. To make their research easier, 10 archaeologists asked drone owners for help, using a website **called** Fossil Finder.

This is how it works: First, citizens capture aerial images of the region with drones. Drone owners can do this without enduring the tough conditions and even from their own homes. (A) The images are 15 evaluated by website members who are trained to identify fossils. (B) After that, archaeologists narrow down the places where they should search for fossils. (C) Then they upload the images to the program on the Fossil Finder website. Thanks to drones, archaeologists can not only save time but also get huge amounts of information. 20 Today, this project has become a way for archaeologists to research wide regions and to interact with the public in a meaningful way.

*archaeologist 고고학자

**Reading Comprehension**

1 **What is the passage mainly about?**
   a. the difficult conditions at Lake Turkana
   b. opinions on using drones to find fossils
   c. why people need to develop new drones
   d. how drones help archaeologists' research

2 **Which is NOT true according to the passage?**
   a. Drones can take pictures from hard-to-reach angles.
   b. The area around Lake Turkana contains a lot of fossils.
   c. Citizens have to go to Lake Turkana to capture the images.
   d. Members of the Fossil Finder website participate in the project.

3 **What is the best order of the sentences (A)~(C)?**
   a. (A) – (C) – (B)                    b. (B) – (C) – (A)
   c. (C) – (A) – (B)                    d. (C) – (B) – (A)

Writing Practice

4 **According to the passage, why is it difficult to work in the area around Lake Turkana?**
   because of the area's _____

---

Q    GRAMMAR **Inside** LEVEL 2                        ≡

현재분사와 과거분사
분사는 형용사처럼 쓰여 명사를 수식하거나 주어나 목적어를 보충 설명하는 보어 역할을 한다. 현재분사
(v-ing)는 '~하는, ~하고 있는'의 의미로 〈능동·진행〉을 나타내며, 과거분사(v-ed)는 '~된, ~한'의 의미로
〈수동·완료〉를 나타낸다. 분사는 보통 명사 앞에서 수식하지만 수식어구와 함께 와서 길어질 때는 명사 뒤에서
수식한다.

These **flying** robots can soar above buildings and treetops and … . 〈현재분사: 능동〉
         이 비행하는 로봇들
I talked to the man **working** at the ticket counter. 〈현재분사: 진행〉
                    매표소에서 일하고 있는 남자
…, using a website **called** Fossil Finder. 〈과거분사: 수동〉
             Fossil Finder라고 불리는 웹 사이트
Hailey found her **lost** book in the school bus. 〈과거분사: 완료〉
                 그녀의 분실한 책

 **Link to …**
Chapter 06
Unit 01

# Special Robots for Autism

**v Mini Quiz**

While you read, check *T* if it is true, or *F* if it is false.

1 Robots can teach autistic children how to pronounce certain words.
☐ T ☐ F

2 Children can learn how to act properly through interaction with robots.
☐ T ☐ F

Anthony is a seven-year-old boy with *autism. Today, he is spending time with a smiling robot. "What is your favorite food?" asks the robot. "Chocolate milk and french fries," replies Anthony. "I love chocolate milk, too!" says the robot. It raises its arm and rubs its belly, and Anthony copies the movement. They are communicating with **each** 5 **other**.

Children with autism struggle to communicate and read facial expressions. As a result of their poor _____ (A) _____, some of them can become isolated. Sadly, treatment is often delayed, as it is difficult to notice their abnormal responses at an early age. 10

To help **autistic children develop their _____ (B) _____, scientists have invented special robots. They feature a highly expressive face that teaches autistic children to identify emotions. Children are asked to choose the emotion matching the robot's facial expression. Meanwhile, their reactions are recorded. Through 15 interaction with the robot, they learn to express empathy and act properly in social situations. Doctors can observe each response and calculate the child's reaction time. This helps them diagnose autism at an early age. These robots are helping many autistic children by acting as a friend, educator, and therapist to them. 20

*autism 자폐증
**autistic 자폐증의

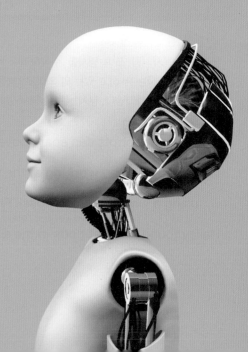

**Reading Comprehension**

1  What is the best title for the passage?
   a. Doctors or Robots: Who Can Diagnose Autism Sooner?
   b. How Interactive Robots Can Help Autistic Children
   c. Robots: The Only Way to Help Autistic Children
   d. New Technologies to Prevent Autism

2  What is the best choice for the blanks (A) and (B)?
   a. social skills                    b. intelligence
   c. language                         d. mental health

3  What is the purpose of measuring the children's reaction time?
   a. to show their growth             b. to communicate better with them
   c. to diagnose autism sooner        d. to improve the systems of the robots

**Writing Practice**

4  According to the passage, what does the underlined part refer to?

_____

---

🔍  GRAMMAR **Inside** LEVEL 2                                    ≡

**부정대명사 표현**
부정대명사란 말 그대로 정해지지 않은 불특정한 사람이나 사물을 가리키는 대명사로서, 특정한 대상을 지칭하는 it, them과 구별된다. 부정대명사를 활용한 표현은 대표적으로 다음과 같다.

**Link to ...**

Chapter 08
Unit 02

• each other / one another: 서로
  They are communicating with **each other**.

• one ~ the other ...: (둘 중의) 하나는 ~, 다른 하나는 …
  one ~, another ...: (셋 이상의 대상 중에) 하나는 ~, 또 다른 (불특정한) 하나는 …
  I bought two gifts. **One** is for my mom, and **the other** is for my dad.
  Each macaron has a different color. **One** is red, and **another** is blue.

• some ~ others ...: 어떤 것[사람]들은 ~, 다른 어떤 것[사람]들은 …
  some ~, the others ...: 어떤 것[사람]들은 ~, 나머지 모든 것[사람]들은 …
  **Some** like chocolate and **others** like candy.
  **Some** are kids, and **the others** are adults.

# VOCABULARY INSIDE

| READING 1 | READING 2 |
|---|---|
| ☐ **take advantage of**<br>to use something so that it helps you<br>syn use | ☐ **feature** (v)<br>to have a particular thing as an important aspect<br>(n) feature |
| ☐ **research** (n)<br>a detailed study of something done in order to find new knowledge about it<br>(v) research   syn investigation, study | ☐ **interaction** (n)<br>two-way communication with someone or something else<br>(v) interact   (a) interactive |
| ☐ **endure** (v)<br>to suffer something difficult for a long time<br>(n) endurance   syn bear | ☐ **properly** (ad)<br>in an acceptable or suitable way<br>(a) proper   syn correctly |
| ☐ **evaluate** (v)<br>to think carefully about something before making a judgment about it<br>(n) evaluation   syn assess, rate | ☐ **observe** (v)<br>to watch something closely<br>(n) observation   syn watch, monitor |
| ☐ **identify** (v)<br>to recognize exactly what something is<br>(n) identification   syn find, discover | ☐ **diagnose** (v)<br>to identify an illness or problem by examining it |

**Check Up**

**Fill in the blanks with the words above. Change the form if necessary.**

1 Let's watch the _____ between the dog and the cat.

2 The scientists are _____ the movements of the wild animals.

3 Cameras were used to _____ the thief.

4 The interviewees were _____ after the interview.

5 This machine is used to help _____ cancer.

6 The mountain climber had to _____ the cold climate.

7 The hotel _____ an outdoor pool.

8 The family decided to _____ the nice weather and went camping.

# UNIT
# 12 | Health

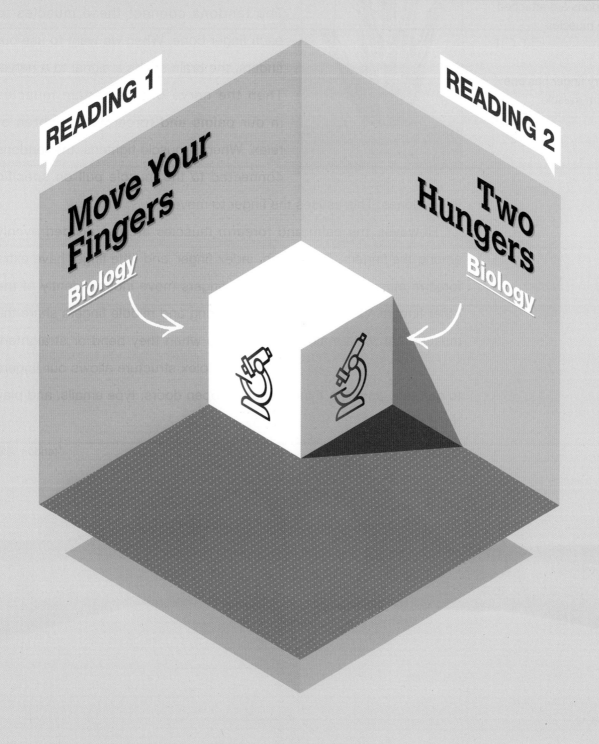

READING 1

## Move Your Fingers

*Biology*

READING 2

## Two Hungers

*Biology*

# Move Your Fingers

Do you know how many finger muscles there are? What if I told you there were none? Surprisingly, it's true! Our fingers have no muscles, but they have *tendons. Tendons are only connective tissue, so they can't move any body parts **by themselves**. How do our fingers move, then? 5

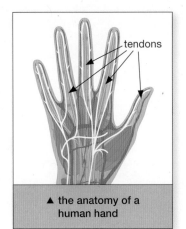

tendons

▲ the anatomy of a human hand

The tendons in our hands are attached to the muscles in our palms and forearms. The tendons connect these muscles to each finger bone. When we want to use our fingers, the brain sends a signal to a nerve. 10 Then the nerve orders certain muscles in our palms and forearms to tighten or relax. When a muscle tightens, the tendons connected to the muscle pull on specific finger bones. This causes the finger to move. 15

However, the palm and forearm muscles are not divided evenly among the fingers. The thumb, index finger, and little finger have extra forearm muscles. This helps these fingers move independently of the other fingers. On the other hand, the ring and middle fingers share the muscle that moves all the fingers. So when they bend or straighten, 20 _____. This complex structure allows our fingers to do many amazing things, such as open doors, type emails, and play the piano!

*tendon 힘줄

**Reading Comprehension**

**1** **What is the passage mainly about?**
a. how to build strong finger muscles
b. why all the fingers move the same way
c. the complex system that makes our fingers move
d. the difference between muscles, tendons, and nerves

**2** **Match the sequence in order from (1) to (3).**

> The brain sends signals to a nerve. → (1) → (2) → (3)

(1) •                          • a. The fingers move.
(2) •                          • b. The tendon pulls on specific finger bones.
(3) •                          • c. The nerve orders certain muscles to tighten or relax.

**3** **What is the best choice for the blank?**
a. the other fingers will, too          b. the little finger will be raised
c. the palm muscles will tighten       d. one finger will cross over another

**Writing Practice**

**4** **According to the passage, what is the difference between the index and middle finger?**
Unlike the middle finger, the index finger has _____,
so it can move _____.

---

**Q    GRAMMAR Inside LEVEL 2    ≡**

**재귀대명사를 포함한 관용 표현**
'~ 자신'이라는 의미를 가지는 재귀대명사(-self[-selves])는 여러 가지 관용 표현으로 쓰인다.
• in itself: 원래, 그 자체가                          • for oneself: 혼자 힘으로
• by oneself: 홀로, 혼자서(= alone), 혼자 힘으로     • beside oneself: 제정신이 아닌
• between ourselves: 우리끼리 이야기인데              • help oneself to: ~을 마음껏 먹다

..., so they can't move any body parts **by themselves**.
                                              그것들만으로

We made dinner **for ourselves**.
                우리들 힘으로

**Link to ...**
Chapter 08
Unit 03

**Check Up**  우리말과 일치하도록 ( ) 안의 말을 이용하여 문장을 완성하시오.
그는 시험에 떨어졌을 때 제정신이 아니었다. (beside)
→ He was _____ _____ when he failed the test.

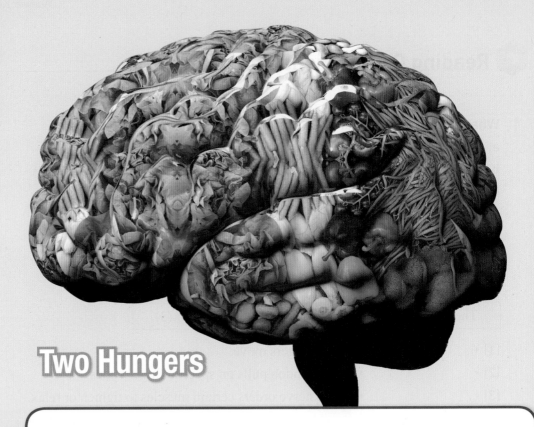

# Two Hungers

People usually feel hunger at least a few times each day. But did you know that there are two different kinds of hunger? Most people think of hunger as the body's physical need for food. If you haven't eaten for a while, your stomach starts to feel empty and makes noises. This means your body needs more calories, and it **is referred to** as 5 *homeostatic hunger.

The other kind of hunger is called **hedonic hunger. Contrary to homeostatic hunger, hedonic hunger is caused by a(n) _____ need. ① For example, when you are stressed, you might have a strong desire for snacks. ② Your body doesn't need these calories, 10 but your brain still tells you to consume them. ③ You should not skip a meal or your body won't function well. ④ This is because you have unconsciously trained yourself to eat snacks under certain situations.

Homeostatic hunger and hedonic hunger are like two ends of the same line. Despite their differences, they aren't completely separate 15 from each other. So it's possible to feel both at the same time. But the next time you feel hungry, don't be tricked into eating for the wrong reasons.

*homeostatic 항상성(恒常性)의
**hedonic 쾌락의

**Reading Comprehension**

1 What is the purpose of this passage?
   a. to explain the need for a balanced diet
   b. to describe the different causes of hunger
   c. to warn people about the danger of snacks
   d. to recommend having healthy eating habits

2 What is the best choice for the blank?
   a. physical          b. emotional          c. natural          d. reasonable

3 Which sentence is NOT needed in the passage?
   a. ①          b. ②          c. ③          d. ④

**Writing Practice**

4 Write *homeostatic* or *hedonic* for each type of hunger.
   (1) When I feel mad, I like to eat spicy food.          _____
   (2) I feel hungry because I skipped breakfast.          _____
   (3) I want to drink some coffee because I am tired.          _____

---

Q     GRAMMAR **Inside** LEVEL 2          ≡

<u>동사구의 수동태</u>
동사구는 수동태로 바꿀 때 하나의 동사로 취급하여 붙여 쓴다.
..., and people **refer to** it as homeostatic hunger.
→ ..., and it **is referred to** as homeostatic hunger (by people).

All students **look up to** the teacher.
→ The teacher **is looked up to** by all students.

아래와 같은 동사구를 예로 들 수 있다.
• take care of: ~을 돌보다          • look after: ~을 돌보다          • laugh at: ~을 비웃다
• look up to: ~을 존경하다          • look down on: ~을 경멸하다          • refer to: ~을 부르다
• put off: ~을 연기하다          • bring up: ~을 키우다

Link to ...
　Chapter 07
　Unit 03

**Check Up** 우리말과 일치하도록 (   ) 안의 말을 이용하여 문장을 완성하시오.
　　그 아이들은 그들의 부모님 대신 그들의 할머니에게 보살핌을 받았다. (take care of)
　　→ The children _____ by their grandmother instead of their parents.

# ⬡ VOCABULARY INSIDE

| READING 1 | READING 2 |
|---|---|
| ☐ **muscle** (n)<br>a type of body tissue that produces movement | ☐ **empty** (a)<br>to have nothing inside<br>(v) empty<br>[syn] hollow, vacant   [ant] full |
| ☐ **connect** (v)<br>to join or link things together<br>(n) connection   (a) connective<br>[syn] link, join, attach   [ant] disconnect | ☐ **desire** (n)<br>a strong feeling of wanting something or wanting to do something<br>(v) desire |
| ☐ **bone** (n)<br>the hard parts that form the frame of the body | ☐ **skip** (v)<br>to leave out a step in a progression<br>[syn] leave out |
| ☐ **signal** (n)<br>a sign that has special meaning; an electrical impulse<br>(v) signal   [syn] sign | ☐ **function** (v)<br>to work in the correct way<br>(n) function   [syn] work, operate |
| ☐ **bend** (v)<br>to fold or curve<br>[syn] twist, curve | ☐ **trick** (v)<br>to make someone believe something is true even though it is not<br>(n) trick   [syn] deceive |

**Check Up** — **Fill in the blanks with the words above. Change the form if necessary.**

1 The referee gave the _____ to stop by blowing the whistle.

2 The machine _____ well now because it was fixed.

3 You can _____ the questions for which you don't know the answers.

4 The magician is able to _____ people's eyes.

5 First, remove the _____ from the chicken, so it's easier to eat.

6 The wires came apart, so she _____ them again.

7 The suitcase is not heavy, because it's almost _____.

8 Slowly _____ over to touch the floor.

# UNIT
# 13 | Maps

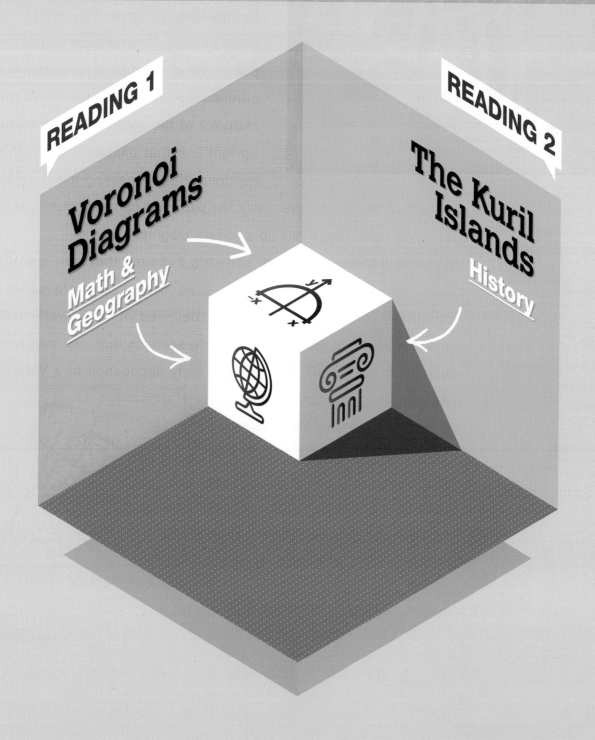

READING 1

Voronoi Diagrams

Math & Geography

READING 2

The Kuril Islands

History

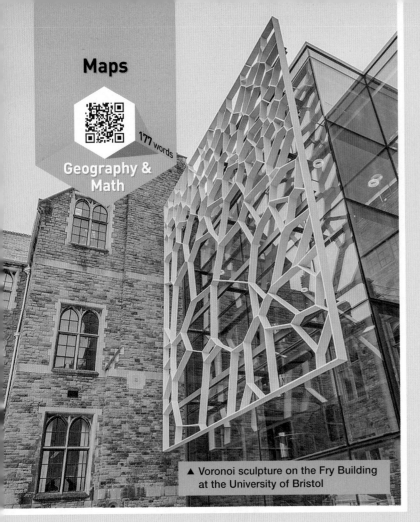

▲ Voronoi sculpture on the Fry Building at the University of Bristol

# Voronoi Diagrams

Voronoi diagrams look random, but they are carefully divided into regions based on distance. To draw one, start **by marking** a number of points on a piece of paper. Then choose two of the 5 points. Next, imagine an invisible line connecting the two points. Find the midpoint of the invisible line. Draw an upright line that passes through this midpoint. Keep repeating this process 10 with sets of two points. Eventually, the paper will contain a multitude of *polygonal cells. They make up a Voronoi diagram.

These diagrams are very valuable because they can identify _____. In 1854, **cholera spread throughout London. Dr. John Snow believed drinking water was 15 the cause of it. He divided London into sections that had their own separate water supply. <u>This</u> was an early application of a Voronoi diagram. The diagram helped him locate the areas with polluted water. The results showed that most deaths were coming from Soho. After removing the pump in Soho, death rates quickly dropped. As you can see, the practice **of** carefully **dividing** a region can be quite powerful.

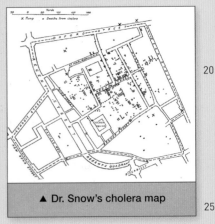

▲ Dr. Snow's cholera map

20

25

*polygonal 다각형의
**cholera 콜레라

## Mini Quiz

Read and underline the answers in the passage.

**Paragraph 1**

1 Find the word in the passage that has the given meaning.

> to think of something in the mind as if it were real

**Paragraph 2**

2 What does "This" refer to in the passage?

**Reading Comprehension**

1  **What is the passage mainly about?**
   a. constructing the Voronoi diagram in maps
   b. the geographic value of Voronoi diagrams
   c. how a Voronoi diagram is drawn and used
   d. where and how the Voronoi diagram was created

2  **What is the best choice for the blank?**
   a. the sources of disease
   b. social problems in cities
   c. fast routes to a destination
   d. where unpolluted areas are

3  **What is the best choice for the blank in the given sentence?**

   By using a Voronoi diagram, Dr. Snow was able to find out which _____.

   a. patients could get medicine
   b. deaths could be prevented
   c. water supplies had been polluted
   d. areas could be provided with water

**Writing Practice**

4  **Complete the process of drawing a Voronoi diagram. Use the words from the passage.**

(1)   (2)   (3)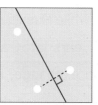

(1) First, _____ many points randomly on a piece of paper and choose two points.
(2) Next, find the _____ of the line connecting the two points.
(3) Last, draw a(n) _____ line that passes through the midpoint.

---

Q  **GRAMMAR Inside** LEVEL 2                                                        ≡

「전치사＋동명사」

• 동명사는 동사의 목적어 뿐 아니라 전치사의 목적어로도 쓰인다.
  To draw one, start **by marking** a number of points on a piece of paper.
  <small>표시하는 것으로 시작해라</small>
  As you can see, the practice **of** carefully **dividing** a region can be quite powerful.
  <small>신중하게 나누는 행위는</small>
• 부정형으로 쓸 때는 동명사 앞에 not을 붙여 쓴다.
  I felt sorry **for not keeping** my promise.

Link to ...
Chapter 05
Unit 01

# The Kuril Islands

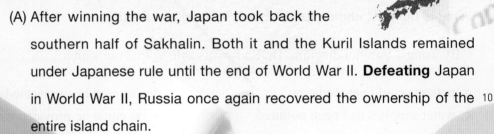

Kuril Islands

Sakhalin

Russia

Japan

**V** Mini Quiz

Find the answers from the passage and write them.

**Paragraph 5**

1 What can Russian ships access year-round through the islands?

→ _____

**Paragraph 5**

2 What has Russia constructed on the islands?

→ _____

The Kuril Islands are a chain of 56 islands. They stretch from Hokkaido in Japan to Russia's Kamchatka Peninsula. For nearly 170 years, the islands have caused significant tension between the two nations.

(A) After winning the war, Japan took back the southern half of Sakhalin. Both it and the Kuril Islands remained under Japanese rule until the end of World War II. **Defeating** Japan in World War II, Russia once again recovered the ownership of the entire island chain.

(B) Ownership of the Kuril Islands was first established by the Treaty of Shimoda in 1855. The treaty gave Japan control of the four southern islands, while Russia gained possession of the rest.

(C) Twenty years later, a new treaty granted Japan the entire island chain. In exchange, Russia gained full control of Sakhalin Island. Over the next three decades, growing competition between the two countries led to *the Russo-Japanese War.

Today the Kuril Islands are home to around 20,000 people. Due to their _____, they have political value for Russia. The **strait does not freeze in winter, allowing Russian ships to access the Pacific Ocean year-round. Russia has also constructed military bases on the islands, which are rich in minerals and precious metals.

*the Russo-Japanese War 러일전쟁
**strait 해협

**Reading Comprehension**

1  **What is the best title for the passage?**
  a. The Tragic Effects of World War II
  b. The History of a Disputed Territory
  c. A Nation's Desire for Ocean Resources
  d. The Kuril Islands as a Tourist Destination

2  **What is the right order of the paragraphs (A)~(C)?**
  a. (A) – (C) – (B)      b. (B) – (A) – (C)
  c. (B) – (C) – (A)      d. (C) – (A) – (B)

3  **What is the best choice for the blank?**
  a. location      b. resources      c. population      d. size

4  **Which CANNOT be answered based on the passage?**
  a. Which country gained control of the Kuril Islands after World War II?
  b. When was ownership of the Kuril Islands first established?
  c. How long did the Russo-Japanese War last?
  d. What kinds of natural resources are there on the Kuril Islands?

---

Q     GRAMMAR **Inside** LEVEL 2                                        ≡

분사구문의 의미 1 (시간)
분사구문은 부사절의 주어와 주절의 주어가 같을 때, 접속사와 주어를 생략하고 부사절의 동사를 분사 형태로
바꿔서 쓴다. 분사구문의 의미에는 여러 가지가 있지만, 그중 〈시간〉을 나타낼 때 '~할 때, ~하는 동안, ~한
후에' 등으로 해석한다.

Link to ...

Chapter 06
Unit 02

**Defeating** Japan in World War II, Russia once again recovered the ownership … .
      제2차 세계대전에서 일본을 이겼을 때
← **When _Russia defeated_** Japan in World War II, _Russia_ once again recovered the ownership … .
**Leaving** his house, he locked the door.
    그의 집을 떠날 때
← **When** _he left_ his house, _he_ locked the door.

Check Up  밑줄 친 부분에 유의하여 다음 문장을 우리말로 해석하시오.
      Cleaning my room, I found some old photos.
      → _____

# 🔷 VOCABULARY INSIDE

| READING 1 | READING 2 |
|---|---|
| ☐ **invisible** ⓐ<br>not able to be seen<br>[ant] visible | ☐ **tension** ⓝ<br>a situation in which people or groups feel fear or anger toward one another |
| ☐ **repeat** ⓥ<br>to do something again and again<br>ⓝ repetition   [syn] replay | ☐ **remain** ⓥ<br>to continue to be in a particular situation<br>[syn] stay |
| ☐ **valuable** ⓐ<br>very important and useful<br>ⓝ value   [syn] important, worthwhile<br>[ant] valueless | ☐ **entire** ⓐ<br>every part of something<br>ⓐⒹ entirely   [syn] full, whole |
| ☐ **separate** ⓐ<br>not joined or related, different from something else<br>ⓥ separate   [syn] individual | ☐ **gain** ⓥ<br>to get or achieve something as a result of effort<br>ⓝ gain   [syn] acquire |
| ☐ **remove** ⓥ<br>to take something away from a place<br>ⓝ removal | ☐ **metal** ⓝ<br>a hard, shiny substance such as iron, gold, or steel<br>ⓐ metallic |

**Check Up**   **Fill in the blanks with the words above. Change the form if necessary.**

1  The wind is _____, but we can feel it.

2  The room has two _____ beds, so we don't have to sleep together.

3  The _____ between the two political parties is growing fierce.

4  _____ the stuff on your desk before taking the test.

5  He _____ silent even though the reporter asked him a question.

6  The CEO donated her _____ salary to charity.

7  The country _____ independence after the war ended.

8  Because the hall was so noisy, I had to _____ the words many times.

# UNIT
# 14 | Paintings

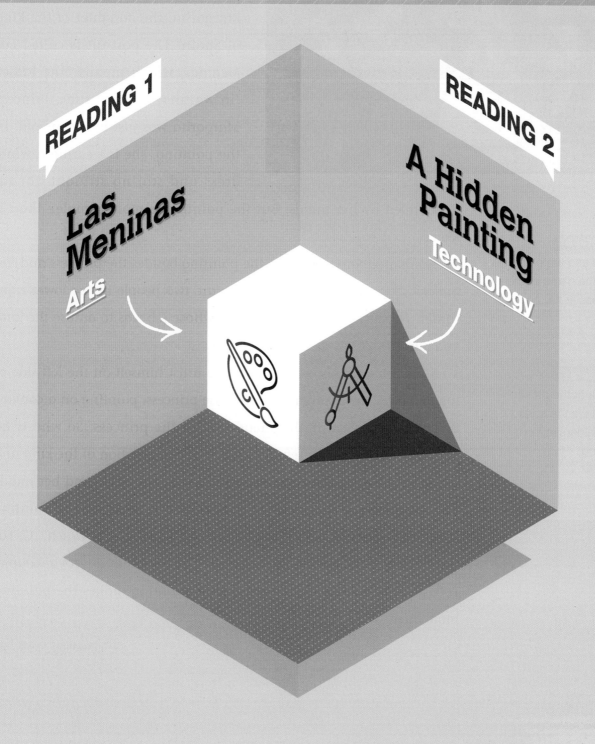

READING 1

Las Meninas

Arts

READING 2

A Hidden Painting

Technology

# Paintings

Arts

# Las Meninas

Diego Velázquez was a 17th-century Spanish painter. One of his most famous portraits was of Princess Margarita, the daughter of the king of Spain. The portrait is called *Las* 5 *Meninas*, which means "the ladies *in waiting." At that time, Princess Margarita was just five years old. In the painting, she is wearing a white dress and staring straight ahead, 10 surrounded by her maids. But the painting is more complex than it seems.

There are many people in the painting besides the princess and her maids. _____, there are two people in the lower right corner. These were royal entertainers **whose** job was to amuse the king 15 and queen.

More interestingly, you can see the artist himself on the left side of the painting. He is standing behind the princess, painting on a canvas. But he is staring straight ahead, not at the princess. So who is he painting? If you look carefully, you can see a reflection of the king and 20 queen in the mirror on the back wall. (A) The princess and her maids were just there to watch. (B) Others, however, think he was painting Margarita, and it was the king and queen who came to watch. (C) For this reason, some people think that he was painting the royal couple. Focusing on the different objects of the painting makes the painting 25 more interesting.

*in waiting 시중을 드는

## Mini Quiz

**Paragraph 1**

1 Find and write what the name of the princess in the portrait is.

→ _____

**Picture**

2 Look at the picture and circle the royal entertainers in the painting.

## Reading Comprehension

1 **What is the passage mainly about?**
   **a.** the details of Velázquez's portrait
   **b.** who Princess Margarita's maids were
   **c.** reasons why Velázquez painted royal families
   **d.** the difficulties faced by a Spanish portrait painter

2 **What is the best choice for the blank?**
   **a.** However          **b.** For example          **c.** Therefore          **d.** On the other hand

3 **What is the right order of the sentences (A)~(C)?**
   **a.** (A) – (C) – (B)                    **b.** (B) – (A) – (C)
   **c.** (C) – (A) – (B)                    **d.** (C) – (B) – (A)

> Writing Practice

4 **According to the passage, who can be seen in the mirror's reflection?**

   _____

---

> **Q   GRAMMAR Inside LEVEL 2**                                        ≡

소유격 관계대명사 whose

whose는 관계사절 내에서 선행사가 소유격의 역할을 할 때 사용하며, 선행사가 사람일 때와 사물일 때 모두 쓸 수 있다.

These were <u>royal entertainers</u> [**whose** job was to amuse the king and queen].
← These were <u>royal entertainers</u>. + <u>Their</u> job was to amuse the king and queen.

There are <u>many buildings</u> [**whose** windows are large].
← There are <u>many buildings</u>. + <u>Their</u> windows are large.

Link to ...

Chapter 11
Unit 01

---

Check Up   관계대명사 whose를 이용하여 다음 두 문장을 한 문장으로 쓰시오.

   **1** Tom is a popular singer. + His songs have stayed at the top of the music charts.
      → _____

   **2** In the school, there are many people. + Their homes were destroyed by the tornado.
      → _____

# Paintings

Technology

202 words

## A Hidden Painting

**Ⓥ Mini Quiz**

Read and underline the answers in the passage.

**Paragraph 3**

1 What is behind Van Gogh's *Patch of Grass*?

**Paragraph 4**

2 When was the portrait painted?

Vincent van Gogh is one of the most beloved artists in history. Interestingly, a new technology has contributed to finding another one of his artworks. And where was it found? It was actually hidden beneath another of Van Gogh's paintings.

The story of the discovery began with Van Gogh's *Patch of Grass*, 5 which was painted in 1887. At first, researchers found the unclear outline of a head in the painting. To find out what it was, they used a new X-ray technique.

The X-ray technique is special because it can show the color as well as the outline of hidden 10 paintings, revealing the image like a color photo. When researchers carefully scanned the deeper layers of the painting, a portrait of a rural Dutch woman finally emerged.

▲ the portrait under *Patch of Grass*

The image of the woman has helped researchers _____ 15 _____. The portrait was painted around two and a half years before *Patch of Grass*. Living in the Netherlands at that time, Van Gogh painted many models to practice color and light techniques. The researchers believe that, **being** poor, he painted grass over the woman to reuse the canvas. This discovery shows how his drawing style and 20 color choice developed. It also proves that even masters need practice!

**Reading Comprehension**

1  **What is the best title for the passage?**

   a. New Technology Helps Painters

   b. Is This a Fake Van Gogh Painting?

   c. Researchers Finally Found Stolen Artwork

   d. A New X-Ray Discovers an Artistic Surprise

2  **What is NOT true according to the passage?**

   a. Researchers saw an unclear head underneath *Patch of Grass*.

   b. The X-ray technique shows images in black and white.

   c. Van Gogh improved his painting style in the Netherlands.

   d. Researchers think that Van Gogh reused his canvas.

3  **What is the best choice for the blank?**

   a. analyze *Patch of Grass*          b. find out how poor Van Gogh was

   c. understand the artwork of Van Gogh    d. prove that Van Gogh was a great artist

**Writing Practice**

4  **Fill in the blank with words from the passage.**

   When he lived in the Netherlands, Van Gogh painted models _____

   _____ .

---

Q    **GRAMMAR Inside** LEVEL 2    ≡

분사구문의 의미 2 (이유, 동시동작)

분사구문은 부사절인 「접속사 + 주어 + 동사」를 분사가 이끄는 부사구로 나타낸 구문이다. 분사구문은 보통 「접속사 + 주어」가 생략되어 있고, 동사는 분사(v-ing, v-ed) 형태이기 때문에, 분사구문의 여러 용법 중 나타내고자 하는 의미가 무엇인지 문맥을 통해서 파악해야 한다.

**Link to ...**

Chapter 06
Unit 02

..., **being poor**, he painted grass over the woman to reuse the canvas. 〈이유〉
  가난했기 때문에

← ... **because** he was poor, he painted grass over the woman ... .

**Hoping** to ride faster, I pushed the pedals as fast as I could. 〈동시동작〉
  더 빠르게 달리길 바라면서

← **As** I hoped to ride faster, I pushed the pedals as fast as I could.

# VOCABULARY INSIDE

| READING 1 | READING 2 |
| --- | --- |
| ☐ **portrait** (n)<br>a painting or photograph of a person | ☐ **artwork** (n)<br>objects such as paintings or sculptures<br>(syn) art |
| ☐ **stare** (v)<br>to look at something directly for a long time<br>(syn) gaze, watch | ☐ **beneath** (prep)<br>directly under something or at a lower level<br>(ad) beneath<br>(syn) under, below    (ant) over, above |
| ☐ **surround** (v)<br>to be all around something | ☐ **outline** (n)<br>the outer shape of something |
| ☐ **royal** (a)<br>related to or connected with a king or a queen<br>(n) royalty | ☐ **reveal** (v)<br>to cause something to be seen<br>(syn) disclose |
| ☐ **amuse** (v)<br>to do or say something to make somebody laugh or smile<br>(n) amusement   (syn) entertain | ☐ **emerge** (v)<br>to come out of something or out from behind something<br>(n) emergence   (syn) come out, appear |

**Check Up**

**Fill in the blanks with the words above. Change the form if necessary.**

1 The _____ palace is full of gold and riches.

2 The soldiers made a shelter _____ the hill.

3 A(n) _____ of the king hangs in the palace.

4 The island is _____ by the sea.

5 The band's performance has _____ the audience.

6 The child drew the _____ of his hand with a crayon.

7 This museum features many traditional _____ of African culture.

8 A woman was _____ at me from across the street.

# The Chocolate Hills

**V Mini Quiz**

Read and underline the answers in the passage.

**Paragraph 2**

1 Find what happened after Arogo's love died in the legend.

**Paragraph 3**

2 Find the word in the passage that has the given meaning.

| causing great surprise or astonishment |

Imagine a thousand chocolate kisses, each as big as a hill. **If** you like the sound of that, then you should visit the Philippines! The "Chocolate Hills" are located on Bohol Island in the Philippines.

▲ lots of chocolate kisses

5

The hills are quite small, mostly 30 to 50 meters high. There are at least 1,300, all standing next to each other. The hills got their name because they look like chocolate when the grass of the hills turns brown in the dry season.

There are many legends about _____. One famous story is that two fighting giants spent days throwing rocks and dirt at each other. When the fight ended, they left without cleaning up their mess, and it became the hills. Another story tells of a giant, Arogo, who fell in love with a human woman. When his true love sadly died, his giant teardrops became the hills.

10

15

Legends aside, scientists believe that the hills were once coral reefs in the ocean before they were *uplifted. Then wind and rain smoothed the hills over thousands of years. This is just a theory, however, as nobody knows for certain how the chocolate hills were made. But that just makes this natural phenomenon even more amazing!

20

*uplift 땅을 융기시키다, 위로 올리다

**Reading Comprehension**

1  **What is the best title for the passage?**
   a. Bohol Island: The Jewel of the Philippines
   b. Ancient Legends about the Chocolate Hills
   c. A Mysterious Natural Phenomenon of the Philippines
   d. The Philippines: Home of the World's Tastiest Chocolates

2  **What is true according to the passage?**
   a. Most of the hills are more than 50 meters high.
   b. Legend says that a giant's teardrops became the hills.
   c. Studies show that wind and rain caused the hills to be uplifted.
   d. Scientists have proven that the hills were once a large coral reef.

3  **What is the best choice for the blank?**
   a. what the hills look like          b. why the hills are not tall
   c. where the hills were made         d. how the hills were formed

Writing Practice
4  **According to the passage, why do the people call the hills the "Chocolate Hills"?**
   because the hills look like chocolates when the grass of the hills _____

---

### GRAMMAR **Inside** LEVEL 2

**조건을 나타내는 접속사**

• 조건을 나타내는 접속사로는 '~한다면, ~라면'의 뜻의 if, '만약 ~하지 않으면'의 뜻의 unless가 있다.
  unless는 if ~ not으로 바꿔 쓸 수 있다.

  **If** you like the sound of that, then you should visit the Philippines!
      만약 그 말이 듣기 좋다면
  **Unless** you call your mom right now, she will be very angry.
        만약 네가 어머니께 지금 당장 전화하지 않는다면
  (= **If** you **don't** call your mom right now)

• 조건을 나타내는 부사절에서는 현재시제가 미래시제를 대신한다.
  If you **miss** the last bus, you will have to take a taxi. (~~If you will miss the last bus~~)

Link to ...
Chapter 10
Unit 02

**Check Up** 두 문장의 의미가 비슷하도록 unless를 사용하여 주어진 문장을 완성하시오.
   If you don't eat some food now, you will get hungry after a while.
   → _____ _____ _____ some food now, you will get hungry after a while.

# Biosphere 2

Could the Earth's environment be recreated on a spaceship? To find the answer, scientists created a futuristic "greenhouse" in the Sonoran Desert in the US. It was built in 1991 to recreate the ecosystems of the Earth. Scientists called it Biosphere 2, as the Earth was Biosphere 1.

Many artificial habitats, such as an ocean, a rainforest, and a 5 desert, were created inside the structure. They were meant to mimic the Earth's ecosystem as closely as possible. The habitats contained over 3,000 species of plants and animals. There were also work and leisure areas for the eight "Biospherians." They **were to grow** their own food and **do** environmental experiments. No outside contact was 10 allowed.

Unfortunately, their mission failed after a short time. Animals and plants died off, and there was a shortage of both food and oxygen. Later, the Biospherians fought among themselves. Poor management also made their experiment worse. 15

Today, however, scientists believe the experiments were worthwhile. They were able to learn many things about the growth of plants and animals. They also learned about human relationships in a closed space. Today, Biosphere 2 is an educational place that helps people understand more about our planet. 20

ⓥ Mini Quiz

Find the answers from the passage and write them.

**Paragraph 1**

1 What is Biosphere 1?

→ _____

**Paragraph 2**

2 What were the people living in Biosphere 2 called?

→ _____

**Reading Comprehension**

1  What is the passage mainly about?
  a. the important missions of astronauts
  b. environmental conditions on other planets
  c. how an ecosystem was created in a spaceship
  d. an experiment that recreated the Earth's ecosystems

2  What were some of the reasons why Biosphere 2 failed? (Choose two.)
  a. a lack of time                   b. poor management
  c. a lack of oxygen                 d. too many animal species

3  Which CANNOT be answered based on the passage?
  a. Why was Biosphere 2 created?
  b. When was Biosphere 2 built?
  c. How long did it take to recreate the habitats for Biosphere 2?
  d. How many Biospherians were there in Biosphere 2?

**Writing Practice**

4  According to the passage, what did scientists learn from the experiments?
  They learned about _____. They also learned about
  _____ in a closed space.

---

**Q   GRAMMAR Inside LEVEL 2**                                    ☰

주어를 설명하는 「be to-v」
to부정사의 형용사적 용법으로는 명사를 수식하는 것뿐만 아니라, 「be to-v」 형태로 주어를 설명할 수 있다.
「be to-v」는 문맥에 따라 〈예정, 가능, 의무, 운명, 의도〉 등을 나타낸다.

The twins **are to enter** the elementary school next year.          〈예정〉
초등학교에 들어갈 예정이다

They **were to grow** their own food and **do** environmental experiments.   〈의무〉
그들의 식량을 재배하고 환경과 관련된 실험을 해야 했다

The man **was to become** a hero.                                    〈운명〉
영웅이 될 운명이었다

Link to ...
Chapter 04
Unit 02

Check Up  우리말과 일치하도록 (  ) 안의 말을 이용하여 문장을 완성하시오.
나는 이 과제를 내일까지 마쳐야 한다. (finish)
→ I _____ _____ _____ this assignment by tomorrow.

# ◆ VOCABULARY INSIDE

| READING 1 | READING 2 |
|---|---|
| ☐ **quite** (ad)<br>very, but not extremely<br>(syn) fairly, pretty | ☐ **create** (v)<br>to make something that didn't exist before<br>(n) creation, creature  (a) creative |
| ☐ **legend** (n)<br>an old story that may or may not be true<br>about a famous person, event, or place<br>(a) legendary  (syn) myth | ☐ **ecosystem** (n)<br>all the plants and animals in a particular area |
| ☐ **mess** (n)<br>something that has been left in a dirty or<br>untidy state<br>(a) messy  (syn) clutter, litter | ☐ **habitat** (n)<br>the type of place that a particular animal or<br>plant usually lives in |
| ☐ **smooth** (v)<br>to make something have a flat and even<br>surface by rubbing it<br>(a) smooth  (ad) smoothly<br>(syn) flatten, level | ☐ **allow** (v)<br>to let someone have or do something<br>(syn) permit |
| ☐ **phenomenon** (n)<br>something interesting that is known to exist<br>or happen | ☐ **worthwhile** (a)<br>useful, important, and worth the time or effort |

**Check Up**  **Fill in the blanks with the words above. Change the form if necessary.**

1 The guards do not _____ anyone to enter the building.

2 The Bible says that God _____ the world.

3 The tigers were returned to their original _____.

4 Many classic novels are based on Greek _____.

5 Rainbows are a beautiful natural _____.

6 Unless you clean the _____ in your room, you will be punished.

7 This _____ contains a wide variety of plant and animal species.

8 Helping others is always _____.

# UNIT
# 16 | Sports

READING 1

**The Veolia Desert Challenge**

*Geography*

READING 2

**Five-a-Side Football**

PE

Geography

197 words

# The Veolia Desert Challenge

Find the answers from the passage and write them.

**Paragraph 1**

1 In which country is the Veolia Desert Challenge held?

→ _____

**Paragraph 3**

2 In "The Night Run," what lights the running course?

→ _____

_____

_____

Imagine running in a desert under the full moon. It's quiet and calm, and the sand glows in the moonlight. You can experience this kind of magical moment every December in the Dead Sea region of Israel. This area has one of the most spectacular desert landscapes in the world. Warm and dry all year round, it is filled with breathtaking valleys 5 and canyons. _____, it was chosen to host one of the world's most unique biking and running events: the Veolia Desert Challenge.

The main event is "The Ride," a mountain bike race with three courses of 23, 46, and 69 km in length. Two-rider teams race through 10 the river valley and alongside Mount Sodom. The cyclists experience spectacular cliffs, salt caves, and white salt rocks.

Another popular attraction is "The Night Run." Runners race for **either** 14 **or** 24 km through the desert at night. The course is lit only by the full moon and the runners' headlamps. Runners must carry 15 their own food and water. They also have to withstand the extreme temperature changes of the desert. These weekend-long events offer a great chance to appreciate **both** the hot days **and** starry nights of the desert.

# Reading Comprehension

**1   What is the passage mainly about?**

a. races held in the Dead Sea region

b. why people visit the Dead Sea region

c. things to prepare for traveling in the desert

d. how to take part in the Veolia Desert Challenge

**2   What is the best choice for the blank?**

a. However                          b. For example

c. For this reason                  d. On the other hand

**3   What is NOT true about the Veolia Desert Challenge?**

a. It's held in a region that is warm throughout the year.

b. In "The Ride," cyclists participate in races of up to 69 km in length.

c. The cyclists in "The Ride" can see cliffs and salt rocks.

d. "The Night Run" finishes when the full moon rises.

**Writing Practice**

**4   Fill in the blanks with words from the passage.**

For "The Night Run," runners have to carry _____.

Also, they must withstand _____ of the desert.

---

Q    **GRAMMAR Inside** LEVEL 3                                ☰

짝으로 이루어진 접속사

• both A and B: A와 B 둘 다

  … to appreciate **both** the hot days **and** starry nights of the desert.

• either A or B: A 또는 B 둘 중 하나

  Runners race for **either** 14 **or** 24 km through the desert at night.

• neither A nor B: A도 B도 아닌

  The novel is **neither** easy **nor** funny.

• not only A but also B: A뿐만 아니라 B도 (= B as well as A)

  The girl is **not only** pretty **but also** smart.

Link to ...

Chapter 08
Unit 02

---

**Check Up** 다음 두 문장을 짝으로 이루어진 접속사를 이용하여 한 문장으로 쓰시오.

I haven't met Tom before. I haven't met Chloe before, either.

→ I have met _____ Tom _____ Chloe before.

# Sports

**PE**

215 words

# Five-a-Side Football

### ✓ Mini Quiz

While you read, check *T* if it is true, or *F* if it is false.

**1** A sighted athlete can't be a goalkeeper.

☐ T ☐ F

**2** The ball makes a sound so that players can find it.

☐ T ☐ F

My little brother is *visually impaired. He loves soccer, but it's not easy for him to play. Every time I play, he has to sit on the bench. But I found an amazing sport for him today! I was watching the **Paralympics on TV, and I saw visually impaired athletes playing soccer! It's called five-a-side football. 5

Five-a-side football has some different rules from soccer in the Paralympics. It is played by two teams of blind or nearly blind players. ( ① ) Each team consists of five players: a goalkeeper, who can be sighted or visually impaired, and four visually impaired field players. ( ② ) The four field players wear eyeshades. ( ③ ) The ball is equipped with 10 a noise-making device to help players find it. ( ④ ) The teams compete over two 25-minute halves, with a 10-minute break at halftime. The playing field is smaller than a regular soccer field, and it is surrounded by a wall.

Referees penalize players who touch their eyeshades or push their 15 opponents. To prevent injuries, players must warn others when they are attempting a tackle. They do this by shouting "voy," which is the Spanish word for "I go."

**If** we **had known** about this sport earlier, my brother **could have joined** a league. Instead, I plan on teaching it to him and all of my 20 friends.

*visually impaired 시각 장애를 가진
**Paralympics 패럴림픽(세계 장애인 올림픽)

**Reading Comprehension**

1  What is the best title for the passage?
   a. Playing Soccer with Blind People
   b. Why Five-a-Side Football Is Popular
   c. The History of the Paralympic Games
   d. Paralympic Soccer for the Visually Impaired

2  Where would the following sentence best fit?

| This guarantees that they cannot see. |
|---|

   a. ①            b. ②            c. ③            d. ④

Writing Practice

3  According to the passage, when do referees penalize players?
   Players are penalized when they _____ or _____.

4  What can be answered based on the passage?
   a. When was five-a-side football first included in the Paralympics?
   b. How can referees warn players when they are tackled?
   c. How long do the players compete in each half?
   d. What is the penalty for touching another player's eyeshade?

---

🔍 **GRAMMAR Inside** LEVEL 2                                    ☰

**가정법 과거와 가정법 과거완료**

• 가정법 과거는 「If + 주어 + 동사의 과거형, 주어 + would[could/might] + 동사원형」으로 나타내며, '만일 ~라면 …할 텐데'의 의미이다. 현재 사실에 반대되거나 실현 가능성이 없는 일을 가정할 때 쓴다. 가정법 과거에서 if절의 be동사는 주어의 인칭에 관계없이 보통 were를 쓴다.

**If I knew** his number, I **would call** him.
　　　　　내가 그의 번호를 안다면, 그에게 전화를 할 텐데.

• 가정법 과거완료는 「If + 주어 + had v-ed, 주어 + would[could/might] + have v-ed」로 나타내며, '만일 ~였다면 …했을 텐데'의 의미이다. 과거 사실과 반대되는 가정을 할 때 쓴다.

**If** we **had known** about this sport earlier, my brother **could have joined** a league.
　　　　우리가 이 스포츠에 대해 더 일찍 알았더라면, 내 동생은 리그에 들어갈 수 있었을 텐데.

Link to ...

📁 Chapter 12
📁 Unit 01

# VOCABULARY INSIDE

| READING 1 | READING 2 |
|---|---|
| ☐ **calm** (a)<br>to be in a quiet and peaceful state; not windy<br>(ad) calmly<br>[syn] still, quiet | ☐ **athlete** (n)<br>someone who takes part in sports<br>[syn] player |
| ☐ **landscape** (n)<br>an area of land that has a particular type of appearance<br>[syn] scenery | ☐ **opponent** (n)<br>someone who you compete with in a game<br>[ant] partner, ally |
| ☐ **host** (v)<br>to provide a place and resources for an event<br>(n) host | ☐ **injury** (n)<br>damage to the body<br>(v) injure   (a) injured<br>[syn] wound |
| ☐ **withstand** (v)<br>to deal with difficult situations<br>[syn] bear, endure, stand up to<br>[ant] give in | ☐ **warn** (v)<br>to tell someone of a possible danger or problem that should be avoided<br>[syn] alert |
| ☐ **extreme** (a)<br>very great in degree<br>(ad) extremely<br>[syn] intense   [ant] mild | ☐ **attempt** (v)<br>to try to do or complete something difficult<br>(n) attempt   [syn] try |

**Check Up**

**Fill in the blanks with the words above. Change the form if necessary.**

1 They took pictures of the beautiful _____.

2 He knocked down his _____ in the competition.

3 Adam is the top _____ on his rugby team.

4 The buildings were constructed to _____ earthquakes.

5 He can't play because of a(n) _____ to his leg.

6 My city _____ a firework festival last week.

7 The boy _____ to steal my wallet, and my friend saw him.

8 This quilted jacket will protect you even in _____ cold.

# WORD LIST

## UNIT 01 Origins

| | | |
|---|---|---|
| O△X | adopt | 동 입양하다; 취하다[차용하다] |
| O△X | attract | 동 마음을 끌다; (어디로) 끌어들이다 |
| O△X | back and forth | 앞뒤로 |
| O△X | bobsled | 명 봅슬레이 동 봅슬레이를 타다 |
| O△X | clever | 형 영리한; 기발한 |
| O△X | come up with | (해답을) 찾아내다, 내놓다 |
| O△X | crash into | ~와 충돌하다 |
| O△X | creative | 형 창의적인 |
| O△X | crowded | 형 붐비는, 복잡한 |
| O△X | endure | 동 견디다, 참다 |
| O△X | essential | 형 필수적인, 극히 중요한 |
| O△X | exhausted | 형 기진맥진한, 탈진한 |
| O△X | fasten | 동 매다 |
| O△X | field | 명 들판, 밭 |
| O△X | fit | 동 맞다, 적합하다 |
| O△X | for free | 무료로 |
| O△X | frustrated | 형 좌절감을 느끼는 |
| O△X | get to | ~에 도착하다[닿다] |
| O△X | hop | 동 뛰다, 뛰어다니다 |
| O△X | immigrant | 명 이민자[이주민] |
| O△X | impress | 동 깊은 인상을 주다 |
| O△X | invent | 동 발명하다 |
| O△X | journey | 명 여정, 여행 |
| O△X | master | 동 숙달하다, 통달하다 |
| O△X | mineral | 명 미네랄, 무기물 |
| O△X | musical instrument | 악기 (= instrument) |
| O△X | on board | 승선한, 탑승한 |
| O△X | pedestrian | 명 보행자 |
| O△X | race | 동 경주하다 |
| O△X | root | 명 (식물의) 뿌리; 기원 |
| O△X | run | 동 달리다; 경영하다 |
| O△X | thanks to | ~ 덕분에 |
| O△X | throughout | 전 도처에 |
| O△X | track | 명 길; 경주로, 트랙 |
| O△X | traditional | 형 전통의 |

## UNIT 02 Numbers

| | | |
|---|---|---|
| O△X | add | 동 더하다 |
| O△X | ancient | 형 고대의 |
| O△X | chart | 명 도표 |
| O△X | comfortable | 형 편한 |
| O△X | construct | 동 건설하다 |
| O△X | double | 동 두 배로 되다[만들다] |
| O△X | especially | 부 특히 |
| O△X | eternity | 명 영원 |
| O△X | everlasting | 형 영원한 |
| O△X | exactly | 부 정확히 |
| O△X | farming | 명 농사 |
| O△X | finally | 부 마침내 |
| O△X | flow | 명 흐름 동 흐르다 |
| O△X | for this reason | 이러한 이유로 |
| O△X | fortune | 명 운; 재산 |
| O△X | hold | 동 잡고 있다; 개최하다 |
| O△X | important | 형 중요한 |
| O△X | include | 동 포함하다 |
| O△X | involve | 동 수반[포함]하다 |
| O△X | mean | 동 ~라는 뜻[의미]이다 |
| O△X | method | 명 방법 |
| O△X | multiplication | 명 곱셈 |
| O△X | practical | 형 실용적인 |
| O△X | purpose | 명 목적 |
| O△X | record | 동 기록하다 |
| O△X | repeatedly | 부 되풀이하여, 여러 차례 |
| O△X | rich | 형 부유한; 비옥한 |
| O△X | ruler | 명 통치자, 지배자 |
| O△X | settle | 동 해결하다; 정착하다 |
| O△X | shape | 명 모양, 형태 |
| O△X | similar to | ~와 비슷한 |
| O△X | smoothly | 부 부드럽게[순조롭게] |
| O△X | suppose | 동 가정하다 |
| O△X | symbol | 명 상징 |
| O△X | wealth | 명 부(富), 재산 |

## UNIT 03 Fiction

| | | |
|---|---|---|
| ⃞Ⓐ⃤Ⓧ amount | 몡 총액; 양 |
| ⃞Ⓐ⃤Ⓧ attack | 동 공격하다 |
| ⃞Ⓐ⃤Ⓧ balanced | 형 균형 잡힌 |
| ⃞Ⓐ⃤Ⓧ based on | ~에 근거하여 |
| ⃞Ⓐ⃤Ⓧ battle | 몡 전투 |
| ⃞Ⓐ⃤Ⓧ capture | 동 붙잡다, 생포하다 |
| ⃞Ⓐ⃤Ⓧ caterpillar | 몡 애벌레 |
| ⃞Ⓐ⃤Ⓧ classic | 형 명작의, 걸작의 |
| ⃞Ⓐ⃤Ⓧ court | 몡 법정, 법원 |
| ⃞Ⓐ⃤Ⓧ creature | 몡 생물, 생명체 |
| ⃞Ⓐ⃤Ⓧ destroy | 동 파괴하다 |
| ⃞Ⓐ⃤Ⓧ discovery | 몡 발견 |
| ⃞Ⓐ⃤Ⓧ escape | 동 탈출하다 |
| ⃞Ⓐ⃤Ⓧ explore | 동 탐험하다 |
| ⃞Ⓐ⃤Ⓧ find out | ~을 알아내다 |
| ⃞Ⓐ⃤Ⓧ fortunately | 부 다행스럽게도 |
| ⃞Ⓐ⃤Ⓧ gifted | 형 재능 있는 |
| ⃞Ⓐ⃤Ⓧ government | 몡 정부 |
| ⃞Ⓐ⃤Ⓧ hide | 동 감추다, 숨기다 |
| ⃞Ⓐ⃤Ⓧ include | 동 포함하다 |
| ⃞Ⓐ⃤Ⓧ local | 형 현지의 |
| ⃞Ⓐ⃤Ⓧ logic | 몡 논리, 논리학 |
| ⃞Ⓐ⃤Ⓧ magical | 형 마법의 |
| ⃞Ⓐ⃤Ⓧ mathematician | 몡 수학자 |
| ⃞Ⓐ⃤Ⓧ normal | 형 보통의, 정상적인 |
| ⃞Ⓐ⃤Ⓧ order | 동 명령하다 몡 명령 |
| ⃞Ⓐ⃤Ⓧ proportion | 몡 (전체의) 부분; (전체에서 차지하는) 비율 |
| ⃞Ⓐ⃤Ⓧ search | 동 찾아보다, 수색하다 |
| ⃞Ⓐ⃤Ⓧ shrink | 동 줄어들다 |
| ⃞Ⓐ⃤Ⓧ strange | 형 이상한, 낯선 |
| ⃞Ⓐ⃤Ⓧ submarine | 몡 잠수함 |
| ⃞Ⓐ⃤Ⓧ suggest | 동 제안하다 |
| ⃞Ⓐ⃤Ⓧ survive | 동 살아남다 |
| ⃞Ⓐ⃤Ⓧ tale | 몡 이야기, 소설 |
| ⃞Ⓐ⃤Ⓧ unexpected | 형 예상 밖의 |

## UNIT 04 Business

| | | |
|---|---|---|
| ⃞Ⓐ⃤Ⓧ advantage | 몡 장점 |
| ⃞Ⓐ⃤Ⓧ affect | 동 영향을 미치다 |
| ⃞Ⓐ⃤Ⓧ aspect | 몡 측면 |
| ⃞Ⓐ⃤Ⓧ at least | 적어도 |
| ⃞Ⓐ⃤Ⓧ banknote | 몡 지폐 |
| ⃞Ⓐ⃤Ⓧ be made of | ~으로 만들어지다 |
| ⃞Ⓐ⃤Ⓧ benefit | 몡 이득; (회사에서 받는) 혜택 |
| ⃞Ⓐ⃤Ⓧ convenient | 형 편리한 |
| ⃞Ⓐ⃤Ⓧ currency | 몡 통화 |
| ⃞Ⓐ⃤Ⓧ decade | 몡 10년 |
| ⃞Ⓐ⃤Ⓧ develop | 동 발달하다 |
| ⃞Ⓐ⃤Ⓧ economy | 몡 경제 |
| ⃞Ⓐ⃤Ⓧ employee | 몡 근로자 |
| ⃞Ⓐ⃤Ⓧ extremely | 부 극도로 |
| ⃞Ⓐ⃤Ⓧ fake | 형 가짜의 |
| ⃞Ⓐ⃤Ⓧ favor | 동 찬성하다; 선호하다 |
| ⃞Ⓐ⃤Ⓧ feature | 몡 특징, 특성 |
| ⃞Ⓐ⃤Ⓧ increase | 동 증가하다 |
| ⃞Ⓐ⃤Ⓧ increasingly | 부 점점 더 |
| ⃞Ⓐ⃤Ⓧ negative | 형 부정적인 |
| ⃞Ⓐ⃤Ⓧ note | 몡 메모; 지폐 |
| ⃞Ⓐ⃤Ⓧ old-fashioned | 형 옛날식의, 구식의 |
| ⃞Ⓐ⃤Ⓧ pandemic | 몡 전세계적인 전염병 |
| ⃞Ⓐ⃤Ⓧ payment | 몡 지불 |
| ⃞Ⓐ⃤Ⓧ rely on | ~에 의존하다 |
| ⃞Ⓐ⃤Ⓧ right | 몡 권리 |
| ⃞Ⓐ⃤Ⓧ security | 몡 보안 |
| ⃞Ⓐ⃤Ⓧ shift | 동 옮기다; 바뀌다 |
| ⃞Ⓐ⃤Ⓧ switch | 동 전환되다, 바뀌다 |
| ⃞Ⓐ⃤Ⓧ take a break | 휴식을 취하다 |
| ⃞Ⓐ⃤Ⓧ tear | 몡 구멍 |
| ⃞Ⓐ⃤Ⓧ temporary | 형 임시의 |
| ⃞Ⓐ⃤Ⓧ term | 몡 용어; 기간 |
| ⃞Ⓐ⃤Ⓧ tough | 형 힘든; 튼튼한 |
| ⃞Ⓐ⃤Ⓧ transparent | 형 투명한 |

# UNIT 05 | Society

| | | |
|---|---|---|
| O△X | afford | 동 (~하거나 살) 여유가 되다 |
| O△X | artificial | 형 인공의 |
| O△X | citizen | 명 시민 |
| O△X | cling | 동 달라붙다 |
| O△X | collector | 명 수집가; 수집기 |
| O△X | connection | 명 관련성[연관성] |
| O△X | date back to | ~으로 (시간을) 거슬러 올라가다 |
| O△X | desperate | 형 자포자기한; 간절히 원하는 |
| O△X | distance | 명 거리 |
| O△X | dry season | 건기(乾期) |
| O△X | effective | 형 효과적인 |
| O△X | emperor | 명 황제 |
| O△X | exact | 형 정확한 |
| O△X | fabric | 명 직물, 천 |
| O△X | fancy | 형 화려한 |
| O△X | fine | 형 좋은; 아주 가는 |
| O△X | gather | 동 모으다[수집하다], 모이다 |
| O△X | harvest | 동 수확하다, 거둬들이다 |
| O△X | material | 명 직물, 천; 재료 |
| O△X | moisture | 명 수분, 습기 |
| O△X | notice | 동 의식하다[알다] |
| O△X | ordinary | 형 보통의, 평범한 |
| O△X | organization | 명 조직, 단체 |
| O△X | portrait | 명 초상화 |
| O△X | process | 명 과정 |
| O△X | rainfall | 명 강우량 |
| O△X | rare | 형 드문, 희귀한 |
| O△X | robe | 명 예복 |
| O△X | royal | 형 왕의[여왕의] |
| O△X | salary | 명 급여, 봉급 |
| O△X | shell | 명 껍데기[껍질] |
| O△X | shortage | 명 부족 |
| O△X | tiny | 형 아주 작은 |
| O△X | valuable | 형 귀중한; 값비싼 |
| O△X | worth | 형 ~의 가치가 있는 |

# UNIT 06 | Animals

| | | |
|---|---|---|
| O△X | adapt to | ~에 적응하다 |
| O△X | assume | 동 추정하다, 추측하다 |
| O△X | care | 명 돌봄[보살핌] |
| O△X | cell | 명 세포 |
| O△X | community | 명 공동체[사회] |
| O△X | conservation | 명 보호, 보존 |
| O△X | consume | 동 소비하다; (음식물을) 섭취하다 |
| O△X | due to | ~ 때문에 |
| O△X | efficient | 형 효율적인 |
| O△X | eventually | 부 결국 |
| O△X | fatty | 형 지방으로 된, 지방이 많은 |
| O△X | flexible | 형 유연한 |
| O△X | form | 동 형성시키다; 모이다[이루다] |
| O△X | horrible | 형 끔찍한 |
| O△X | hunt | 동 사냥하다 |
| O△X | illegal | 형 불법적인 |
| O△X | locate | 동 ~의 위치를 찾아내다 |
| O△X | maintain | 동 유지하다 |
| O△X | massive | 형 거대한; (수량 등이) 엄청난 |
| O△X | orphan | 동 고아로 만들다 명 고아 |
| O△X | practice | 명 실행; 관행 |
| O△X | protect | 동 보호하다 |
| O△X | protection | 명 보호 |
| O△X | raise | 동 들어올리다; 키우다[기르다] |
| O△X | rescue | 동 구하다, 구조하다 |
| O△X | source | 명 원천 |
| O△X | store | 동 저장하다 |
| O△X | sweat | 동 땀을 흘리다 |
| O△X | target | 명 목표; 표적, 목표물 |
| O△X | temperature | 명 온도 |
| O△X | tragic | 형 비극적인 |
| O△X | traumatic | 형 대단히 충격적인 |
| O△X | unique | 형 독특한 |
| O△X | unit | 명 단일체, 단위 |
| O△X | weak | 형 약한, 힘이 없는 |

# WORD LIST

## UNIT 07 Social Media

| | | |
|---|---|---|
| ☐△☒ | access | 명 접근 |
| ☐△☒ | active | 형 활동적인 |
| ☐△☒ | communicate | 동 의사소통 하다 |
| ☐△☒ | compare | 동 비교하다 |
| ☐△☒ | connect | 동 연결하다 |
| ☐△☒ | consider | 동 사려[고려]하다 |
| ☐△☒ | cooperation | 명 협력 |
| ☐△☒ | customer | 명 고객, 소비자 |
| ☐△☒ | depression | 명 우울증 |
| ☐△☒ | donate | 동 기부[기증]하다 |
| ☐△☒ | effect | 명 영향 |
| ☐△☒ | emotional | 형 정서적인 |
| ☐△☒ | host | 명 사회자, 진행자 |
| ☐△☒ | importance | 명 중요성 |
| ☐△☒ | launch | 동 시작[개시]하다 |
| ☐△☒ | limit | 명 제한, 한계 |
| ☐△☒ | mental | 형 정신의 |
| ☐△☒ | negatively | 부 부정적으로 |
| ☐△☒ | pay attention to | ~에 주의를 기울이다 |
| ☐△☒ | post | 명 우편; (인터넷) 게시글 |
| ☐△☒ | probably | 부 아마도 |
| ☐△☒ | product | 명 상품, 제품 |
| ☐△☒ | profit | 명 이익, 이윤 |
| ☐△☒ | psychologist | 명 심리학자 |
| ☐△☒ | purchase | 명 구입[구매] 동 구입[구매]하다 |
| ☐△☒ | raise | 동 (자금 등을) 모으다 |
| ☐△☒ | reach | 동 ~에 이르다[닿다] |
| ☐△☒ | real | 형 실제의 |
| ☐△☒ | recently | 부 최근에 |
| ☐△☒ | require | 동 요구하다[필요로 하다] |
| ☐△☒ | restore | 동 회복시키다; 복원하다 |
| ☐△☒ | slow down | 둔화되다 |
| ☐△☒ | social media | 소셜 미디어 |
| ☐△☒ | trend | 명 트렌드, 추세 |
| ☐△☒ | usage | 명 사용; 사용량 |

## UNIT 08 Psychology

| | | |
|---|---|---|
| ☐△☒ | actually | 부 실제로, 정말로 |
| ☐△☒ | at the same time | 동시에 |
| ☐△☒ | attach | 동 붙이다, 첨부하다 |
| ☐△☒ | average | 명 평균 |
| ☐△☒ | breathe | 동 호흡하다, 숨을 쉬다 |
| ☐△☒ | case | 명 경우; 사례 |
| ☐△☒ | condition | 명 상태, 질환 |
| ☐△☒ | dip | 동 (액체에) 살짝 담그다 |
| ☐△☒ | drop | 동 떨어지다 |
| ☐△☒ | emotion | 명 감정 |
| ☐△☒ | empathy | 명 감정 이입, 공감 |
| ☐△☒ | exist | 동 존재하다 |
| ☐△☒ | experience | 동 겪다, 경험하다 |
| ☐△☒ | frozen | 형 얼어붙은 |
| ☐△☒ | heartbeat | 명 심장 박동 |
| ☐△☒ | imagine | 동 상상하다 |
| ☐△☒ | influence | 동 영향을 주다 |
| ☐△☒ | last | 동 지속하다[되다] |
| ☐△☒ | lower | 동 내리다[낮추다] |
| ☐△☒ | measure | 동 측정하다[재다] |
| ☐△☒ | physical | 형 육체[신체]의 |
| ☐△☒ | psychological | 형 정신[심리]의, 정신[심리]적인 |
| ☐△☒ | react | 동 반응하다 |
| ☐△☒ | relationship | 명 관계 |
| ☐△☒ | report | 동 알리다; 보고하다 |
| ☐△☒ | researcher | 명 연구원 |
| ☐△☒ | sensitive | 형 세심한; 감성 있는; 민감한 |
| ☐△☒ | significant | 형 중요한; 주목할 만한 |
| ☐△☒ | situation | 명 상황 |
| ☐△☒ | symptom | 명 증상 |
| ☐△☒ | syndrome | 명 증후군 |
| ☐△☒ | volunteer | 명 자원봉사자; 지원자 |
| ☐△☒ | wander | 동 거닐다[돌아다니다] |
| ☐△☒ | wonder | 동 궁금하다, 궁금해하다 |
| ☐△☒ | worsen | 동 악화되다, 악화시키다 |

# UNIT 09 Winter

| O△X | adaptation | 명 적응 |
| O△X | appear | 동 ~처럼 보이다 |
| O△X | bottom | 명 맨 아래; 바닥 |
| O△X | century | 명 세기, 100년 |
| O△X | condition | 명 상태; 환경 |
| O△X | convince | 동 확신시키다; 설득하다 |
| O△X | cope with | ~에 대처하다 |
| O△X | custom | 명 관습 |
| O△X | decorate | 동 장식하다[꾸미다] |
| O△X | display | 동 전시하다 |
| O△X | edge | 명 가장자리, 모서리 |
| O△X | enemy | 명 적 |
| O△X | evolve | 동 발달시키다; 진화하다 |
| O△X | expose | 동 드러내다 |
| O△X | feature | 동 특징으로 하다; 특집으로 다루다 |
| O△X | grip | 명 움켜쥠 |
| O△X | historian | 명 역사학자 |
| O△X | holy | 형 신성한 |
| O△X | hoof | 명 발굽 ((pl.) hooves) |
| O△X | migrate | 동 이주하다 |
| O△X | native | 명 원주민 |
| O△X | originate | 동 유래하다 |
| O△X | pray | 동 기도하다 |
| O△X | publication | 명 출판(물) |
| O△X | reflect | 동 반사하다 |
| O△X | region | 명 지역 |
| O△X | reindeer | 명 순록 |
| O△X | religious | 형 종교의 |
| O△X | represent | 동 대표하다; 나타내다 |
| O△X | seasonal | 형 계절의 |
| O△X | slip | 동 미끄러지다 |
| O△X | survivor | 명 생존자 |
| O△X | tough | 형 힘든; 거친 |
| O△X | tradition | 명 전통 |
| O△X | various | 형 다양한 |

# UNIT 10 People

| O△X | achievement | 명 업적, 성취 |
| O△X | admire | 동 존경하다; 감탄하다 |
| O△X | anniversary | 명 기념일 |
| O△X | announce | 동 발표하다 |
| O△X | athlete | 명 운동 선수 |
| O△X | barrier | 명 장벽 |
| O△X | behavior | 명 행동 |
| O△X | brilliantly | 부 찬란히; 뛰어나게 |
| O△X | chat | 동 이야기를 나누다 |
| O△X | complex | 형 복잡한 |
| O△X | composer | 명 작곡가 |
| O△X | design | 명 디자인; 설계 |
| O△X | dramatic | 형 극적인 |
| O△X | engineer | 명 기술자 |
| O△X | except | 전 ~을 제외하고 |
| O△X | fall in love with | ~와 사랑에 빠지다 |
| O△X | fight for | ~을 위해 싸우다 |
| O△X | influence | 동 영향을 미치다 |
| O△X | inspire | 동 영감을 주다 |
| O△X | insult | 동 모욕하다 |
| O△X | mighty | 형 힘센; 장대한 |
| O△X | movement | 명 움직임; (조직적으로 벌이는) 운동 |
| O△X | nonviolent | 형 비폭력적인 |
| O△X | overwhelming | 형 압도적인 |
| O△X | passion | 명 열정 |
| O△X | past | 전 ~을 지나서 |
| O△X | popularity | 명 인기 |
| O△X | produce | 동 생산하다; 만들어내다 |
| O△X | railway | 명 철로 |
| O△X | rush | 동 돌진하다 |
| O△X | symphony | 명 교향곡 |
| O△X | technical | 형 기술적인 |
| O△X | threat | 명 협박, 위협 |
| O△X | threaten | 동 협박[위협]하다 |
| O△X | victory | 명 승리 |

# WORD LIST

| | | |
|---|---|---|
| O△X | abnormal | 형 비정상적인 |
| O△X | aerial | 형 항공기에 의한 |
| O△X | calculate | 동 계산하다 |
| O△X | capture | 동 포획하다; 정확히 포착하다[담아내다] |
| O△X | delay | 동 지연시키다 |
| O△X | diagnose | 동 진단하다 |
| O△X | educator | 명 교육자 |
| O△X | evaluate | 동 평가하다 |
| O△X | expression | 명 표현; 표정 |
| O△X | facial | 형 얼굴의 |
| O△X | fossil | 명 화석 |
| O△X | identify | 동 확인하다[알아보다] |
| O△X | interact | 동 상호 작용을 하다 |
| O△X | interaction | 명 상호 작용 |
| O△X | isolated | 형 고립된 |
| O△X | landscape | 명 풍경; 지표, 지형 |
| O△X | match | 동 일치하다 |
| O△X | meaningful | 형 의미 있는 |
| O△X | meanwhile | 부 그 동안에 |
| O△X | narrow down | 좁히다[줄이다] |
| O△X | observe | 동 보다[관찰하다] |
| O△X | owner | 명 주인, 소유주 |
| O△X | properly | 부 제대로, 적절히 |
| O△X | reaction | 명 반응 |
| O△X | reply | 동 대답하다 |
| O△X | research | 명 연구, 조사 동 연구[조사]하다 |
| O△X | response | 명 대답; 반응 |
| O△X | rub | 동 문지르다[비비다] |
| O△X | soar | 동 급증하다; (하늘 높이) 날아오르다 |
| O△X | social | 형 사회의, 사회적인 |
| O△X | struggle | 동 애쓰다, 힘겹게 나아가다 |
| O△X | surface | 명 표면[표층] |
| O△X | take advantage of | ~을 이용하다 |
| O△X | tough | 형 힘든, 어려운 |
| O△X | treatment | 명 치료 |

| | | |
|---|---|---|
| O△X | bend | 동 굽히다 |
| O△X | certain | 형 확실한; 어떤 |
| O△X | completely | 부 완전히 |
| O△X | contrary to | ~와 반대로[달리] |
| O△X | desire | 명 욕구 |
| O△X | despite | 전 ~에도 불구하고 |
| O△X | difference | 명 차이(점) |
| O△X | divide | 동 나뉘다[나누다] |
| O△X | empty | 형 비어 있는 |
| O△X | evenly | 부 고르게 |
| O△X | extra | 형 추가의[여분의] |
| O△X | for a while | 한동안 |
| O△X | forearm | 명 팔뚝 |
| O△X | function | 동 작동하다 |
| O△X | independently | 부 독립하여 |
| O△X | index finger | 집게손가락(검지) |
| O△X | muscle | 명 근육 |
| O△X | need | 명 필요, 욕구 |
| O△X | nerve | 명 신경 |
| O△X | palm | 명 손바닥 |
| O△X | physical | 형 신체적인 |
| O△X | possible | 형 가능한 |
| O△X | reason | 명 이유 |
| O△X | relax | 동 휴식을 취하다; 긴장을 풀다 |
| O△X | separate | 형 분리된 |
| O△X | signal | 명 신호 |
| O△X | skip | 동 깡충깡충 뛰다; 거르다 |
| O△X | specific | 형 구체적인; 특정한 |
| O△X | straighten | 동 똑바르게 하다 |
| O△X | structure | 명 구조 |
| O△X | such as | ~와 같은 |
| O△X | thumb | 명 엄지손가락 |
| O△X | tighten | 동 팽팽해지다[팽팽하게 하다] |
| O△X | trick | 동 속이다 |
| O△X | unconsciously | 부 무의식적으로 |

O△X  O = I know this word and its meaning.
△ = I know either the word spelling or its meaning.
X = I've never seen this word before.
• Study the words that you've checked △ or X.

# UNIT 13 Maps

| | | |
|---|---|---|
| O△X | a number of | 얼마간의; 다수의 |
| O△X | access | 동 접근하다 |
| O△X | application | 명 적용 |
| O△X | area | 명 지역 |
| O△X | cell | 명 세포; 칸 |
| O△X | construct | 동 건설하다; 구성하다 |
| O△X | defeat | 동 패배시키다[이기다] |
| O△X | dispute | 동 논쟁하다; (소유권) 분쟁을 벌이다 |
| O△X | distance | 명 거리 |
| O△X | establish | 동 설립[수립]하다 |
| O△X | gain | 동 얻다 |
| O△X | identify | 동 확인하다; 찾다 |
| O△X | invisible | 형 보이지 않는 |
| O△X | mark | 동 표시하다 |
| O△X | multitude | 명 다수 |
| O△X | ownership | 명 소유권 |
| O△X | political | 형 정치적인 |
| O△X | possession | 명 소유(권) |
| O△X | precious | 형 귀중한 |
| O△X | random | 형 무작위의 |
| O△X | rate | 명 비율 |
| O△X | recover | 동 회복되다; 되찾다 |
| O△X | remain | 동 계속 ~이다 |
| O△X | remove | 동 제거하다 |
| O△X | repeat | 동 반복하다 |
| O△X | result | 명 결과 |
| O△X | rule | 명 규칙; 통치 |
| O△X | separate | 형 별개의 |
| O△X | significant | 형 상당한 |
| O△X | source | 명 근원 |
| O△X | stretch | 동 늘이다; 뻗어 있다 |
| O△X | tension | 명 긴장 |
| O△X | territory | 명 영토 |
| O△X | upright | 형 수직의 |
| O△X | value | 명 가치 |

# UNIT 14 Paintings

| | | |
|---|---|---|
| O△X | ahead | 부 앞에 |
| O△X | amuse | 동 즐겁게 하다 |
| O△X | artwork | 명 미술품 |
| O△X | at that time | 그 당시에 |
| O△X | begin with | ~으로 시작하다 |
| O△X | beneath | 전 ~ 아래에 |
| O△X | besides | 전 ~ 외에 |
| O△X | carefully | 부 주의 깊게, 신중히 |
| O△X | choice | 명 선택 |
| O△X | detail | 명 세부 사항 |
| O△X | develop | 동 성장[발달]하다 |
| O△X | discover | 동 발견하다 |
| O△X | drawing | 명 그림 |
| O△X | emerge | 동 나오다[모습을 드러내다] |
| O△X | face | 동 ~을 마주보다; (상황에) 직면하다 |
| O△X | focus on | ~에 집중하다, 초점을 맞추다 |
| O△X | hidden | 형 숨겨진, 숨은 |
| O△X | interestingly | 부 흥미롭게도 |
| O△X | layer | 명 막[층] |
| O△X | lower | 형 더 낮은 쪽의 |
| O△X | master | 명 주인; 대가 |
| O△X | object | 명 물체; 대상 |
| O△X | outline | 명 개요; 윤곽 |
| O△X | portrait | 명 초상화 |
| O△X | practice | 명 연습 |
| O△X | prove | 동 입증하다 |
| O△X | reflection | 명 (거울 등에 비친) 상[모습] |
| O△X | reuse | 동 재사용하다 |
| O△X | reveal | 동 드러내다 |
| O△X | royal | 형 왕실의 |
| O△X | rural | 형 시골의, 지방의 |
| O△X | scan | 동 살피다; 정밀 촬영하다 |
| O△X | stare | 동 응시하다 |
| O△X | straight | 부 똑바로 |
| O△X | surround | 동 둘러싸다 |

O = I know this word and its meaning.
Δ = I know either the word spelling or its meaning.
X = I've never seen this word before.
• Study the words that you've checked Δ or X.

# WORD LIST

## UNIT 15 | Places

| | | |
|---|---|---|
| O Δ X | allow | 통 허락하다; 용납하다 |
| O Δ X | amazing | 형 놀라운 |
| O Δ X | aside | 부 옆에; 제쳐두고[접어두고] |
| O Δ X | closely | 부 가깝게 |
| O Δ X | contact | 명 접촉 |
| O Δ X | contain | 통 ~이 들어 있다 |
| O Δ X | create | 통 창조하다 |
| O Δ X | die off | 차례대로[하나하나] 죽다 |
| O Δ X | dirt | 명 먼지, 흙 |
| O Δ X | educational | 형 교육의, 교육적인 |
| O Δ X | environment | 명 환경 |
| O Δ X | experiment | 명 실험 |
| O Δ X | for certain | 확실히 |
| O Δ X | futuristic | 형 미래의, 미래를 상상하는 |
| O Δ X | greenhouse | 명 온실 |
| O Δ X | habitat | 명 서식지 |
| O Δ X | legend | 명 전설 |
| O Δ X | leisure | 명 여가 |
| O Δ X | management | 명 경영[관리] |
| O Δ X | mess | 명 엉망인 상태 |
| O Δ X | mimic | 통 모방하다 |
| O Δ X | mission | 명 임무 |
| O Δ X | mostly | 부 주로, 일반적으로 |
| O Δ X | once | 부 한 번; 언젠가[한때] |
| O Δ X | oxygen | 명 산소 |
| O Δ X | phenomenon | 명 현상 |
| O Δ X | planet | 명 행성 |
| O Δ X | quite | 부 꽤, 상당히 |
| O Δ X | rainforest | 명 (열대) 우림 |
| O Δ X | recreate | 통 되살리다[재현하다] |
| O Δ X | smooth | 통 매끈하게 하다 |
| O Δ X | teardrop | 명 눈물 |
| O Δ X | theory | 명 이론, 학설 |
| O Δ X | throw | 통 던지다 |
| O Δ X | worthwhile | 형 가치 있는 |

## UNIT 16 | Sports

| | | |
|---|---|---|
| O Δ X | appreciate | 통 진가를 알아보다; 감상하다 |
| O Δ X | athlete | 명 운동 선수 |
| O Δ X | attempt | 통 시도하다 |
| O Δ X | attraction | 명 명소[명물] |
| O Δ X | blind | 형 앞을 보지 못하는 |
| O Δ X | break | 명 휴식 시간 |
| O Δ X | breathtaking | 형 숨이 멎는 듯한 |
| O Δ X | calm | 형 고요한, 차분한; 바람이 없는 |
| O Δ X | canyon | 명 협곡 |
| O Δ X | challenge | 명 도전 |
| O Δ X | cliff | 명 절벽 |
| O Δ X | compete | 통 경쟁하다; ~와 겨루다 |
| O Δ X | desert | 명 사막 |
| O Δ X | device | 명 장치 |
| O Δ X | equip | 통 장비를 갖추다 |
| O Δ X | extreme | 형 극도의[극심한] |
| O Δ X | field | 명 들판; 경기장 |
| O Δ X | glow | 통 빛나다 |
| O Δ X | guarantee | 통 보장하다; 확실하게 하다 |
| O Δ X | half | 명 반; (경기의) 전반, 후반 |
| O Δ X | host | 통 주최하다 |
| O Δ X | injury | 명 부상[상처] |
| O Δ X | length | 명 길이 |
| O Δ X | nearly | 부 거의 |
| O Δ X | offer | 통 제의하다; 제공하다 |
| O Δ X | opponent | 명 (게임·대회 등의) 상대 |
| O Δ X | penalize | 통 벌칙을 주다 |
| O Δ X | prevent | 통 막다, 방지하다 |
| O Δ X | referee | 명 심판 |
| O Δ X | regular | 형 보통의 |
| O Δ X | spectacular | 형 장관을 이루는 |
| O Δ X | take part in | ~에 참여하다 (= participate in) |
| O Δ X | valley | 명 계곡, 골짜기 |
| O Δ X | warn | 통 경고하다 |
| O Δ X | withstand | 통 견뎌내다 |

## Photo Credits

| PAGE | PHOTO | SOURCE |
|---|---|---|
| p. 62 | Sandberg, Bob. *Jackie Robinson as a member of the Brooklyn Dodgers, circa 1954*. Photograph. *LOOK*, February 1955. | https://commons.wikimedia.org/wiki/File:Jrobinson.jpg |
| p. 80 | Oatley, George. *Voronoi Sculpture*. 1909. Photograph by Pamaths. Fry Building, University of Bristol. October 2020. | https://commons.wikimedia.org/wiki/File:Voronoi-Fry.jpg |
| p. 86 | Velázquez, Diego. *Las Meninas*. 1656. Oil on canvas. Museo del Prado, Madrid. | https://commons.wikimedia.org/wiki/File:Diego_Vel%C3%A1zquez_Las_Meninas_Die_Hoffr%C3%A4ulein.jpg |
| p. 88 | Van Gogh, Vincent. *Grasgrond[Patch of grass]*. 1887. Oil on canvas. Kröller-Müller Museum, Otterlo. | https://commons.wikimedia.org/wiki/File:Vincent_van_Gogh_-_Patch_of_grass_-_Google_Art_Project.jpg |
| p. 88 | Van Gogh, Vincent. *Portrait of a woman under Grasgrond[Patch of grass]*.1884-1885. Oil on canvas. Kröller-Müller Museum, Otterlo. | https://commons.wikimedia.org/wiki/File:Van_Gogh_portrait_under_Grasgrond.jpg |
| others |  | www.shutterstock.com |

지은이

**NE능률 영어교육연구소**

NE능률 영어교육연구소는 혁신적이며 효율적인 영어 교재를 개발하고
영어 학습의 질을 한 단계 높이고자 노력하는 NE능률의 연구조직입니다.

# Reading Inside 〈Level 2〉

펴 낸 이　주민홍
펴 낸 곳　서울특별시 마포구 월드컵북로 396(상암동) 누리꿈스퀘어 비즈니스타워 10층
　　　　　㈜NE능률 (우편번호 03925)
펴 낸 날　2022년 9월 15일 개정판 제1쇄 발행
　　　　　2024년 6월 15일 제6쇄
전　　화　02 2014 7114
팩　　스　02 3142 0356
홈페이지　www.neungyule.com
등록번호　제1-68호
I S B N　979-11-253-4032-4 53740
정　　가　15,500원

**NE** 능률

**고객센터**

교재 내용 문의 : contact.nebooks.co.kr (별도의 가입 절차 없이 작성 가능)

제품 구매, 교환, 불량, 반품 문의 : 02-2014-7114

☎ 전화문의는 본사 업무시간 중에만 가능합니다.

# READING Inside

## LEVEL 2

A 4-level curriculum
integration reading course

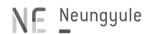

NE Neungyule

# Answer Key

# READING
# Inside

# LEVEL 2

## READING 1   Caspar Badrutt

**◎ Mini Quiz**
  1 T    2 F

▶ **Reading Comprehension**
  1 b    2 a    3 b    4 "bobbed" back and forth

▶ **Grammar Inside LEVEL 2**
  Check Up   to watch

**해석**   시속 150킬로미터까지 이르는 4인승 봅슬레이는 흥미진진한 동계 스포츠이다. 그런데 당신은 이 초고속 스포츠가 기발한 호텔 경영자 Caspar Badrutt 덕분에 발명되었다는 것을 알았는가?

  19세기에, Badrutt는 스위스 생모리츠에서 호텔을 운영했다. 생모리츠는 미네랄 온천으로 유명했다. 여름 동안에는 많은 투숙객들이 온천을 즐기러 왔지만, Badrutt는 추운 겨울 동안에는 아무도 오지 않는 것에 좌절감을 느꼈다. 방문객을 끌어들이기 위해, Badrutt는 한 가지 아이디어를 내놓았다. 그는 투숙객들에게 겨울 휴가에 만족하지 않는다면, 그들에게 방을 무료로 제공하기로 결정했다.

  곧, Badrutt의 호텔은 붐비게 되었고, 투숙객들은 그들이 바깥의 눈 속에서 노는 것을 아주 좋아한다는 것을 알게 되었다. 어떤 창의적인 투숙객들은 네 명에게 맞는 썰매를 만들기 위해 작은 썰매 두 대를 함께 맸다. 그러고 나서, 그들은 팀을 이루어 길을 내려오는 경주를 했다. 썰매가 더 빨리 가게 하려고, 팀들은 앞뒤로 '흔들었는데', 그래서 그 스포츠는 봅슬레이로 알려지게 되었다. 하지만 한 가지 다른 문제가 있었는데, 바로 그 썰매가 종종 보행자들과 충돌한다는 것이었다. 그 문제를 해결하기 위해 Badrutt는 하프파이프 경주로를 만들었고, 투숙객들이 안전하게 썰매를 탈 수 있게 되었다. 이것이 최초의 봅슬레이 트랙이었으며, 이것은 오늘날에도 여전히 사용된다.

**어휘**   bobsled 몡 봅슬레이 통 봅슬레이를 타다   invent 통 발명하다   thanks to ~ 덕분에   clever 혱 영리한; *기발한   hotelier 몡 호텔 경영자   run 통 달리다; *경영하다   mineral 몡 미네랄, 무기물   spa 몡 온천   frustrated 혱 좌절감을 느끼는   come up with (해답을) 찾아내다, 내놓다   for free 무료로   be satisfied with ~에 만족하다   crowded 혱 붐비는, 복잡한   creative 혱 창의적인   fasten 통 매다   sled 몡 썰매 통 썰매를 타다   fit 통 맞다, 적합하다   back and forth 앞뒤로   crash into ~와 충돌하다   pedestrian 몡 보행자   halfpipe 몡 하프파이프 (U사형 구소물이나 홈)   track 몡 길; *경주로, 트랙   [문제] attract 통 마음을 끌다; *(어디로) 끌어들이다[끌어모으다]   race 통 경주하다

**구문**   2행 But did you **know** [that this super-fast sport was invented thanks to *a clever hotelier*, *Caspar Badrutt*]?
    → [ ]는 동사 know의 목적어 역할을 하는 명사절이며, that은 명사절을 이끄는 접속사이다.
    → a clever hotelier와 Caspar Badrutt는 동격 관계이다.

  7행 ..., but Badrutt was **frustrated** [that no one came during the cold winter].
    → [ ]는 감정(frustrated)의 원인을 나타낸다.

  9행 He decided to give guests rooms for free **if** they weren't satisfied with their winter vacation.
    → if는 '만약 ~한다면'의 의미로 〈조건〉을 나타내는 접속사이다.

[12행] Some creative guests fastened two small sleds together **to make** *a sled* [that fit four people].
→ to make는 '만들기 위해'의 의미로 〈목적〉을 나타내는 부사적 용법의 to부정사이다.
→ [ ]는 선행사 a sled를 수식하는 주격 관계대명사절이다.

[14행] To **make the sleds go** faster, the teams "bobbed" back and forth, so the sport became known as bobsled.
→ 「make+목적어+동사원형」은 '~가 …하게 하다[만들다]'라는 의미이며, 이때 동사원형 go는 사역동사 make의 목적격 보어로 쓰였다.

## READING 2 The Ukulele

**Mini Quiz**
1 Portugal 2 João Fernandes

**Reading Comprehension**
1 d 2 a 3 a 4 hopped like fleas

**해석** 130년이 넘도록, 예술가에서부터 와이키키 해변의 소년들에 이르기까지 하와이 사람들은 그들의 전통 악기인 우쿨렐레를 통달하도록 배워 왔다. 우쿨렐레가 하와이에서 가장 인기 있는 악기지만, 이것은 사실 포르투갈에 기원을 둔다.

1879년에, Ravenscrag 호가 하와이 호놀룰루에 도착했다. 400명의 포르투갈인들이 탑승해 있었다. 그들은 사탕수수밭에 일하러 온 이주민들이었다. 그들은 포르투갈에서부터 호놀룰루에 도착하기까지 바다에서 4개월을 견뎠다. 15,000마일의 어려운 여정 끝에, 포르투갈인들은 신났고 마침내 도착하게 되어 안도했다. 그들이 해변에 도달하자, João Fernandes라는 이름의 한 남자가 배에서 뛰어내렸다. 그는 포르투갈의 전통 악기인 마체테로 민요를 연주하기 시작했다.

Fernandes의 연주는 해변에서 듣고 있던 하와이 사람들에게 깊은 인상을 주었다. 그들은 그의 손가락이 벼룩처럼 악기를 뛰어다닌다고 생각했다. 그래서, 그들은 그 악기를 하와이 단어로 '뛰는 벼룩'인 '우쿨렐레'라고 불렀고, 하와이 문화로 받아들였다.

오늘날 그 악기는 여전히 인기 있다. 하와이 도처에 우쿨렐레 축제와 학교가 있다. 심지어 우쿨렐레를 연주하는 아이들로 구성된 오케스트라도 있다! 그 악기는 포르투갈에서 왔지만, 지금 그것은 하와이 문화의 필수적인 부분이다.

**어휘** master [동] 숙달하다, 통달하다 traditional [형] 전통의 musical instrument 악기 (= instrument) Hawaii [명] 하와이 (Hawaiian [형] 하와이의 [명] 하와이 사람) Portuguese [형] 포르투갈의 [명] 포르투갈인 (Portugal [명] 포르투갈) root [명] (식물의) 뿌리; *기원 on board 승선한, 탑승한 immigrant [명] 이민자[이주민] sugarcane [명] 사탕수수 field [명] 들판, 밭 endure [동] 견디다, 참다 get to ~에 도착하다[닿다] Honolulu [명] 호놀룰루 (미국 하와이주의 주도) journey [명] 여정, 여행 relieved [형] 안도하는 shore [명] 해안[해변] jump off ~에서 뛰어내리다 folk song 민요 impress [동] 깊은 인상을 주다 hop [동] 뛰다, 뛰어다니다 flea [명] 벼룩 adopt [동] 입양하다; *취하다[차용하다] throughout [전] 도처에 orchestra [명] 오케스트라, 관현악단 essential [형] 필수적인, 극히 중요한 [문제] exhausted [형] 기진맥진한, 탈진한 amazed [형] 놀란 embarrassed [형] 당황스러운

**구문** [1행] For more than 130 years, Hawaiians–**from** artists **to** Waikiki beach boys–have learned to master *their traditional musical instrument*, *the ukulele*.
→ 「from A to B」는 'A부터 B까지'의 의미이다.
→ their traditional musical instrument와 the ukulele는 동격 관계이다.

5행 In 1879, **a ship** [named the *Ravenscrag*] arrived in Honolulu, Hawaii.
→ [ ]는 a ship을 수식하는 과거분사구이다.

6행 They were immigrants who came **to work** in the sugarcane fields.
→ to work는 '일하기 위해'의 의미로, 〈목적〉을 나타내는 부사적 용법의 to부정사이다.

7행 They **had endured** four months at sea to get to Honolulu from Portugal.
→ had endured는 과거완료(had v-ed)로 과거의 특정 시점(호놀룰루에 도착)까지 지속되었던 일을 가리킨다.

15행 Therefore, they **called** the instrument **a "ukulele,"** the Hawaiian word … .
→ 「call A B」는 'A를 B로 부르다'의 의미이며, 이때 a "ukulele"는 동사 called의 목적격 보어이다.

---

● **VOCABULARY INSIDE**

*Check Up*
| 1 adopted | 2 immigrants | 3 creative | 4 Fasten |
| 5 impressed | 6 essential | 7 invent | 8 instrument |

---

# UNIT 02 | **Numbers**                                              pp. 13-18

## READING 1    Chinese Numbers

◎ **Mini Quiz**
1 T    2 T

▶ **Reading Comprehension**
1 c    2 d    3 (1) 6  (2) 9  (3) 8    4 b

---

해석    중국 문화에서는, 모든 숫자들이 각각의 의미를 지닌다. 어떤 숫자들은 특별히 운이 좋고, 좋은 의미를 가지고 있다. 게다가, 중국인들은 이 숫자들을 반복해서 여러 번 쓰는 것은 더 많은 운을 가져온다고 생각한다. 그렇다면 이 숫자들은 무엇일까?

첫째, 중국인들은 숫자 6이 편한 삶을 가져온다고 믿는다. 중국어로 '6'을 뜻하는 단어는 '흐름'이라는 뜻의 단어와 비슷한 소리가 나서, 사람들은 숫자 6이 모든 일을 순조롭게 흘러가도록 해준다고 말한다. (A) 게다가, '6'에 해당하는 단어는 '행운'과 '도로'를 뜻하는 단어와 비슷한 소리가 나기도 한다. 이런 이유로, 오토바이 번호판 AW6666은 매우 비싼 값인 34,000달러에 팔렸다.

숫자 9는 영원을 의미한다. 고대에, 중국 통치자들은 궁궐이 영원히 지속되기를 바랐기 때문에 북경 자금성에 9,999칸의 방을 만들었다. 오늘날에는, 숫자 9는 낭만적인 방식으로 사용되기도 한다. 예를 들면, 중국 남성들은 영원한 사랑의 상징으로 여성들에게 종종 99송이나 999송이의 장미를 보낸다.

모든 숫자들 중 가장 행운의 숫자는 8인데, 그 (8이라는) 단어가 '부'를 뜻하는 단어와 비슷한 소리가 나기 때문이다. 사람들은 종종 숫자 8을 포함하는 날짜에 중요한 행사를 개최한다. (B) 예를 들어, 베이징 올림픽은 정확히 2008년의 8번째 달, 8번째 날, 8시 8분 8초에 시작되었다.

어휘 meaning [명] 뜻[의미] (mean [동] ~라는 뜻[의미]이다) especially [부] 특히 repeatedly [부] 되풀이하여, 여러 차례 comfortable [형] 편한 flow [명] 흐름 [동] 흐르다 smoothly [부] 부드럽게[순조롭게] similar to ~와 비슷한 for this reason 이러한 이유로 eternity [명] 영원 ancient [형] 고대의 ruler [명] 통치자, 지배자 palace [명] 궁전, 왕실 romantic [형] 로맨틱한, 낭만적인 symbol [명] 상징 everlasting [형] 영원한 wealth [명] 부(富), 재산 hold [동] 잡고 있다; *개최하다 important [형] 중요한 include [동] 포함하다 exactly [부] 정확히 [문제] method [명] 방법 indicate [동] 나타내다 fortune [명] 운; *재산 riches [명] 부, 재물

구문 [2행] Moreover, the Chinese **think** [**(that)** *using these numbers repeatedly brings* more luck].

→ [ ]는 동사 think의 목적어 역할을 하는 명사절로 접속사 that이 생략되었다.

→ using ... repeatedly는 명사절 내에서 주어 역할을 하는 동명사구로, 명사절의 동사는 brings이다. 동명사구 주어는 단수 취급한다.

[6행] In Chinese, the word for "six" **sounds like** the word for "flow," so people *say* [(*that*) the number six makes everything flow smoothly].

→「sound like」는 '~처럼 들리다'의 의미이다.

→ [ ]는 동사 say의 목적어 역할을 하는 명사절로, 앞에 접속사 that이 생략되었다.

→「make+목적어+동사원형」은 '~가 …하게 하다[만들다]'라는 의미이며, 이때 동사원형 flow는 사역동사 makes의 목적격 보어로 쓰였다.

[9행] ..., the motorcycle plate number AW6666 **was sold** for a very high price of $34,000.

→ was sold는 '팔렸다'의 의미로「be v-ed」의 수동태이다.

[17행] People often hold important events on **dates** [that include the number eight].

→ [ ]는 선행사 dates를 수식하는 주격 관계대명사절이다.

## READING 2 Egyptian Math

**Mini Quiz**

1 to record the changes of the moon's shape for farming and to construct their grand pyramids 2 doubling and adding numbers

**Reading Comprehension**

1 d 2 b 3 a, c 4 (1) 4, 12 (2) 144, 288

해석 기원전 6,000년 경부터, 초기 이집트인들은 비옥한 나일 계곡에 정착하기 시작했다. 체계적인 사회를 건설하기 위해, 그들은 실용적인 목적으로 수학을 사용했다. 그들은 농사를 위해 달의 형태 변화를 기록하고 그들의 웅장한 피라미드를 건설하기 위해 수학을 사용했다. 그들은 '두 배로 만들기'라고 불리는 곱셈법을 이용함으로써 이 과업들을 수행했다. 이 방법은 숫자들을 두 배로 만들고 더하기를 포함한다. 여기 한 가지 예가 있다.

문제 24×25를 풀어보자. 우선, 아래와 같이 표를 만들어라. 다음으로, 두 개의 숫자들 중 하나를 골라라. 24를 고른다고 가정하자. 왼쪽 단에, 1부터 시작해서 이 숫자를 계속 두 배로 만들어라. 다음 두 배가 된 숫자가 24보다 커지면 두 배로 만드는 것을 멈춰라. 그래서, 32가 24보다 크므로 16에서 멈춰야 한다. 다음으로, 왼쪽 단에서 합계가 24가 되는 숫자들을 찾아라. 이 숫자는 8과 16이다. 오른쪽 단에서는, 25부터 시작하고 이 숫자를 두 배로 만들어라. 그러고 나서, 8과 16의 맞은편에 있는 오른쪽 단의 숫자들을 더하는데, 그것들은 200과 400이다. 마침내 600이 나올 것인데, 그것이 25×24의 답이다! 고대 이집트인들이 수학에 대해 이렇게 깊이 이해하고 있었다는 것이 놀랍지 않은가?

어휘 Egyptian [형] 이집트의 [명] 이집트인 early [형] 초기의 settle [동] 해결하다; *정착하다 rich [형] 부유한; *비옥한 organized [형] 조직화된, 체계적인 practical [형] 실용적인 purpose [명] 목적 record [동] 기록하다 shape [명] 모양, 형태 farming [명] 농사 construct [동] 건설하다 grand [형] 웅장한 multiplication [명] 곱셈 involve [동] 수반[포함]하다 double [동] 두 배로 되다[만들다] add [동] 더하다 chart [명] 도표 suppose [동] 가정하다 column [명] 기둥; *(세로) 단 add up to 총 ~가 되다 across from ~의 맞은편에 finally [부] 마침내 understanding [명] 이해

구문 [3행] They used it [**to record** the changes of the moon's shape for farming] and [**to construct** their grand pyramids].

→ to record와 to construct는 〈목적〉을 나타내는 부사적 용법의 to부정사이며, 이들이 이끄는 두 개의 [ ]는 접속사 and로 병렬 연결되어 있다.

[11행] Next, find ***the numbers*** **in the left column** [that add up to 24].

→ in the left column은 the numbers를 수식하는 전치사구이다.

→ [ ]는 선행사 the numbers를 수식하는 주격 관계대명사절이다.

[14행] Finally, you'll get **600, which** is the answer to 25X24!

→ 「, which」는 선행사 600을 부연 설명하는 계속적 용법의 주격 관계대명사이다.

[15행] Aren't you **surprised** [that ancient Egyptians had such a deep understanding …]?

→ [ ]는 감정(surprised)의 이유를 나타낸다.

**● VOCABULARY INSIDE**

*Check Up* 1 constructed 2 practical 3 eternity 4 involves 5 settling 6 meaning 7 ancient 8 comfortable

## UNIT 03 | Fiction

pp. 19-24

### READING 1 Alice in Wonderland

**Mini Quiz**

1 mathematician 2 people more than a mile high

**▶ Reading Comprehension**

1 c 2 a 3 c 4 eat balanced amounts

**▶ Grammar Inside LEVEL 1**

[Check Up] have to prepare

해석 많은 사람들이 루이스 캐럴을 1865년에 출간된 명작 아동 문학 「이상한 나라의 앨리스」를 집필한 영국 작가로 알고 있다. 독자들은 마법의 세계를 통한 앨리스와 그녀의 여정이 담긴 그의 이야기를 좋아한다. 하지만, 사람들은 캐럴이 또

한 재능 있는 수학자였다는 것은 잘 모를 것이다. 그는 대학생들에게 수학과 논리학을 가르쳤고, 수학에 관한 책들을 출간하였다. 몇몇 연구가들은 그가 그의 이야기에 숫자와 수학적인 아이디어를 숨기기를 좋아했다고 말한다.

한 가지 예가 「이상한 나라의 앨리스」의 제5장에서 발견된다. 앨리스는 키를 3인치로 줄게 하는 케이크를 먹는다. 그녀는 정상 크기로 돌아가고 싶어서, 애벌레에게 도움을 요청한다. 애벌레는 그녀가 크기를 변화시킬 수 있는 버섯을 먹어야한다고 제안한다. 그는 그것의 한쪽 면은 그녀를 더 크게 만들어주지만, 다른 쪽은 그녀를 더 작게 만들 것이라고 말한다. 이 말은 앨리스가 적절한 비율에 도달하기 위해서는 균형 잡힌 양을 먹어야만 한다는 것을 의미한다. 캐럴은 이 장에 등장하는 아이디어를 전통 기하학 법칙에서 빌려왔다.

캐럴은 또한 숫자 42를 좋아했던 것으로 보이는데, 그래서 이 숫자는 이 이야기에 자주 등장한다. 예를 들어, 여왕은 '규정 제42조'에 근거하여 앨리스에게 떠날 것을 명령한다. 그 규정은 키가 1마일이 넘는 사람은 법정을 떠나야 한다고 말하고 있다. 책에는 심지어 42개의 삽화가 있다.

「이상한 나라의 앨리스」는 예기치 않은 놀라움으로 가득 차 있고, 이런 수학적 미스터리들은 더욱 재미를 더한다!

**어휘** classic [형] 명작의, 걸작의 tale [명] 이야기, 소설 journey [명] 여행[여정] magical [형] 마법의 gifted [형] 재능 있는 mathematician [명] 수학자 (mathematics [명] 수학 (= math) mathematical [형] 수학적인) logic [명] 논리, 논리학 publish [동] 출판하다 hide [동] 감추다, 숨기다 shrink [동] 줄어들다 normal [형] 보통의, 정상적인 caterpillar [명] 애벌레 suggest [동] 제안하다 balanced [형] 균형 잡힌 amount [명] 총액; *양 proportion [명] (전체의) 부분; *(전체에서 차지하는) 비율 order [동] 명령하다 [명] 명령 based on ~에 근거하여 state [동] 말하다; *명시하다 court [명] 법정, 법원 be full of ~으로 가득 차다 unexpected [형] 예상 밖의 add [동] 더하다

**구문**

[10행] **She** wants to **return herself** to normal size, so she *asks for* help from a caterpillar.
→ herself는 She(Alice)를 대신하는 재귀대명사로, return의 목적어로 쓰였다.
→ 「ask for」는 '~을 요청하다'의 의미이다.

[13행] The caterpillar **suggests** (**that**) she **should eat** *a mushroom* [that can change her size].
→ 동사 suggests 뒤에 접속사 that이 생략되었다. suggest처럼 〈주장·제안〉을 나타내는 동사 뒤에 이어지는 명사절의 내용이 '~해야 한다'의 의미를 나타낼 경우, 명사절의 동사는 「(should+)동사원형」이 되어야 한다.
→ [ ]는 선행사 a mushroom을 수식하는 주격 관계대명사절이다.

[15행] ... **one** side of it will make her bigger, but **the other** will make her smaller.
→ 두 개 중 하나는 one으로, 나머지 다른 하나는 the other로 나타낸다.

[15행] It means Alice must eat balanced amounts **to reach** the right proportions.
→ to reach는 '도달하기 위해'의 의미로, 〈목적〉을 나타내는 to부정사의 부사적 용법이다.

[17행] Carroll **borrowed** the ideas in this chapter **from** traditional rules of geometry.
→ 「borrow A from B」는 'B로부터 A를 빌리다[차용하다]'의 의미이다.

[19행] Carroll also **seemed to like** the number 42, so it often appears in the story.
→ 「seem to-v」는 '~인 것 같다'의 의미이다.

ⓥ **Mini Quiz**
  1 T   2 F

▶ **Reading Comprehension**
  1 b   2 c   3 a   4 a submarine called the Nautilus

▶ **Grammar Inside LEVEL 2**
  `Check Up`  1 the teacher whom Michael likes   2 the article that his friend wrote

**해석**
    1866년, 이상한 바다 괴물이 전 세계의 배들을 공격하고 있다. 그리하여 미국 정부는 그 괴물을 사냥하기 위해 탐험 대를 보낸다. 탐험대에는 피에르 아로낙스라는 이름의 과학자, 그의 하인 콩세유, 네드 랜드라는 사냥꾼이 포함되어 있다.

(B) 몇 달 후, 탐험대는 자신들이 찾고 있던 그 사나운 생물을 발견한다. 하지만 배를 공격해 오던 그 괴물은 사실 노틸러 스라는 잠수함이다. 짧은 전투 끝에, 아로낙스, 콩세유, 네드는 붙잡힌다. 그 남자들은 잠수함으로 안내된다. 그리고 그들은 잠수함의 지휘관인 네모 선장을 만난다.

(C) 네모는 그들이 절대 떠날 수 없다는 점을 분명히 하지만, 포로들이 노틸러스호를 탐험하도록 내버려 둔다. 그러고 나 서 그는 그들을 많은 모험에 데리고 간다. 그들은 상어를 사냥하고, 거대한 오징어를 물리치고, 심지어 환상의 땅 아 틀란티스를 방문한다. 그 남자들은 이러한 탐험을 즐기지만, 여전히 탈출해서 자신들의 삶으로 돌아가고 싶어 한다.

(A) 어느 날, 노틸러스호가 노르웨이 근처의 소용돌이로 빨려 들어간다. 노틸러스호가 파괴될 것 같다. 다행히도, 그 세 남자는 배를 타고 탈출한다. 그들은 현지인들에 의해 구조되지만, 네모 선장과 그의 놀라운 잠수함이 살아남았는지 결코 알지 못한다.

**어휘**
strange ⑱ 이상한, 낯선   attack ⑧ 공격하다   government ⑲ 정부   expedition ⑲ 탐험; 탐험대   include ⑧ 포함하다   name ⑧ 이름을 짓다[부르다]   servant ⑲ 하인   suck ⑧ (입으로) 빨다; *(기계 등이) 빨아들이다   destroy ⑧ 파괴하다   fortunately ⑨ 다행스럽게도   local ⑲ 현지의   find out ~을 알아내다   submarine ⑲ 잠수함   survive ⑧ 살아남다   fierce ⑲ 사나운   creature ⑲ 생물   search ⑧ 찾아보다, 수색하다   brief ⑲ 짧은   battle ⑲ 전투   capture ⑧ 붙잡다, 생포하다   guide ⑧ (안내하여) 데려가다   commander ⑲ 지휘관   captive ⑲ 포로   explore ⑧ 탐험하다   fight off ~을 물리치다   squid ⑲ 오징어   fantasy ⑲ 환상, 공상   escape ⑧ 탈출하다   [문제] discovery ⑲ 발견   crew ⑲ 승무원, 선원   creature ⑲ 생명체

**구문**
  `2행` So the US government sends an expedition **to hunt** the monster.
    → to hunt는 '사냥하기 위해'의 의미로, 〈목적〉을 나타내는 to부정사의 부사적 용법이다.

  `7행` They are saved by local people, but they never **find out** [**if** Captain Nemo and his amazing submarine survived].
    → [ ]는 find out의 목적어 역할을 하는 명사절로, '~인지 아닌지'라는 의미의 접속사 if가 쓰였다.

  `10행` However, **the monster** [that has been attacking ships] **is** actually *a submarine* {called the Nautilus}.
    → [ ]는 문장의 주어인 선행사 the monster를 수식하는 주격 관계대명사절이며, 동사는 is이다.
    → { }는 a submarine을 수식하는 과거분사구이다.

  `15행` Nemo **lets the captives explore** the Nautilus, *though* he makes it clear that they can never leave.
    → 「let+목적어+동사원형」은 '~가 …하게 두다'의 의미이며, 이때 동사원형 explore는 사역동사 lets의 목적격

보어이다.

→ though는 〈양보〉를 나타내는 접속사로 '비록 ~이지만'의 의미이다.

→ it은 가목적어, that they can never leave가 진목적어이다.

**17행** They **hunt** sharks, **fight off** a giant squid, and even **visit** *Atlantis, a land of fantasy.*

→ hunt, fight off, visit이 접속사 and로 병렬 연결되어 있다.

→ Atlantis와 a land of fantasy는 동격 관계이다.

---

## ● VOCABULARY INSIDE

---

# UNIT 04 | Business

pp. 25-30

## READING 1   The Gig Economy

**Ⓥ Mini Quiz**

1 T   2 F

▶ **Reading Comprehension**

1 a   2 c   3 d   4 the pandemic

▶ **Grammar Inside LEVEL 2**

**Check Up**  can't miss

---

**해석**

최근 많은 나라에서 gig 경제가 발달했다. 그런데 gig 경제가 무엇일까? 'gig'이라는 단어는 음악 산업에서 왔으며 단기 일자리를 가리킨다. 그래서 gig 경제에서는 기업들이 임시직 또는 시간제 근로자에게 의존한다. 이 직원들은 그들이 하는 일의 양에 대한 보수를 받는다. 개인 교사, 베이비시터, 승차 서비스 운전사가 gig 근로자의 예이다.

gig 경제는 많은 이점을 가지고 있다. 예를 들어, 기업들은 gig 앱으로 수많은 사람들 중에서 근로자를 고를 수 있다. 이는 그들이 숙련된 근로자를 빨리 찾을 수 있게 해준다. 근로자들은 스스로 일정을 짤 수 있기 때문에 gig 일자리가 편리하다고 생각한다. 게다가, 그들은 원하는 만큼 일할 수 있다.

이런 장점들에도 불구하고, gig 경제는 부정적인 측면도 있다. gig 경제에서는 근로자들이 장기적인 경력을 쌓기 어렵다. 게다가, 그들은 회사의 (복지) 혜택을 받지 않는다. 예를 들어, 그들은 병가를 내지 않는다. (그들은 또한 자주 휴식을 취할 수 있다.)

그럼에도 불구하고, 연구는 세계적인 전염병 기간 동안 gig 일자리의 수가 크게 증가했다는 것을 보여준다. 사실, 세계에는 5백만 명이 넘는 승차 서비스 운전사들이 있으므로 그것들에 대한 수요가 틀림없이 있다. gig 경제가 그저 지나가는 유행일 리가 없다는 것은 분명하다.

**어휘**

gig 몡 (특히 임시로 하는) 일   economy 몡 경제   develop 통 발달하다   industry 몡 산업   refer to ~을 가리키다

term 몡 용어; *기간   rely on ~에 의존하다   temporary 혱 임시의   employee 몡 근로자 (employment 몡 고용

employ 통 고용하다)   amount 몡 양   private 혱 개인적인   tutor 몡 가정교사   advantage 몡 장점

a number of 많은 ~   skilled 혱 숙련된   convenient 혱 편리한   schedule 몡 일정   negative 혱 부정적인

aspect 몡 측면   career 몡 경력   furthermore 묑 게다가   benefit 몡 이득; *(회사에서 받는) 혜택   take a break

휴식을 취하다   nevertheless 묑 그럼에도 불구하고   increase 통 증가하다   significantly 묑 상당히   pandemic

몡 전세계적인 전염병   demand 몡 수요   [문제] right 몡 권리

**구문**

**2행** The word "gig" **comes** from the music industry and **refers** to short-term work.
→ 동사 comes와 refers가 접속사 and로 병렬 연결되어 있다.

**4행** These employees **get paid** for the amount of *work* [(*that*) they do].
→ 「get v-ed」는 '~하게 되다'의 의미로 수동태이다.
→ [ ]는 선행사 work를 수식하는 목적격 관계대명사절로, 관계대명사 that이 생략되었다.

**5행** [Private tutors, babysitters, and drivers for ride services] **are** examples of gig workers.
→ [ ]는 주어이고, are가 동사이다. Private tutors, babysitters, drivers for ride services가 접속사 and로 병렬 연결되어 있다.

**9행** This **allows them to find** skilled workers quickly.
→ 「allow+목적어+to-v」는 '~가 …하게 하다'의 의미이며, 이때 to find는 동사 allows의 목적격 보어이다.

**13행** In gig economies, **it**'s difficult *for workers* **to develop long-term careers.**
→ it은 가주어이며, to develop long-term careers는 진주어, for workers는 to develop long-term careers의 의미상의 주어이다.

---

**READING 2   Polymer Money**

**Mini Quiz**
1 form   2 security features

**Reading Comprehension**
1 d   2 d   3 b   4 holograms and transparent windows

**Grammar Inside LEVEL 2**
**Check Up** two times as heavy as

**해석**   세상은 종이를 쓰지 않고 (돈을) 지불하는 것으로 바뀌고 있지만, 많은 사람들이 여전히 손에 종이 현금을 쥐는 것을 선호한다. 그러나, 점점 돈은 더는 종이로 만들어지지 않는다. 세계의 은행들이 최첨단 플라스틱 폴리머로 만들어진 돈으로 전환하면서 돈의 형태가 바뀌고 있다. 예를 들어, 호주는 수십 년 동안 폴리머 돈을 사용해 왔고, 영국도 또한 최근에 모든 지폐를 폴리머로 교체했다. 뉴질랜드, 루마니아, 캐나다도 폴리머 지폐를 사용하기 시작했다.

폴리머 돈은 얇고 투명한 플라스틱 필름으로 제작된다. 이것에 홀로그램과 투명창과 같은 보안상의 특징이 더해져 있다. 이것들은 위조지폐를 만드는 것을 매우 어렵게 한다.

게다가, 폴리머 지폐는 구식의 종이 지폐보다 더 튼튼하다. 그것은 찢김이나 구멍 나는 것의 영향을 덜 받아서, 종이 화폐보다 적어도 2.5배는 더 오래간다. 폴리머 지폐는 또한 종이돈보다 더 깨끗한데, 그것은(종이돈은) 박테리아와 바이러스를 며칠씩 가지고 다닐 수 있다.

이러한 많은 이점들 때문에, 많은 은행들이 폴리머를 돈의 미래라고 본다. 언젠가, 한국을 포함해 어디서나 폴리머 지폐를 보게 될 수 있을 것이다!

**구문**　4행 It is changing form **as** banks around the world switch to *money* [made of high-tech plastic polymers].
→ as는 〈때〉를 나타내는 접속사로, '~함에 따라, ~하면서'의 의미이다.
→ [ ]는 money를 수식하는 과거분사구이다.

10행 These **make *it*** extremely **difficult** *to produce fake money*.
→ 「make+목적어+형용사」는 '~을 …하게 만들다'의 의미이며, 이때 형용사 difficult는 동사 make의 목적격 보어이다.
→ it은 가목적어, to produce fake money는 진목적어이다.

14행 Polymer banknotes are also cleaner than **paper money, which** can carry bacteria and viruses for days.
→ 「, which」는 paper money를 선행사로 하는 계속적 용법의 주격 관계대명사이다.

---

● **VOCABULARY INSIDE**

| *Check Up* | 1 affect | 2 temporary | 3 carry | 4 payment |
|---|---|---|---|---|
| | 5 convenient | 6 switch | 7 demand | 8 career |

---

# UNIT 05 | Society

pp. 31-36

## READING 1　The Color Purple

**♡ Mini Quiz**
1 because purple dye was rare　2 much more than the monthly salary of an ordinary person

**▶ Reading Comprehension**
1 c　2 a　3 b, d　4 (the first) artificial dyes

해석 초상화에서 왕과 왕비가 보라색 옷을 자주 입고 있다는 것을 알았는가? 보라색과 왕족과의 관련성은 고대까지 거슬러 올라간다. 비잔틴 제국에서, 통치자들은 화려한 보라색 예복을 입었다. (A) 이러한 이유로, 사람들은 왕족의 자녀들이 '보라색으로 태어났다'고 말했다. 심지어 로마 시민들은 황제에 의해 보라색 옷을 입는 것을 금지당했다.

그럼 보라색은 왜 왕족의 색깔로 여겨졌는가? 이것은 보라색 염료가 희귀했기 때문이었다. 수 세기 동안, 보라색 염료는 티레의 페니키아에서 생산되었다. 염료 제조업자들은 그것을 티레 인근의 지중해에서만 발견될 수 있는 작은 바다 우렁이에서 얻었다. 염료를 만드는 과정 또한 매우 어려웠다. 우선, 우렁이의 껍데기를 깨뜨려 열고, 정확한 시간 동안 햇볕에 놓아야 했다. 1그램의 보라색 염료를 만들기 위해 무려 9,000마리나 되는 바다 우렁이가 필요했다. (B) 그리하여, 이것이 염료를 너무 비싸게 만들어서 오직 왕족만 보라색 직물을 살 여유가 되었다. 한때, 1파운드의 보라색 모직은 보통 사람의 월급보다 훨씬 높은 가치가 있었다. 하지만 19세기 중반에, 최초의 인공 염료가 만들어졌다. 이것이 보라색을 더 널리 이용되게 했다.

어휘 notice [동] 의식하다[알다] portrait [명] 초상화 connection [명] 관련성[연관성] between A and B A와 B 사이에 royalty [명] 왕족(들) (royal [형] 왕의[여왕의]) date back to ~으로 (시간을) 거슬러 올라가다 empire [명] 제국 ruler [명] 통치자, 지배자 fancy [형] 화려한 robe [명] 예복 citizen [명] 시민 ban A from B A가 B하는 것을 금지하다 emperor [명] 황제 rare [형] 드문, 희귀한 Mediterranean Sea 지중해 process [명] 과정 shell [명] 껍데기[껍질] crack [동] 갈라지다; *깨뜨리다 exact [형] 정확한 afford [동] (~하거나 살) 여유가 되다 fabric [명] 직물, 천 wool [명] 털, 모직 worth [형] ~의 가치가 있는 salary [명] 급여, 봉급 ordinary [형] 보통의, 평범한 artificial [형] 인공의 widely [부] 널리, 폭넓게 [문제] valuable [형] 귀중한; *값비싼 available [형] 구할[이용할] 수 있는

구문 [9행] Dye makers got it from **a small sea snail** [that *can* only be found in the Mediterranean Sea near Tyre].

→ [ ]는 a small sea snail을 선행사로 하는 주격 관계대명사절이다.

→ 문장의 전체 시제는 과거이지만, 선행사인 바다 우렁이(a small sea snail)가 현재에도 지중해에서 발견되므로, 주격 관계대명사절 내에서는 현재 시제(can)가 쓰였다.

[11행] First, the snails' shells **had to be cracked** open and **(be) put** in the sunlight … .

→ 조동사 had to 뒤에 be cracked와 (be) put이 접속사 and로 병렬 연결되어 있다.

[13행] **It took** *as many as* 9,000 sea snails **to make** one gram of purple dye.

→ 「it takes+시간[노력/재료]+to-v」는 '~하는 데 …가 들다[필요로 하다]'의 의미이다.

→ 「as+ 형용사[부사]의 원급+as」는 '~만큼 …한[하게]'의 의미이다.

[14행] Therefore, this made the dye **so** expensive **that** only royalty **could** afford purple fabric.

→ 「so ~ that … can」은 '너무 ~해서 …할 수 있다'의 의미이다.

[15행] At one time, one pound of purple wool was worth **much** more than the monthly salary of an ordinary person.

→ much는 '훨씬'의 의미로 비교급을 강조하는 부사이며, a lot, even, far 등으로 바꿔 쓸 수 있다.

**◊ Mini Quiz**
　1 T　　2 F

▶ **Reading Comprehension**
　1 a　　2 b　　3 b　　4 40 liters of water

해석　　예멘의 산악 마을인 마나하에는 물이 드물다. 건기에는, 마을 사람들은 저수지에서 물을 얻기 위해 먼 거리를 이동한다. 이 물이 깨끗하진 않지만, 사람들은 절박하다. 비록 이 마을에는 강수량이 아주 적지만, 항상 많은 안개가 있다. 그리고 안개는 사실 물로 이루어져 있는데, 그것은 작은 물방울 구름이다. 이런 이유로, 마나하의 물 부족을 해결하기 위해 몇몇 단체들은 안개에서 수분을 '채집하려고' 노력하기 시작하였다.

　　그 단체들은 안개를 잡아서 물로 바꾸는 특수 그물을 개발해냈다. (B) 그 그물은 배구 네트처럼 생겼고, 촘촘한 나일론으로 만들어져 있다. (A) 이 물질은 물방울을 채집하는 데 효과적이다. (C) 안개가 그물을 통과할 때, 작은 물방울들이 그곳에 달라붙어 서로 모인다. 물방울이 충분히 커지면, 그것들은 아래에 있는 물탱크에 떨어진다.

　　안개 수집기를 세우는 비용은 15달러 미만이다. 이것은 마나하 주민들이 수백 개를 설치할 만큼 충분히 저렴하다. 각 그물은 하루에 물 40리터 이상을 모을 수 있는데, 이것은 7명의 가족이 마시기에 충분한 양이다. 이 기술로, 마나하의 사람들은 안개에서 깨끗한 물을 채집할 수 있다.

어휘　　collector 뗑 수집가; *수집기　　rare 뼹 드문, 희귀한　　dry season 건기(乾期)　　distance 뗑 거리　　gather 똥 모으다[수집하다], 모이다　　desperate 뼹 자포자기한; *간절히 원하는　　rainfall 뗑 강우량　　tiny 뼹 아주 작은　　organization 뗑 조직, 단체　　harvest 똥 수확하다, 거둬들이다　　moisture 뗑 수분, 습기　　shortage 뗑 부족　　material 뗑 직물, 천; *재료　　effective 뼹 효과적인　　capture 똥 붙잡다　　volleyball 뗑 배구　　fine 뼹 좋은; *아주 가는　　cling 똥 달라붙다　　cost 똥 (값·비용이) 들다　　set up ~을 세우다[설치하다]

구문　　**1행** During the dry season, villagers travel long distances **to gather** water from reservoirs.
　　→ to gather는 '얻기 위해'의 의미로, 〈목적〉을 나타내는 to부정사의 부사적 용법이다.

　　**5행** And fog **is** actually **made up of** water … .
　　→ 「be made (up) of」는 '~으로 구성되다[이루어지다]'라는 의미로, 재료의 물리적 변화를 나타낼 때 쓰인다. 「be made from」도 동일한 의미이지만, 재료의 화학적 변화를 나타낼 때 주로 쓴다.

　　**8행** The organizations developed **special nets** [that capture fog and turn it into water].
　　→ [ ]는 선행사 special nets를 수식하는 주격 관계대명사절이다.

　　**9행** This material is effective **in capturing** water drops.
　　→ 「in v-ing」는 '~하는 데 있어서'의 의미이며, 이때 capturing은 전치사 in의 목적어로 쓰인 동명사이다.

　　**14행** [Building a fog collector] **costs** less than $15.
　　→ [ ]는 주어 역할을 하는 동명사구이고, costs가 동사이다. 동명사구 주어는 단수 취급한다.

　　**15행** Each net can collect more than 40 liters of water a day, **which** is enough *for a family of seven to drink*.
　　→ 「, which」는 앞 절 전체를 선행사로 하는 계속적 용법의 주격 관계대명사이다.
　　→ for a family of seven은 to drink의 의미상의 주어이다.

**● VOCABULARY INSIDE**

*Check Up* 1 gather 2 shortage 3 desperate 4 afford
5 rare 6 royalty 7 worth 8 organization

# UNIT 06 | Animals

pp. 37-42

## READING 1 Orphaned Elephants

**Mini Quiz**
1 T 2 F

**▶ Reading Comprehension**
1 d 2 b 3 d 4 elephants, ivory

**해석** 2002년에, 사람들은 숲에서 홀로 있는 새끼 코끼리를 발견했다. 스트레스를 받고 탈진한 이 동물은 태어난 지 겨우 일주일이 되었다. 슬프게도, 그 코끼리는 엄마가 죽임을 당하는 것을 보았고, 이것이 그녀에게는 대단히 충격적이었다. 그녀는 웬디라는 이름이 주어졌다. 웬디와 그녀의 엄마에게 무슨 일이 벌어진 걸까?

15분마다 야생 코끼리 한 마리가 사냥꾼에게 죽임을 당한다. 코끼리 상아는 채집되어 불법 시장에서 팔린다. 그래서, 많은 양의 상아를 가진 성체 코끼리가 보통 표적이 된다. 그러나 성체 코끼리를 사냥하는 것은 그들의 공동체 전체에 영향을 미친다. 어미 코끼리가 죽임을 당하면, 어린 새끼들은 먹이, 보호, 또는 보살핌 없이 고아로 남겨진다.

다행히도, 동물 보호단체들은 이 심각한 상황을 더 나아지게 하려고 노력하고 있다. 그들은 웬디같은 코끼리 고아들을 구조해서 탄자니아에 있는 코끼리 고아원으로 보낸다. 그 코끼리들은 그곳에서 9년에서 14년 동안 머문다. 어리고 약한 코끼리들은 24시간 내내 보살핌을 받는다. 점차 자라면서, 그들은 자신들만의 사회적 단위를 형성하며 마침내 보호구역으로 풀려난다.

비록 고아원이 굉장한 일을 수행하긴 하지만, 새끼 코끼리는 어미에 의해 길러져야 한다. 그 끔찍한 관행이 멈춰지지 않는다면, 이러한 비극적인 상황은 계속될 것이다.

**어휘** orphan [동] 고아로 만들다 [명] 고아 (orphanage [명] 고아원) exhausted [형] 탈진한 traumatic [형] 대단히 충격적인 hunter [명] 사냥꾼 (hunt [동] 사냥하다) illegal [형] 불법적인 massive [형] 거대한; *(수량 등이) 엄청난 target [명] 목표; *표적, 목표물 affect [동] 영향을 미치다 community [명] 공동체[사회] protection [명] 보호 (protect [동] 보호하다) care [명] 돌봄[보살핌] conservation [명] 보호, 보존 rescue [동] 구하다, 구조하다 weak [형] 약한, 힘이 없는 around-the-clock 24시간 내내[밤낮으로] form [동] 형성시키다; *모이다[이루다] unit [명] 단일체, 단위 eventually [부] 결국 release [동] 풀어 주다 raise [동] 들어올리다; *키우다[기르다] horrible [형] 끔찍한 practice [명] 실행; *관행 tragic [형] 비극적인

**구문** [5행] The elephant ivory **is taken** and **(is) sold** in illegal market.
→ 수동태로 쓰인 동사 is taken과 (is) sold가 접속사 and로 병렬 연결되어 있다.

[7행] But **hunting** adult elephants **affects** their whole community.

→ 동명사(hunting)가 주어인 경우 항상 단수 취급하여 뒤에 단수 동사(affects)가 쓰인다.

[15행] **As** they *grow older*, they form their own social units and … .

→ as는 〈때〉를 나타내는 접속사로, '~함에 따라, ~하면서'의 의미이다.

→ 「grow+형용사」는 '~하게 되다'의 의미이다.

[18행] **Unless** the horrible practice **is** stopped, this tragic situation will continue.

→ unless는 '만약 ~하지 않는다면'의 의미의 〈조건〉을 나타내는 접속사로, 〈시간·조건〉을 나타내는 부사절에서는 현재시제가 미래시제를 대신한다.

## READING 2 Camels in the Desert

**Mini Quiz**

1 one of its humps begins to shrink 2 survive

▶ **Reading Comprehension**

1 c 2 d 3 b 4 oval-shaped blood cells

해석 낙타는 몇 달 동안 물 없이 지내는 것으로 알려져 왔다. 많은 사람들은 낙타의 혹이 물로 가득 차 있다고 추측하지만, 그것은 사실이 아니다. 낙타는 혹에 물이 아닌 지방을 저장한다. 그들의 혹은 지방 조직으로 이루어져 있는데, 지방 조직은 에너지원으로 저장된다. 낙타가 사막에서 먹을 것 없이 지낼 때, 그것의 혹들 중 하나는 줄어들기 시작한다. 낙타의 혹은 또한 체온을 유지하는 것을 돕는다. 낮 동안에, 그들의 혹에 있는 지방은 낮의 더위를 막는 데 도움을 준다. 그것은 낙타들이 과열되고 땀을 흘리는 것을 방지한다. 반대로, 그것은 밤에 낙타를 따뜻하게 해준다.

비록 혹이 물을 저장하지는 않지만, 낙타는 여전히 물을 사용하는 데 효율적이다. 이것은 그들의 혈액 세포의 독특한 특징 때문이다. 혈액 세포는 타원형이다. 타원형의 혈액 세포는 낙타가 한 번에 30갤런이나 되는 물을 섭취하는 것을 가능하게 한다. 그 세포들은 유연하고 쉽게 모양을 바꿀 수 있다. 그것들은 체내 수분이 떨어질 때 혈액이 더 쉽게 흐르도록 한다. 낙타가 혹 없이는 사막에서 살아남을 수 없다는 것은 사실이다. 하지만 여전히 그렇게 많은 물을 저장하도록 돕는 것은 혹이 아니라 타원형의 혈액 세포이다.

어휘 assume [동] 추정하다, 추측하다 be filled with ~으로 가득 차다 store [동] 저장하다 fat [명] 지방 (fatty [형] 지방으로 된, 지방이 많은) be made of ~으로 구성되다 source [명] 원천 shrink [동] 줄어들다 daytime [명] 낮, 주간 overheat [동] 과열되다 sweat [동] 땀을 흘리다 conversely [부] 정반대로 efficient [형] 효율적인 due to ~ 때문에 unique [형] 독특한 blood [명] 혈액 cell [명] 세포 consume [동] 소비하다; *(음식물을) 섭취하다 gallon [명] 갤런(액량 단위) at a time 한 번에 flexible [형] 유연한 flow [동] 흐르다 survive [동] 살아남다 [문제] locate [동] ~의 위치를 찾아내다 source [명] 원천 reinforce [동] 강화하다 strength [명] 힘 adapt to ~에 적응하다 maintain [동] 유지하다 temperature [명] 온도

구문 [1행] Camels **have *been known*** *to go* for months without water.

→ have been known은 '알려져 왔다'의 의미로, 〈계속〉을 나타내는 현재완료의 수동태(have been v-ed)이다.

→ 「be known to-v」는 '~한 것으로 알려지다'의 의미이다.

[2행] Many people **assume** [**that** the humps of a camel are filled with water], but it's not true.

→ that은 명사절을 이끄는 접속사로, [ ]는 동사 assume의 목적어 역할을 한다.

6행 Their humps are made of **fatty tissue, which** is stored *as* a source of energy.
→「, which」는 fatty tissue를 선행사로 하는 계속적 용법의 주격 관계대명사이다.
→ as는 '~으로'의 의미인 전치사이다.

11행 It **prevents** them **from** *overheating* and *sweating*.
→「prevent A from B」는 'A가 B하는 것을 막다'의 의미이다.
→ 동명사 overheating과 sweating이 접속사 and로 병렬 연결되어 있다.

12행 Conversely, it **keeps camels warm** at night.
→「keep+목적어+형용사」는 '~을 …한 상태로 유지하다'의 의미이며, 이때 형용사 warm은 keeps의 목적격 보어이다.

15행 The oval-shaped blood cells make **it** possible **for camels** [to consume *as much as* *30 gallons of water* at a time].
→ it은 가목적어, [ ]는 진목적어이다. for camels는 [ ]의 의미상의 주어이다.
→「as much as ~」는 양이 많은 것을 강조하는 원급 비교 표현이다.

18행 **It** is true **that** *camels could not survive* in the desert *without* their humps.
→ It은 가주어, that 이하가 진주어이다.
→ that 이하는 가정법 과거로서, '만약 ~가 없다면, …할 것이다'로 해석하며 현재 사실에 반대되거나 실현 가능성이 전혀 없는 일을 가정한다. 이때 without은 '~가 없다면'의 의미로 가정법의 if를 대신하고, that절은 「주어+could+동사원형」의 형태로 쓰였다.

● **VOCABULARY INSIDE**

| *Check Up* | 1 community | 2 illegal | 3 stores | 4 protection |
| | 5 efficient | 6 flexible | 7 release | 8 conversely |

# UNIT 07 | Social Media

READING 1    The Effects of Social Media

Ⓥ **Mini Quiz**
1 T   2 T

▶ **Reading Comprehension**
1 c   2 a   3 d   4 emotional problems[loneliness and depression], social media detox [detoxification]

▶ **Grammar Inside LEVEL 2**
Check Up  have lost

**사회자:** 최근에 사람들은 매일 몇 시간을 온라인에서 보내는 것 같습니다. 하지만 이것이 건강에 좋을까요? 오늘, 우리는 심리학자 레베카 스탠포드를 이 쇼에 초대했습니다. 스탠포드 박사님, 소셜 미디어의 영향에 대해 이야기해보죠. 소셜 미디어의 유행이 둔화되진 않았죠, 그렇죠?

**스탠포드 박사:** 아니, 그렇지 않아요. 사람들은 소셜 미디어를 일상생활의 중요한 부분으로 만들었어요. 그것은 뉴스와 정보에 접근하게 해주죠. 또한 그것은 가족, 친구, 그리고 심지어 유명 인사들과 소통하는 아주 좋은 방법입니다. 하지만 소셜 미디어에는 또 다른 측면도 있습니다.

**사회자:** 소셜 미디어가 어떻게 우리에게 부정적인 영향을 미칠 수 있을까요?

**스탠포드 박사:** 연구들은 소셜 미디어가 정서적인 문제를 일으킬 수 있다는 것을 알아냈어요. 사람들은 자신의 게시물에 있는 '좋아요'에 대해 걱정합니다. 그리고 그들은 무언가를 놓치는 것을 두려워하기 때문에 끊임없이 소셜 미디어를 확인하지요. 게다가 그들은 계속해서 자신을 소셜 미디어상의 다른 사람들과 비교합니다. 이는 외로움과 심지어 우울증으로 이어질 수 있습니다. 이런 일이 일어나면, 소셜 미디어 해독이 필요합니다.

**사회자:** 소셜 미디어 해독이 무엇인가요?

**스탠포드 박사:** 소셜 미디어 해독은 소셜 미디어를 사용하는 것으로부터 잠시 쉬는 시간입니다. 우선, 여러분이 온라인에서 활동하는 시간에 주의를 기울이고 스스로 제한을 설정하세요. 또한, 여러분의 실제 생활에 다시 접속하세요. 여러분이 즐기는 장소에 가고 사람들을 방문하세요. (요즈음 점점 더 많은 곳이 무료 인터넷 서비스를 제공합니다.) 실제 세계에 더, 소셜 미디어에는 덜 집중하세요!

어휘

effect 명 영향   social media 소셜 미디어   host 명 사회자, 진행자   recently 부 최근에   psychologist 명 심리학자   trend 명 트렌드, 추세   slow down 둔화되다   important 형 중요한 (importance 명 중요성)   daily 형 일상적인   access 명 접근   communicate 동 의사소통 하다   celebrity 명 유명 인사   emotional 형 정서적인   post 명 우편; *(인터넷) 게시글   constantly 부 끊임없이   compare 동 비교하다   loneliness 명 외로움   depression 명 우울증   take a break 잠시 휴식을 취하다   pay attention to ~에 주의를 기울이다   active 형 활동적인   limit 명 제한, 한계   connect 동 연결하다   real 형 실제의   [문제] harm 동 해치다   negatively 부 부정적으로   affect 동 영향을 미치다

구문

**1행** Recently, it **seems like** people spend hours every day online.
→ 「seem like」는 '~인 것 같다, ~처럼 보이다'의 의미이다.

**7행** Also, it's **a great way** [to communicate with family, friends, and even celebrities].
→ [ ]는 a great way를 수식하는 형용사적 용법의 to부정사구이다.

**13행** Moreover, they **keep** *comparing* themselves *with* others on social media.
→ 「keep v-ing」는 '계속 ~하다'의 의미이며, keep은 동명사(comparing)를 목적어로 취하는 동사이다.
→ 「compare A with B」는 'A를 B와 비교하다'의 의미이다.

**17행** A social media detoxification is **a time** [when you take a break *from using* social media].
→ [ ]는 선행사 a time을 수식하는 관계부사절이다.
→ using은 전치사 from의 목적어로 쓰인 동명사이다.

**18행** First, **pay** attention to *the time* [(*when*) you are active online] and **set** limits for yourself.
→ 동사 pay와 set이 접속사 and로 병렬 연결되어 있다.
→ [ ]는 선행사 the time을 수식하는 관계부사절로, 관계부사 when이 생략되었다.

## READING 2 Cause Marketing

**Mini Quiz**

1 organization  2 They can reach millions of customers in a matter of hours, and it requires less money and effort

**Reading Comprehension**

1 c  2 b  3 d  4 (1) Nonprofit organizations (2) Customers (3) Companies

**해석**

물건을 구입함으로써 세상을 도울 수 있다면 당신은 어떻게 느낄까? 당신은 아마 기분이 좋고, 그 물건을 다시 사는 것을 고려할 것이다. 이것이 코즈 마케팅이 기초를 둔 아이디어이다. 고객들이 구매하면, 기업은 비영리 단체에 기부를 한다. 이런 방식으로, 고객들은 비영리 단체를 돕고 기업들은 그들의 이익을 늘릴 수 있다.

요즘에는, 소셜 미디어가 코즈 마케팅을 훨씬 더 효과적으로 만든다. 고객들은 단지 소셜 네트워킹 사이트에 정보를 공유하는 것만으로 기업들이 기부하도록 할 수 있다. 이것은 기업에도 이득이다. 그들은 몇 시간 내에 수백만 명의 고객들에게 다가갈 수 있는데, 이것은 더 적은 돈과 노력을 필요로 한다.

코즈 마케팅의 아이디어는 American Express에 의해 1983년에 처음 도입되었다. 그 당시에, 그들은 고객들에게 자금을 요청하는 새로운 캠페인에 착수했다. 그 돈은 자유의 여신상을 복구하기 위해 모금되었다. 고객이 American Express의 카드를 사용할 때마다 1센트가 복구 작업에 기부되었다. American Express와 고객들의 이러한 협동으로 170만 달러가 모였다. 게다가, 그 회사는 카드 사용량이 28퍼센트 증가함을 보였다.

**어휘**

product [명] 상품, 제품  probably [부] 아마도  consider [동] 사려[고려]하다  customer [명] 고객, 소비자  purchase [명] 구입[구매] [동] 구입[구매]하다  donation [명] 기부, 기증 (donate [동] 기부[기증]하다)  nonprofit organization 비영리 단체  profit [명] 이익, 이윤  effective [형] 효과적인  benefit [동] 유익[유용]하다 [명] 혜택, 이득  reach [동] ~에 이르다[닿다]  a matter of (적은 수량 등에 쓰여) 단 몇 ~  require [동] 요구하다[필요로 하다]  effort [명] 수고; 노력  launch [동] 시작[개시]하다  raise [동] (자금 등을) 모으다  restore [동] 회복시키다; *복원하다 (restoration [명] 복원, 복구)  usage [명] 사용; *사용량  [문제] cooperation [명] 협력  competition [명] 경쟁  concept [명] 개념

**구문**

[8행] Nowadays, social media **makes cause marketing** *even* **more effective**.

→ 「make+목적어+형용사」는 '~을 …하게 만들다'의 의미이며, 이때 more effective는 비교급으로 동사 makes의 목적격 보어이다.

→ even은 '훨씬, 더욱'의 의미로, 비교급을 수식하는 부사이다.

[15행] The money was raised **to restore** the Statue of Liberty.

→ to restore는 '복구하기 위해'의 의미로 〈목적〉을 나타내는 부사적 용법의 to부정사이다.

[18행] **This cooperation** [between American Express and its customers] **raised** $1.7 million.

→ [ ]는 문장의 주어인 This cooperation을 수식하는 전치사구이며, 동사는 raised이다.

**VOCABULARY INSIDE**

*Check Up*

1 compare  2 required  3 effects  4 donation

5 customers  6 access  7 communicate  8 considering

# UNIT 08 | Psychology

## READING 1　Stendhal Syndrome

**⊙ Mini Quiz**
　1 T　2 F

▶ **Reading Comprehension**
　1 c　2 b　3 c　4 Extremely sensitive people

▶ **Grammar Inside LEVEL 2**
　**Check Up**　where to go

---

**해석**　**에이미:** 박사님, 지난주 제가 피렌체에서 휴가를 보내던 중에 이상한 일이 일어났어요. 저는 미켈란젤로의 작품을 보려고 갤러리를 돌아다니고 있었어요. 저는 그렇게 아름다운 것이 존재할 거라고는 상상도 못 했어요. 바로 그때, 갑자기 숨을 쉬기가 힘들었어요. 어지러웠고 땀이 났어요. 저는 무엇을 해야 할지 몰랐어요. 저에게 무슨 일이 일어난 걸까요?

**로버트 박사:** 음, 당신의 증상에 대해 걱정하지 않아도 됩니다. 그것들은 심각하지 않아요. 그것들은 당신이 스탕달 증후군을 겪었음을 시사합니다. 스탕달 증후군의 다른 증상에는 빠른 심장 박동과 실신이 포함됩니다. 사람들은 놀랄 만큼 아름다운 예술을 경험할 때 이런 식으로 반응할 수 있어요.

이 증후군은 프랑스 작가 Marie-Henri Beyle의 이름에서 따왔습니다. 그의 필명은 스탕달이었어요. (그는 스탕달 이외에 다른 필명들도 가지고 있었습니다.) 1800년대에, 스탕달은 피렌체의 산타 크로체 성당의 아름다움에 몹시 놀랐습니다. 그 감정은 너무나 강렬해서 그는 자신이 정신적인 문제를 겪고 있다고 생각했어요. 100건이 넘는 유사한 사례가 보고된 이후에 이 상태는 스탕달 신드롬이라는 이름이 붙었습니다. 이는 극도로 감성적인 사람들에게 발생할 수 있어요. 시차 또한 상황을 악화시킬 수 있어요. 하지만 증상은 오래가지 않아요. 며칠 휴식을 취하면 정상으로 돌아갈 겁니다.

**어휘**　syndrome 몡 증후군　wander 툉 거닐다[돌아다니다]　imagine 툉 상상하다　exist 툉 존재하다　all of a sudden 갑자기　trouble 몡 문제　breathe 툉 호흡하다, 숨을 쉬다　dizzy 혱 어지러운　sweaty 혱 땀투성이의, 땀에 젖은　symptom 몡 증상　serious 혱 심각한　heartbeat 몡 심장 박동　fainting 몡 기절　react 툉 반응하다　amazingly 톈 놀랍게도 (amazed 혱 대단히 놀란)　apart from ~을 제외하고; *~ 이외에도　extremely 톈 극도로, 극히　psychological 혱 정신[심리]의, 정신[심리]적인　condition 몡 상태, 질환　case 몡 경우; *사례　report 툉 알리다; *보고하다　sensitive 혱 세심한; *감성 있는; 민감한　jet lag (비행기 여행) 시차증　worsen 툉 악화되다, 악화시키다 (worse 혱 더 나쁜)　situation 몡 상황　last 툉 지속하다[되다]　normal 혱 평범한; *정상적인　rest 몡 휴식

**구문**　**1행** Doctor, **something strange** happened last week when I was on vacation in Florence.
　→ -thing, -one, -body로 끝나는 대명사는 형용사가 뒤에서 수식한다.

**4행** Just then, all of a sudden, I **had trouble breathing**.
　→ 「have trouble v-ing」는 '~하는 데 어려움을 겪다'의 의미이다.

**15행** The feeling was **so strong that** he *thought* [(that) he was having psychological problems].
　→ 「so+형용사+that」은 '매우 ~해서 …하다'의 의미이다.
　→ [ ]는 동사 thought의 목적어 역할을 하는 명사절로, 접속사 that이 생략되었다.

[17행] This condition **was named** Stendhal syndrome after more than 100 similar cases *had been reported*.

→「A be named B」는 'A가 B로 명명되다'의 의미로, 「name A B」의 수동태이다.

→ had been reported는 「had been v-ed」 형태의 과거완료 수동태로, 스탕달 신드롬이라고 이름 지어진 때(과거의 특정 시점)까지 보고되었던 것을 말한다.

## READING 2 Do You Feel What I Feel?

**[V] Mini Quiz**

1 temperature 2 Surprisingly, the temperature of their hands dropped by an average of 0.2˚C while they were watching the video.

▶ **Reading Comprehension**

1 c 2 watching someone feeling cold 3 b 4 c

▶ **Grammar Inside LEVEL 2**

[Check Up] 1 after 2 until

**해석** 어느 날, 닐 해리슨 박사는 영화를 보는 동안 추위를 느꼈다. 그것은 특히 어느 한 장면 동안 일어났다. 그 장면에서, 벌거벗은 한 남자가 얼어붙은 북극에서 뛰고 있었다. 해리슨 박사는 어떤 사람이 추워하는 것을 보는 것이 실제로 자신의 체온을 낮췄는지 궁금해졌다.

해리슨 박사와 다른 연구자들은 이것을 실험해보기로 했다. 연구를 위해, 그들은 36명의 지원자들을 찾아 그들의 손에 작은 체온계를 부착했다. 그러고 나서 그들은 그 그룹에 비디오를 보여줬다. 비디오에서, 사람들은 얼음물에 손을 담그고 있었다. 동시에 지원자들의 체온 변화가 측정되었다. 놀랍게도, 그들이 비디오를 보고 있는 동안에 그들의 손 온도는 평균 섭씨 0.2도 떨어졌다. 이것은 작지만 주목할 만한 수치이다.

연구자들은 이 체온 변화가 감정 이입 때문이라고 말한다. 감정 이입은 우리가 다른 사람들의 감정을 이해하고 공유하게 한다. 하지만 그 연구는 감정 이입이 감정의 변화뿐만 아니라 신체적인 변화까지도 일으킬 수 있다는 것을 보여준다. 우리가 누군가가 차갑거나 따뜻한 온도를 경험하는 것을 볼 때, 우리의 신체 온도는 실제로 변할지도 모르며, 이것은 우리가 그들이 어떻게 느끼는지를 경험하도록 한다.

**어휘** scene [명] 장면 in particular 특히 naked [형] 벌거벗은 frozen [형] 얼어붙은 wonder [동] 궁금하다, 궁금해하다 actually [부] 실제로, 정말로 lower [동] 내리다[낮추다] temperature [명] 온도 researcher [명] 연구원 volunteer [명] 자원봉사자; *지원자 attach [동] 붙이다, 첨부하다 thermometer [명] 온도계, 체온계 dip [동] (액체에) 살짝 담그다 measure [동] 측정하다[재다] at the same time 동시에 drop [동] 떨어지다 average [명] 평균 significant [형] 중요한; *주목할 만한 due to ~ 때문에 empathy [명] 감정 이입, 공감 emotion [명] 감정 (emotional [형] 감정의) experience [동] 겪다, 경험하다 [문제] relationship [명] 관계 curiosity [명] 호기심 influence [동] 영향을 주다 physical [형] 육체[신체]의

**구문** [3행] Dr. Harrison wondered **whether** *watching someone feeling cold had* actually *lowered* his own body temperature.

→ whether는 명사절을 이끄는 접속사로, '~인지 아닌지'의 의미이다.

→ 명사절 내 주어는 동명사구(watching someone feeling cold)이며, 동사는 had lowered이다.

→「watch+목적어+v-ing」는 '~가 …하고 있는 것을 보다'의 의미이며, 이때 현재분사 feeling은 watching의

목적격 보어이다.

**14행** Empathy **allows us to understand** and **(to) share** others' emotions.
→ 「allow+목적어+to-v」는 '~가 …하게 하다'라는 의미이다. to understand와 (to) share는 동사 allows의 목적격 보어이며, and로 병렬 연결되었다.

**15행** But the study **shows** [that empathy can lead to physical *changes* as well as emotional *ones*].
→ [ ]는 동사 shows의 목적어 역할을 하는 명사절이다.
→ ones는 앞서 나온 명사 changes의 반복을 피하기 위해 쓰인 대명사이다.

**17행** ..., our body temperature may actually change, **which** *lets us experience* [how they feel].
→ 「, which」는 앞 절 전체를 선행사로 하는 계속적 용법의 주격 관계대명사이다.
→ 「let+목적어+동사원형」은 '~가 …하게 하다[두다]'라는 의미이며, 이때 동사원형 experience는 사역동사 lets의 목적격 보어이다.
→ [ ]는 「의문사+주어+동사」 어순의 간접의문문으로, experience의 목적어 역할을 한다.

---

● **VOCABULARY INSIDE**

| *Check Up* | 1 symptoms | 2 wonder | 3 measure | 4 react |
| | 5 exist | 6 attached | 7 imagine | 8 volunteers |

---

## UNIT 09 | Winter

pp. 55-60

**READING 1**　**Christmas Trees**

ⓥ **Mini Quiz**
　1 T　2 F

▶ **Reading Comprehension**
　1 b　2 d　3 (1), (3), (4), (2)　4 The royal family, The influence of media publications

**해석**　　다양한 크리스마스 전통 중에서, 크리스마스트리를 세우는 것보다 더 인기 있는 것은 없다. 이 전통은 어떻게 시작되었을까? 역사학자들은 최초의 크리스마스트리가 독일에서 유래되었다고 믿는다. 723년에 한 영국인 선교사가 종교적인 이유로 독일로 여행을 갔다. 도착하고 나서, 그는 몇몇 원주민들이 그들의 신 토르에게 기도하기 위해 떡갈나무에 모여 있는 것을 지켜보았다. 선교사는 그 나무를 베어 넘어뜨렸다. 그다음에 그는 사람들이 근처의 상록수를 그들의 신성한 나무로 대신 숭배하도록 설득했다.

　　중세 시대 동안, 독일 사람들은 12월 24일에 그 나무를 자신들의 집에 전시하기 시작했다. 그들은 에덴동산을 나타내는 사과와 다른 장식품들을 추가했다. 16세기에 마틴 루터는 나무에 양초들을 매달았다. 이것이 크리스마스 조명의 첫 등장이었다. (하지만 이 전통은 유럽의 숲에 부정적인 영향을 미치기 시작했다.)

독일인들이 영국으로 이주하면서, 그들은 그들의 관습을 가지고 갔다. 조지 3세의 독일인 부인은 윈저 성에 나무가 장식되도록 했다. 나중에, 빅토리아 여왕과 앨버트 공은 크리스마스트리를 그들의 휴일 기념행사의 공식적인 부분으로 만들었다. 왕실은 심지어 그들의 나무와 함께 신문과 잡지에 특집으로 실렸다. 미디어 출판물의 영향은 그 후 계속 그 전통이 살아있도록 해 왔다.

**어휘** various [형] 다양한 tradition [명] 전통 put up 세우다 historian [명] 역사학자 originate [동] 유래하다 Germany [명] 독일 (German [명] 독일인 [형] 독일인의) missionary [명] (외국에 파견되는) 선교사 religious [형] 종교의 native [명] 원주민 oak tree 떡갈나무 pray [동] 기도하다 chop down 베어 넘기다 convince [동] 확신시키다; *설득하다 holy [형] 신성한 display [동] 전시하다 decoration [명] 장식(품) (decorate [동] 장식하다[꾸미다]) represent [동] 대표하다; *나타내다 century [명] 세기, 100년 appearance [명] 외모; *등장 have an impact on ~에 영향을 주다[미치다] negative [형] 부정적인 European [형] 유럽의 migrate [동] 이주하다 custom [명] 관습 celebration [명] 기념행사 feature [동] 특징으로 하다; *(영화·잡지 등에서) 특집으로 다루다 influence [명] 영향 publication [명] 출판(물) [문제] beloved [형] 인기 많은 ornament [명] 장식품

**구문**

[2행] Historians **believe** [(**that**) the first Christmas tree originated in Germany].

→ [ ]는 동사 believe의 목적어 역할을 하는 명사절로 접속사 that이 생략되었다.

[4행] **Having arrived**, he *watched some natives gathering* at an oak tree to pray to their god, Thor.

→ Having arrived는 〈때〉를 나타내는 분사구문이며, 선교사가 도착한 것이 원주민들이 모여 있는 것을 본 것보다 먼저 일어난 일이므로 완료형 분사구문(having v-ed)이 쓰였다.

→ 「watch+목적어+v-ing」는 '~가 …하고 있는 것을 지켜보다'의 의미이다. 이때 현재분사 gathering은 지각동사 watched의 목적격 보어이다.

[11행] Later, they added **apples and other decorations** [representing the Garden of Eden].

→ [ ]는 apples and other decorations를 수식하는 현재분사구이다.

[19행] The German wife of King George III **had trees decorated** at Windsor Castle.

→ 「have+목적어+v-ed」는 '~가 …되게 하다'의 의미이다. 사역동사 have는 목적격 보어로 동사원형을 쓰지만, 목적어 trees와의 관계가 수동이므로 과거분사인 decorated가 쓰였다.

[21행] … Prince Albert **made** Christmas trees [an official part of their holiday celebrations].

→ 5형식 동사 make는 '~을 …으로 만들다'의 의미로, 이때 명사구 [ ]는 made의 목적격 보어이다.

## READING 2 The Reindeer: An Arctic Survivor

**Mini Quiz**

1 First, scientists have recently found that reindeer's eyes change color from gold to blue in winter., The second adaptation is reindeer's hooves. They have spongy pads on the bottom. 2 these pads shrink to expose the sharp edges of the hoof

**Reading Comprehension**

1 b 2 c 3 b, d 4 (1) blue (2) enemies (3) sharp edges (4) on the ice

**해석**

순록은 지구상에서 가장 척박한 환경인 북극에 산다. 그곳의 기온은 섭씨 영하 40도만큼이나 낮으며, 겨울에는 밤이 수개월 동안 계속될 수 있다. 이러한 환경에 대처하기 위해, 순록은 두 가지 흥미로운 적응 방법을 진화시켜 왔다.

첫째, 최근 과학자들은 순록의 눈이 겨울에는 금색에서 푸른색으로 변한다는 것을 알아냈다. 여름에는, 그들의 눈은 망막을 통해 대부분의 빛을 반사해서 금색으로 보인다. (A) 그러나, 겨울에는, 그들의 눈은 빛을 아주 약간만 반사하도록 변하여, 푸른색으로 된다. 이것은 순록의 눈을 빛에 더 민감하게 만들고 그들이 더 잘 볼 수 있게 도와준다. 결과적으로, 그들은 어두운 북극의 겨울에 먹이를 찾고 적들을 알아챌 수 있다.

두 번째 적응은 순록의 발굽이다. 그들은 발굽 바닥에 스펀지 같은 발바닥을 가지고 있다. 그 발바닥은 여름에 순록이 부드럽고 젖은 땅 위에서 마찰력을 가지도록 해준다. 다시 말해서, 순록은 미끄러지지 않고 달릴 수 있고 빠르고 쉽게 움직일 수 있다. (B) 그러나, 겨울에는, 이 발바닥이 오그라들어서 발굽의 날카로운 가장자리가 드러나게 된다. 이것은 순록이 눈 위를 달리고 얼음을 꽉 붙잡도록 해준다.

**어휘**

reindeer [명] 순록 Arctic [형] 북극의 (the Arctic 북극) survivor [명] 생존자 tough [형] 힘든; 거친 temperature [명] 온도, 기온 last [동] 계속되다; 지속하다 cope with ~에 대처하다 condition [명] 상태; *환경 evolve [동] 발달시키다; *진화하다 adaptation [명] 적응 recently [부] 최근에 reflect [동] 반사하다 appear [동] ~처럼 보이다 sensitive [형] 세심한; *민감한 enemy [명] 적 hoof [명] 발굽 ((*pl.*) hooves) pad [명] 패드; *발바닥 bottom [명] 맨 아래; 바닥 slip [동] 미끄러지다 shrink [동] 줄어들다[오그라지다] expose [동] 드러내다 edge [명] 가장자리, 모서리 grip [명] 움켜쥠 [문제] region [명] 지역 seasonal [형] 계절의 endangered [형] 멸종 위기에 처한

**구문**

[3행] **To cope with** these conditions, reindeer *have evolved* two interesting adaptations.

→ To cope with는 '…에 대처하기 위해'의 의미로, 〈목적〉을 나타내는 to부정사의 부사적 용법이다.

→ have evolved는 〈결과〉를 나타내는 현재완료이다.

[7행] ..., their eyes change to reflect only a little light, **turning** blue.

→ turning은 '변하면서'의 의미로 〈연속동작〉을 나타내는 분사구문이다.

[8행] This **makes the reindeer's eyes more sensitive** to light and *helps them see* better.

→ 「make+목적어+형용사」는 '~을 …하게 만들다'의 의미이며, 이때 more sensitive는 형용사의 비교급으로 동사 makes의 목적격 보어이다.

→ 「help+목적어+동사원형[to-v]」은 '~가 …하는 것을 돕다'의 의미이며, 이때 동사 helps의 목적격 보어로 동사원형(see)이 쓰였다.

[13행] In other words, reindeer can **run** *without slipping* and **move** around quickly and easily.

→ 동사 run과 move가 접속사 and로 병렬 연결되어 있다.

→ 「without v-ing」는 '~하지 않은 채'의 의미이다.

[14행] However, in winter, these pads shrink **to expose** the sharp edges of the hoof.

→ to expose는 〈결과〉를 나타내는 to부정사의 부사적 용법이다.

**VOCABULARY INSIDE**

*Check Up* 1 displayed 2 evolve 3 represent 4 reflect[reflecting] 5 condition 6 sensitive 7 religious 8 exposed

# UNIT 10 | People

pp. 61-66

## READING 1 Jackie Robinson

**[V] Mini Quiz**

1 in 1955 2 he tried to fight for the rights of African Americans

**▶ Reading Comprehension**

1 c 2 were not welcome to play 3 d 4 d

**▶ Grammar Inside LEVEL 2**

[Check Up] 1 그 정보가 사실이 아니었음에도 불구하고, 모두 그것을 믿었다.
2 집에서 일찍 나섰음에도 불구하고, 제인은 학교에 늦었다.

**해석** 20세기 초에, 미국의 흑인 야구선수들이 메이저 리그 야구(MLB)에서 경기하는 것은 환영받지 못했다. 하지만 1947년 4월 15일, 재키 로빈슨이 브루클린 다저스팀에 입단함으로써 야구의 인종 장벽은 깨졌다. 로빈슨은 뛰어난 재능이 있는 선수였다. 메이저 리그 첫해에, 그는 12개의 홈런을 쳤고 내셔널 리그 챔피언쉽에서 다저스팀이 우승하도록 도왔다. 1949년에, 그는 내셔널 리그의 최우수 선수(MVP)에 지명되었다. 그는 또한 1955년에 그의 팀을 첫 번째 월드 시리즈 승리로 이끌었다. 그의 인기는 심지어 '재키 로빈슨이 그 공을 치는 것을 봤나요?'라는 노래에 영감을 주었다.

로빈슨이 뛰어난 선수임에도 불구하고, 그의 팀 동료들 중 일부는 그와 함께 뛰고 싶어 하지 않았다. 그는 종종 모욕을 당했고 혐오 메일과 죽음의 위협을 받았는데, 그저 그가 흑인이었기 때문이다. 그러나, 그는 절대 화내거나 반격하지 않았다. 그의 행동은 흑인뿐만 아니라 백인에게도 깊은 인상을 주었으며, 비폭력 미국 흑인 평등권 운동에 영향을 끼쳤다. (그 운동은 1960년대 내내 지속되었다.) 1957년에 은퇴한 이후로, 그는 흑인 인권을 위해 싸우려고 애썼다. 그의 메이저 리그 입단 50주년을 맞아, MLB는 그의 등 번호인 42번을 영구결번으로 하고, 재키 로빈슨 날인 4월 15일 이외에 어떤 선수도 그 숫자를 착용해서는 안 된다고 발표했다.

**어휘** barrier [명] 장벽 brilliantly [부] 찬란히; *뛰어나게 talented [형] 재능이 있는 athlete [명] 운동 선수 valuable [형] 귀중한 lead [동] 이끌다 victory [명] 승리 popularity [명] 인기 even [부] 심지어 inspire [동] 영감을 주다 insult [동] 모욕하다 threat [명] 협박, 위협 (threaten [동] 협박[위협]하다) fight back 반격하다 behavior [명] 행동 impress [동] 깊은 인상을 주다 influence [동] 영향을 미치다 nonviolent [형] 비폭력적인 right [명] 권리, 권한 movement [명] 움직임; *(사람들이 조직적으로 벌이는) 운동 throughout [전] 도처에; *~동안 죽, 내내 fight for ~을 위해 싸우다 anniversary [명] 기념일 retire [동] 은퇴하다; *(등 번호를) 영구결번으로 하다 announce [동] 발표하다 except [전] ~을 제외하고

**구문** [7행] In 1949, he **was named** the National League's Most Valuable Player (MVP).

→「A be named B」는 'A가 B로 불리다[지명되다]'의 의미로, 「name A B」의 수동태이다.

[14행] His behavior **impressed** whites *as well as* blacks and **influenced** the nonviolent Civil Rights Movement.

→ 동사 impressed와 influenced가 접속사 and에 의해 병렬 연결되어 있다.

→「B as well as A」는 'A뿐만 아니라 B도'의 의미로, 「not only A but also B」로 바꿔 쓸 수 있다.

[18행] ..., MLB retired his number, 42, and **announced** [**that** no other player could wear it except on *April 15, which* is Jackie Robinson Day].

→ that은 명사절을 이끄는 접속사로, [ ]는 announced의 목적어 역할을 한다.

→「, which」는 April 15를 선행사로 하는 계속적 용법의 주격 관계대명사이다.

## READING 2 Antonín Dvořák

**[V] Mini Quiz**

1 T 2 F

▶ **Reading Comprehension**

1 a 2 b 3 c 4 many instruments working together

▶ **Grammar Inside LEVEL 2**

[Check Up] 그 뉴스는 민감한 문제이다. 우리는 그에 관해 침묵을 지키는 것이 낫다.

**해석** 비록 클래식 음악을 좋아하지 않더라도, 아마 '신세계로부터'라는 곡은 들어봤을지도 모른다. 그것은 19세기 체코 출신의 작곡가인 안토닌 드보르작의 세계적으로 유명한 교향곡이다. 드보르작은 그의 아름다운 교향곡들로 유명하지만, 흥미롭게도, 그에게는 또 다른 열정이 있었는데, 그것은 바로 기차였다.

그가 아홉 살 때, 새로운 철로가 그의 고향을 바로 통과하여 지어졌다. 어느 봄날, 거대한 증기 기관차가 압도적인 소리를 내며 그를 지나쳐 돌진했다. 그날, 어린 드보르작은 기차와 사랑에 빠졌다. 기차에 대한 드보르작의 애정은 그의 평생에 걸쳐 지속되었다. 기차로 여행할 때마다, 그는 열차 시간표를 살피는 데 시간을 보냈다. 그리고 역에서 기차를 갈아탈 때마다, 그는 기차에 관해 기관사들과 이야기하곤 했다.

기차에 대한 그의 애정은 그의 음악에도 영감을 주었다. 예를 들어, 그의 교향곡 7번은 기차역에서 탄생하였다. 그가 프라하의 기차역에 서 있었을 때, 한 멜로디가 그에게 떠올랐다. 이것은 그의 가장 멋진 작품 중 하나가 되었다. 드보르작은 기차의 복잡한 설계와 기술적인 업적에도 감탄했다. 기차의 여러 부품들처럼, 드보르작의 교향곡은 극적인 효과를 만들어내기 위해 함께 연주하는 많은 악기를 사용한다.

**어휘** world-famous [형] 전세계적으로 유명한 symphony [명] 교향곡 composer [명] 작곡가 be famous for ~으로 유명하다 passion [명] 열정 railway [명] 철로 hometown [명] 고향 mighty [형] 힘센; *장대한 rush [동] 돌진하다 past [전] ~을 지나서 overwhelming [형] 압도적인 fall in love with ~와 사랑에 빠지다 last [동] (특정 시간 동안) 계속되다 lifetime [명] 일생 chat [동] 이야기를 나누다 engineer [명] 기술자 admire [동] 존경하다; *감탄하다 complex [형] 복잡한 design [명] 디자인; 설계 technical [형] 기술적인 achievement [명] 업적, 성취 part [명] 부분[일부]; *부품 instrument [명] 기구; *악기 produce [동] 생산하다; *만들어내다 dramatic [형] 극적인 effect [명] 영향, 효과 [문제] motivate [동] 동기를 부여하다

**구문** [1행] **Even if** you don't like classical music, you *may have heard* "From the New World."

→ Even if는 '비록 ~일지라도'의 의미로, 〈양보〉를 나타내는 접속사이다.

→ 「may have v-ed」는 '~했을지도 모른다'는 과거의 불확실한 추측을 나타낸다.

6행 One spring day, a mighty steam train rushed past him, **making** an overwhelming sound.

→ making 이하는 〈동시동작〉을 나타내는 분사구문으로, 이 경우 '~하면서'라고 해석한다.

9행 **Whenever** he traveled by train, he *spent hours studying* train schedules.

→ Whenever는 '~할 때마다'의 의미인 복합관계부사로, 시간의 부사절을 이끈다.

→ 「spend+시간+v-ing」는 '~하는 데 (시간을) 보내다'의 의미이다.

15행 This became **one of his greatest works.**

→ 「one of (the)+형용사의 최상급+복수 명사」는 '가장 ~한 … 중 하나'의 의미이다.

17행 ..., Dvořák's symphonies use **many instruments** [working together] to produce a dramatic effect.

→ [ ]는 many instruments를 수식하는 현재분사구이다.

---

● **VOCABULARY INSIDE**

*Check Up*     1 popularity    2 passion    3 inspired    4 talented
   5 dramatic    6 lasts    7 admired    8 rushed

---

# UNIT 11 | **Machines**     pp. 67-72

## READING 1   Fossil Finder

**Ⓥ Mini Quiz**

1 search    2 Thanks to drones, archaeologists can not only save time but also get huge amounts of information.

▶ **Reading Comprehension**

1 d    2 c    3 c    4 rough landscape and high temperatures

---

해석    드론은 장난감 비행기 이상의 것이다. 이 비행 로봇은 건물과 나무 꼭대기 위로 날아올라서 접근하기 어려운 각도에서 사진이나 영상을 찍을 수 있다. 대부분의 사람들이 단지 취미로 드론을 날리는 것을 즐기는 반면에, 고고학자들은 이제 연구를 위해 그것을 이용할 수 있다.

한 가지 좋은 예시가 투르카나 호수 지역 조사이다. 그 지역 표층에는 화석이 풍부하다. 그러나, 그곳의 거친 지형과 높은 온도는 이 지역에서 일하는 것을 어렵게 만든다. 연구를 더 쉽게 하기 위해, 고고학자들은 Fossil Finder라고 불리는 웹 사이트를 이용하여 드론 소유자들에게 도움을 요청했다.

그것의 원리는 다음과 같다. 첫째, 시민들은 드론으로 그 지역의 항공 이미지를 포착한다. 드론 소유자들은 힘든 환경을 견디지 않고 심지어 자신의 집에서 이 일을 할 수 있다. (C) 그리고 나서, 그들은 Fossil Finder 웹 사이트에 있는 프로그램에 그 이미지를 올린다. (A) 그 이미지들은 화석을 확인하도록 훈련받은 웹 사이트 회원들에 의해 평가된다.

(B) 그다음에, 고고학자들은 자신들이 화석을 찾아야 할 장소를 좁혀나간다. 드론 덕택에, 고고학자들은 시간을 절약할 수 있을 뿐만 아니라, 엄청난 양의 정보를 얻을 수 있다. 오늘날 이 프로젝트는 고고학자들이 광범위한 지역을 조사하고, 의미 있는 방식으로 대중과 상호 작용하는 방법이 되고 있다.

**어휘** fossil 몡 화석   drone 몡 드론, 무인 항공기   soar 통 급증하다; *(하늘 높이) 날아오르다   capture 통 포획하다; *정확히 포착하다[담아내다]   hard-to-reach 접근하기 어려운   take advantage of ~을 이용하다   research 몡 연구, 조사 통 연구[조사]하다   surface 몡 표면[표층]   rough 몡 거친   landscape 몡 풍경; *지표, 지형   owner 몡 주인, 소유주   citizen 몡 시민   aerial 몡 항공기에 의한   region 몡 지방, 지역   endure 통 견디다[참다]   tough 몡 힘든, 어려운   evaluate 통 평가하다   trained 몡 훈련받은, 숙달된   identify 통 확인하다[알아보다]   narrow down 좁히다[줄이다]   upload 통 업로드하다   thanks to ~ 덕택에   interact 통 상호 작용을 하다   meaningful 몡 의미 있는

**구문**

9행 However, its rough landscape and high temperatures make **it** difficult **to work in**.
→ it은 가목적어, to work in이 진목적어이다. 목적어가 길어질 때는 가목적어 it을 쓰고, 진목적어는 뒤에 둔다.

11행 ..., archaeologists asked drone owners for help, **using** a website called Fossil Finder.
→ using은 '사용하면서'의 의미로, 〈동시동작〉을 나타내는 분사구문이다.

13행 This is **how** it works: ... .
→ how는 〈방법〉을 나타내는 관계부사로, 선행사 the way와 함께 쓰지 않는다.

15행 The images are evaluated by **website members** [who are trained to identify fossils].
→ [ ]는 선행사 website members를 수식하는 주격 관계대명사절이다.

17행 ..., archaeologists narrow down **the places** [where they should search for fossils].
→ [ ]는 선행사 the places를 수식하는 관계부사절이다.

19행 Thanks to drones, archaeologists can **not only** save time **but also** get huge amounts of information.
→ 「not only A but also B」는 'A뿐만 아니라 B도'의 의미이다.

21행 Today, this project **has become** *a way for archaeologists* [*to research* wide regions and *to interact* with the public in a meaningful way].
→ has become은 「have v-ed」 형태의 〈계속〉을 나타내는 현재완료이다.
→ [ ]는 a way를 수식하는 형용사적 용법의 to부정사로, for archaeologists가 의미상의 주어이다. to research와 to interact가 접속사 and로 병렬 연결되어 있다.

## READING 2   Special Robots for Autism

**Ⓥ Mini Quiz**
1 F   2 T

**▶ Reading Comprehension**
1 b   2 a   3 c   4 children with autism[autistic children]

해석 앤터니는 자폐가 있는 일곱 살 소년이다. 오늘 그는 웃고 있는 로봇과 함께 시간을 보내고 있다. "네가 가장 좋아하는 음식은 무엇이니?"라고 로봇이 묻는다. "초콜릿 우유와 감자튀김이야."라고 앤터니는 대답한다. "나도 초콜릿 우유를 좋아해!"라고 로봇이 말한다. 로봇이 자신의 팔을 올려서 배를 문지르니, 앤터니가 그 움직임을 따라 한다. 그들은 서로 의사소통하고 있다.

자폐가 있는 아이들은 의사소통하고 표정을 읽는 데 어려움을 겪는다. 그들의 부족한 사회성의 결과로, 그들 중 일부는 고립될 수 있다. 안타깝게도, 어린 나이일 때 비정상적인 반응을 알아채는 것이 힘들어서 치료가 종종 지연된다.

자폐 아동의 사회성이 발달하도록 돕기 위해서, 과학자들은 특수 로봇을 발명했다. 그 로봇들은 자폐 아이들에게 감정을 알아보는 것을 알려줄 대단히 풍부한 얼굴 표정을 특징으로 한다. 아이들은 로봇의 표정과 일치하는 감정을 선택하라고 요구된다. 그러는 동안 그들의 반응은 기록된다. 로봇과의 상호 작용을 통해서, 그들은 사회적 상황에서 공감을 표현하고 적절하게 행동하는 법을 배운다. 의사들은 각각의 반응을 관찰하고 아이의 반응 시간을 계산할 수 있다. 이것이 그들이 어린 나이일 때 자폐를 진단하는 것을 돕는다. 이 로봇은 많은 자폐 아동들에게 친구, 교육자, 그리고 치료사 역할을 함으로써 그들을 돕고 있다.

어휘 reply [동] 대답하다 rub [동] 문지르다[비비다] movement [명] 움직임 communicate [동] 의사소통을 하다 struggle [동] 애쓰다, 힘겹게 나아가다 facial [형] 얼굴의 expression [명] 표현; *표정 (expressive [형] 나타내는; *표정이 있는 express [동] 표현하다) as a result 결과적으로 isolated [형] 고립된 treatment [명] 치료 delay [동] 지연시키다 notice [동] 의식하다; *알아채다 abnormal [형] 비정상적인 response [명] 대답; *반응 feature [동] 특징으로 삼다 highly [부] 크게, 대단히 identify [동] 확인하다[알아보다] match [동] 일치하다 meanwhile [부] 그 동안에 reaction [명] 반응 interaction [명] 상호 작용 (interactive [형] 상호 작용을 하는) empathy [명] 공감, 감정 이입 properly [부] 제대로, 적절히 observe [동] 보다[관찰하다] calculate [동] 계산하다 diagnose [동] 진단하다 educator [명] 교육자 therapist [명] 치료사 [문제] social [형] 사회의, 사회적인 intelligence [명] 지능 language [명] 언어 growth [명] 성장

구문 [7행] **Children** [with autism] ***struggle*** *to communicate* and (*to*) *read* facial expressions.

→ [ ]는 문장의 주어인 Children을 수식하는 전치사구이며, 동사는 struggle이다.

→ 「struggle to-v」는 '~하려고 애쓰다, ~하는 데 어려움을 겪다'의 의미이며, to communicate와 (to) read가 접속사 and로 병렬 연결되어 있다.

[9행] Sadly, treatment is often delayed, **as** *it* is difficult *to notice their abnormal responses at an early age.*

→ as는 '~ 때문에'의 의미로, 〈이유〉를 나타내는 접속사이다.

→ it은 가주어, to notice 이하가 진주어이다.

[11행] **To *help*** *autistic children develop* their social skills, scientists have invented special robots.

→ To help는 '돕기 위해'의 의미로, 〈목적〉을 나타내는 부사적 용법의 to부정사이다.

→ 「help+목적어+동사원형[to-v]」은 '~가 …하도록 돕다'의 의미이며, 이때 동사원형 develop은 help의 목적격 보어로 쓰였다.

[14행] Children are asked to choose **the emotion** [matching the robot's facial expression].

→ [ ]는 the emotion을 수식하는 현재분사구이다.

*Check Up*  **1** interaction  **2** observing  **3** identify  **4** evaluated
**5** diagnose  **6** endure  **7** features  **8** take advantage of

# UNIT 12 | Health

pp. 73-78

## READING 1  Move Your Fingers

### ♥ Mini Quiz
1 T  2 F

### ▶ Reading Comprehension
1 c  2 (1) c  (2) b  (3) a  3 a  4 extra forearm muscles, independently (of the other fingers)

### ▶ Grammar Inside LEVEL 2
Check Up  beside himself

**해석**  손가락 근육이 몇 개 있는지 알고 있는가? 하나도 없다고 말한다면 어떨까? 놀랍게도, 그건 사실이다! 우리의 손가락에는 근육은 없지만, 힘줄이 있다. 힘줄은 결합 조직일 뿐이어서, 스스로는 어떤 신체 일부도 움직이게 할 수 없다. 그렇다면 우리의 손가락은 어떻게 움직이는 것일까?

우리 손에 있는 힘줄은 우리의 손바닥과 팔뚝의 근육에 붙어 있다. 힘줄은 이 근육들을 각각의 손가락뼈에 연결한다. 우리가 손가락을 사용하고 싶을 때, 뇌는 신경에 신호를 보낸다. 그러면, 신경은 우리의 손바닥과 팔뚝에 있는 어떤 근육에게 팽팽하거나 느슨해지도록 지시한다. 근육이 팽팽해지면, 근육에 연결된 힘줄은 특정 손가락뼈를 당긴다. 이것이 손가락을 움직이게 한다.

그러나, 손바닥과 팔뚝의 근육은 손가락들에 균등하게 나뉘어 있지 않다. 엄지, 검지, 새끼손가락에는 여분의 팔뚝 근육이 있다. 그것은 이 손가락들이 다른 손가락들과는 독립적으로 움직이게 도와준다. 반면에 약지와 중지는 모든 손가락들을 움직이게 하는 근육을 공유하고 있다. 그래서 그 손가락들을 굽히거나 펼 때, 다른 손가락들도 그렇게 된다. 이 복잡한 구조는 우리의 손가락이 문을 열고, 이메일을 쓰고, 피아노를 연주하는 것과 같은 많은 놀라운 일을 하게 한다!

**어휘**  muscle 명 근육  connective 형 연결[결합]하는 (connect 동 잇다, 연결하다)  tissue 명 조직  attach 동 붙이다  palm 명 손바닥  forearm 명 팔뚝  bone 명 뼈  signal 명 신호  nerve 명 신경  certain 형 확실한; *어떤  tighten 동 팽팽해지다[팽팽하게 하다]  relax 동 휴식을 취하다; *긴장을 풀다  specific 형 구체적인; *특정한  divide 동 나뉘다[나누다]  evenly 부 고르게  thumb 명 엄지손가락  index finger 집게손가락(검지)  little finger 새끼손가락  extra 형 추가의[여분의]  independently 부 독립하여  ring finger 넷째 손가락(약지)  bend 동 굽히다  straighten 동 똑바르게 하다  complex 형 복잡한  structure 명 구조  such as ~와 같은

**구문**  1행 **What if** I told you there were *none*?
→ What if는 '~하면 어떨까?'라는 의미이다.
→ none은 '아무도 ~ 않다, 하나도 없다'의 의미이며, 그 자체로 부정의 뜻을 나타내는 대명사이다.

11행 Then the nerve **orders** *certain muscles* [in our palms and forearms] **to tighten or relax**.

→ 「order+목적어+to-v」는 '~가 …하도록 지시[명령]하다'의 의미이며, 이때 to tighten or relax는 동사 orders의 목적격 보어이다.

→ [ ]는 certain muscles를 수식하는 전치사구이다.

13행 **When** a muscle tightens, *the tendons* [connected to the muscle] pull on specific finger bones.

→ When은 '~할 때'의 의미로, 〈때〉를 나타내는 접속사이다.

→ [ ]는 the tendons를 수식하는 과거분사구이다.

19행 On the other hand, the ring and middle fingers share **the muscle** [that moves all the fingers].

→ [ ]는 the muscle을 선행사로 하는 주격 관계대명사절이다.

20행 So when they bend or straighten, the other fingers **will (bend or straighten)**, too.

→ 조동사 will 뒤에는 이미 언급된 내용의 반복을 피하기 위해 동사구 bend or straighten이 생략되었다.

---

## READING 2  Two Hungers

### ☑ Mini Quiz
1 This is because you have unconsciously trained yourself to eat snacks under certain situations.   2 separate

### ▶ Reading Comprehension
1 b   2 b   3 c   4 (1) hedonic  (2) homeostatic  (3) hedonic

### ▶ Grammar Inside LEVEL 2
Check Up  were taken care of

---

해석  사람들은 보통 하루에 적어도 몇 번은 배고픔을 느낀다. 하지만 당신은 두 가지 다른 종류의 배고픔이 있다는 것을 알고 있었는가? 대부분의 사람들은 배고픔을 음식에 대한 몸의 신체적 필요로 생각한다. 만약 당신이 한동안 먹지 않았다면, 당신의 배는 비어있음을 느끼기 시작하고, 소리를 낸다. 이것은 당신의 몸이 더 많은 열량을 필요로 한다는 것을 의미하며, 그것은 항상성 허기라고 불린다.

다른 종류의 배고픔은 쾌락성 허기라고 불린다. 항상성 허기와 반대로 쾌락성 허기는 정서적 필요에 의해 일어난다. 예를 들어, 스트레스를 받을 때, 당신은 간식에 대한 강한 욕구를 가질 수 있다. 당신의 몸은 이러한 칼로리를 필요로 하지 않지만, 당신의 뇌는 여전히 당신에게 그것들을 먹으라고 말한다. (당신은 식사를 거르면 안 된다. 그렇지 않으면 당신의 몸이 잘 작동하지 않을 것이다.) 이것은 당신이 무의식적으로 특정 상황에서 간식을 먹도록 스스로를 훈련시켰기 때문이다.

항상성 허기와 쾌락성 허기는 동일선상의 양 끝과 같다. 그들의 차이에도 불구하고, 그들은 서로 완전히 분리되어 있지 않다. 그래서 동시에 두 가지를 느끼는 것이 가능하다. 하지만 다음번에 당신이 배고픔을 느낄 때, 잘못된 이유로 먹도록 속아서는 안 된다.

어휘  hunger 명 굶주림, 허기 (hungry 형 배고픈)   at least 적어도   think of A as B A를 B로 생각하다   physical 형 신체적인   need 명 필요, 욕구   for a while 한동안   empty 형 비어 있는   calorie 명 열량, 칼로리   be referred

to as ~으로 불리다　contrary to ~와 반대로[달리]　desire 몡 욕구　brain 몡 뇌　consume 동 소비하다; *먹다
skip 동 깡충깡충 뛰다; *거르다　function 동 작동하다　unconsciously 뿐 무의식적으로　certain 톙 확신하는;
*특정의　situation 몡 상황　difference 몡 차이(점)　despite 쩐 ~에도 불구하고　completely 뿐 완전히
separate 톙 분리된　possible 톙 가능한　at the same time 동시에　trick 동 속이다　wrong 톙 잘못된
reason 몡 이유　[문제] balanced 톙 균형 잡힌　diet 몡 식사, 식습관　emotional 톙 정서적인　reasonable 톙
타당한, 합리적인

**구문**

**1행** But did you **know** [**that** there are two different kinds of hunger]?
→ that은 명사절을 이끄는 접속사로, [ ]는 동사 know의 목적어 역할을 한다.

**3행** **If** you haven't eaten for a while, your stomach *starts* to feel empty and *makes* noises.
→ if는 '만약 ~한다면'의 의미로 〈조건〉을 나타내는 접속사이다.
→ 동사 starts와 makes가 접속사 and로 병렬 연결되어 있다.

**5행** This **means** [(**that**) your body needs more calories], and it is referred to as homeostatic hunger.
→ [ ]는 동사 means의 목적어 역할을 하는 명사절로 접속사 that이 생략되었다.

**10행** Your body doesn't need these calories, but your brain still **tells you to consume** them.
→ 「tell+목적어+to-v」는 '~에게 …하라고 말하다'의 의미이며, 이때 to consume은 동사 tells의 목적격 보어이다.

**16행** So **it's** possible **to feel *both* at the same time**.
→ it은 가주어, to feel 이하가 진주어이다.
→ both는 '둘 다'를 의미하는 대명사로, 여기서는 homeostatic hunger와 hedonic hunger를 가리킨다.

● **VOCABULARY INSIDE**

| *Check Up* | 1 signal | 2 functions | 3 skip | 4 trick |
| | 5 bones | 6 connected | 7 empty | 8 bend |

# UNIT 13 | Maps

pp. 79-84

**READING 1**　**Voronoi Diagrams**

◎ **Mini Quiz**
1 imagine　2 He divided London into many sections that had their own separate water supply.

▶ **Reading Comprehension**
1 c　2 a　3 c　4 (1) mark　(2) midpoint　(3) upright

**해석** 보로노이 다이어그램은 무작위로 보이지만 거리에 따른 지역으로 신중하게 나뉘어 있다. 보로노이 다이어그램을 그리려면, 종이에 여러 개의 점을 표시하는 것으로 시작하라. 그런 다음 두 점을 선택하라. 다음으로, 그 두 점을 연결하는 보이지 않는 선을 상상하라. 그 보이지 않는 선의 중심점을 찾아라. 이 중심점을 통과하는 수직선을 그려라. 두 점의 세트들로 이 과정을 계속 반복하라. 결국 종이는 다수의 다각형 칸들을 담게 될 것이다. 그것들이 보로노이 다이어그램을 구성한다.

이 다이어그램은 질병의 근원을 찾을 수 있기 때문에 매우 귀중하다. 1854년에 콜레라가 런던 전역에 퍼졌다. 존 스노우 박사는 식수(食水)가 그것의 원인이라고 믿었다. 그는 런던을 별도의 급수 시설이 있는 지역들로 나누었다. 이것이 보로노이 다이어그램의 초기의 적용이었다. 그 다이어그램은 그가 물이 오염된 지역을 찾는 것을 도왔다. 그 결과는 대부분의 사망자가 소호에서 나오고 있다는 것을 보여주었다. 소호에서 펌프를 제거한 후, 사망률은 급락했다. 보다시피, 지역을 신중하게 나누는 행위는 꽤 강력한 일이다.

**어휘** diagram [명] 도표; *도식 random [형] 무작위의 region [명] 지역 based on ~에 근거하여 distance [명] 거리 mark [동] 표시하다 a number of 얼마간의; *다수의 imagine [동] 상상하다 invisible [형] 보이지 않는 connect [동] 연결하다 midpoint [명] 중간점 upright [형] 수직의 repeat [동] 반복하다 process [명] 과정 eventually [부] 결국 multitude [명] 다수 cell [명] 세포; *칸 valuable [형] 귀중한 identify [동] 확인하다; *찾다 section [명] 부분 separate [형] 별개의 water supply 수도 공급 시설, 상수도 application [명] 적용 area [명] 지역 polluted [형] 오염된 result [명] 결과 remove [동] 제거하다 rate [명] 비율 practice [명] 실행 [문제] construct [동] 건설하다; *구성하다 geographic [형] 지리(학)의, 지리(학)상의 source [명] 근원 social [형] 사회의 route [명] 길[경로] destination [명] 목적지[도착지] be provided with ~을 제공받다

**구문**

[6행] Next, imagine **an invisible line** [connecting the two points].
→ [ ]는 an invisible line을 수식하는 현재분사구이다.

[8행] Draw **an upright line** [that passes through this midpoint].
→ [ ]는 선행사 an upright line을 수식하는 주격 관계대명사절이다.

[15행] Dr. John Snow **believed** [(**that**) drinking water was the cause of it].
→ [ ]는 동사 believed의 목적어 역할을 하는 명사절로 접속사 that이 생략되었다.

[16행] He **divided** London **into** *sections* [that had their own separate water supply].
→ 「divide A into B」는 'A를 B로 나누다'의 의미이다.
→ [ ]는 선행사 sections를 수식하는 주격 관계대명사절이다.

[18행] The diagram **helped him locate** *the areas* [with polluted water].
→ 「help+목적어+동사원형[to-v]」은 '~가 …하도록 돕다'의 의미이며, 이때 동사원형 locate는 동사 helped의 목적격 보어이다.
→ [ ]는 the areas를 수식하는 전치사구이다.

## READING 2 The Kuril Islands

**[V] Mini Quiz**
1 the Pacific Ocean 2 military bases

▶ **Reading Comprehension**
1 b 2 c 3 a 4 c

▶ **Grammar Inside LEVEL 2**
[Check Up] 내 방을 치울 때, 나는 오래된 사진 몇 장을 찾았다.

**해석** 쿠릴 열도는 일련의 56개의 섬이다. 그 섬들은 일본의 홋카이도에서 러시아의 캄차카반도까지 뻗어 있다. 거의 170년 동안, 그 섬들은 두 국가 사이에 상당한 긴장을 불러일으켰다.

(B) 쿠릴 열도의 소유권은 1855년 시모다 조약에 의해 처음 확립되었다. 그 조약은 일본에 남부의 섬 네 개에 대한 통제권을 준 반면, 러시아는 나머지를 점유했다.

(C) 20년 후, 새로운 조약이 일본에 열도 전체를 부여했다. 그 대신 러시아는 사할린섬의 완전한 통제권을 얻었다. 그 후 30년에 걸쳐, 두 나라 사이의 심화되는 경쟁은 러일전쟁으로 이어졌다.

(A) 전쟁에서 승리한 후, 일본은 사할린의 남쪽 절반을 되찾았다. 그곳과 쿠릴 열도 모두는 제2차 세계 대전이 끝날 때까지 일본의 통치하에 있었다. 제2차 세계 대전에서 일본을 이겼을 때, 러시아는 다시 한번 열도 전체의 소유권을 되찾았다.

오늘날 쿠릴 열도는 약 2만 명의 사람들의 주거지이다. 쿠릴 열도의 위치 때문에, 그것들은 러시아에 정치적인 가치가 있다. 해협이 겨울에 얼지 않아 러시아 선박들이 일 년 내내 태평양에 접근할 수 있다. 러시아는 또한 그 섬들에 군사 기지를 건설했는데, 그 섬에는 광물과 귀금속이 풍부하다.

**어휘** a chain of 일련의 stretch [동] 늘이다; *뻗어 있다 peninsula [명] 반도 significant [형] 상당한 tension [명] 긴장 southern [형] 남쪽의, 남향의 remain [동] 계속 ~이다 rule [명] 규칙; *통치 defeat [동] 패배시키다[이기다] recover [동] 회복되다; *되찾다 ownership [명] 소유권 entire [형] 전체의 establish [동] 설립[수립]하다 treaty [명] 조약 gain [동] 얻다 possession [명] 소유(권) grant [동] 부여하다 in exchange 그 대신[답례로] decade [명] 10년 competition [명] 경쟁 political [형] 정치적인 value [명] 가치 access [동] 접근하다 the Pacific Ocean 태평양 year-round [부] 일 년 내내[연중 내내] construct [동] 건설하다 military base 군사 기지 mineral [명] 광물 precious [형] 귀중한 metal [명] 금속 [문제] tragic [형] 비극적인[비극의] dispute [동] 논쟁하다; *(소유권을 두고) 분쟁을 벌이다 territory [명] 영토 resource [명] 자원[재원]

**구문** [4행] For nearly 170 years, the islands **have caused** significant tension between the two nations.

→ have caused는 「have v-ed」 형태의 〈계속〉을 나타내는 현재완료이다.

[12행] **Ownership** [of the Kuril Islands] **was** first established by the Treaty of Shimoda in 1855.

→ [ ]는 Ownership을 수식하는 전치사구이며, Ownership이 문장의 주어이므로 단수 동사 was가 쓰였다.

[13행] The treaty **gave Japan control of the four southern islands**, *while* Russia gained possession of the rest.

→ gave는 4형식 동사로 간접목적어(Japan)와 직접목적어(control of the four southern islands)를 취한다.

→ while은 '~인 반면에'의 의미로, 〈대조〉를 나타내는 접속사이다.

**17행** Over the next three decades, ***growing competition*** [between the two countries] **led** to the Russo-Japanese War.

→ growing competition이 문장의 주어이고, led가 동사이다.

→ growing은 competition을 수식하는 현재분사이며, [ ]는 growing competition을 수식하는 전치사구이다.

**20행** The strait does not freeze in winter, ***allowing*** Russian ships to access the Pacific Ocean year-round.

→ allowing 이하는 〈결과〉를 나타내는 분사구문이다.

→ 「allow+목적어+to-v」는 '~가 …하게 하다'의 의미이며, to access는 allowing의 목적격 보어이다.

**22행** Russia has also constructed military bases on **the islands, which** are rich in minerals and precious metals.

→ 「, which」는 the islands를 선행사로 하는 계속적 용법의 주격 관계대명사이다.

---

### ● VOCABULARY INSIDE

| *Check Up* | | | |
|---|---|---|---|
| **1** invisible | **2** separate | **3** tension | **4** Remove |
| **5** remained | **6** entire | **7** gained | **8** repeat |

---

# UNIT 14 | Paintings

pp. 85-90

### READING 1  Las Meninas

#### ⓥ Mini Quiz
1 Margarita   2

#### ▶ Reading Comprehension
1 a   2 b   3 c   4 the king and queen[the royal couple]

#### ▶ Grammar Inside LEVEL 2
**Check Up** 1 Tom is a popular singer whose songs have stayed at the top of the music charts.

2 In the school, there are many people whose homes were destroyed by the tornado.

---

**해석**     디에고 벨라스케스는 17세기 스페인 화가였다. 그의 가장 유명한 초상화 중 하나는 스페인 왕의 딸인 마르가리타 공주의 것이었다. 그 초상화는 「라스 메니나스」라고 불리는데, 이것은 '시중드는 숙녀들'을 의미한다. 그 당시, 마르가리타

공주는 고작 다섯 살이었다. 그림에서 그녀는 흰색 드레스를 입고 시녀들에 의해 둘러싸인 채 정면을 똑바로 응시하고 있다. 그러나 그림은 보이는 것보다 더 복잡하다.

공주와 그녀의 시녀 외에 그림에는 많은 사람들이 있다. 예를 들어, 오른쪽 아래 모퉁이에 두 사람이 있다. 이들은 왕과 왕비를 즐겁게 하는 것이 직업인 왕실의 광대들이었다.

더욱 흥미롭게도, 당신은 그림 왼쪽에 있는 화가 자신을 볼 수 있다. 그는 캔버스에 그림을 그리면서, 공주 뒤에 서 있다. 그러나 그는 공주가 아닌 정면을 똑바로 응시하고 있다. 그렇다면 그는 누구를 그리고 있는가? 당신이 주의 깊게 본다면, 뒤쪽 벽에 있는 거울에 왕과 왕비가 비친 모습을 볼 수 있다. (C) 이러한 이유로, 몇몇 사람들은 그가 왕족 부부를 그리고 있는 것이라고 생각한다. (A) 공주와 시녀들은 그저 구경하려고 그곳에 있었던 것이다. (B) 그러나, 다른 사람들은 그가 마르가리타를 그리고 있으며, 구경하러 온 것은 왕과 왕비라고 생각한다. 그림의 각기 다른 대상에 집중하는 것은 그 그림을 더욱 흥미롭게 만든다.

어휘 | **portrait** 몡 초상화  **at that time** 그 당시에  **stare** 통 응시하다  **straight** 튀 똑바로  **ahead** 튀 앞에  **surround** 통 둘러싸다  **maid** 몡 하녀[시녀]  **complex** 혱 복잡한  **besides** 젠 ~ 외에  **lower** 혱 더 낮은 쪽의  **royal** 혱 왕실의  **entertainer** 몡 연예인; *광대  **amuse** 통 즐겁게 하다  **interestingly** 튀 흥미롭게도 (**interesting** 혱 흥미로운)  **carefully** 튀 주의 깊게, 신중히  **reflection** 몡 (거울 등에 비친) 상[모습]  **focus on** ~에 집중하다, 초점을 맞추다  **object** 몡 물체; *대상  [문제] **detail** 몡 세부 사항  **face** 통 ~을 마주보다; *(상황에) 직면하다

구문 | **2행** **One of his most famous portraits was** of *Princess Margarita, the daughter of the king of Spain.*
→ 「one of (the)+형용사의 최상급+복수 명사」는 '가장 ~한 …들 중 하나'의 의미이다. 문장의 주어가 One이므로, 단수 동사 was가 쓰였다.
→ Princess Margarita와 the daughter of the king of Spain은 동격 관계이다.

**9행** ..., she is wearing a white dress and staring straight ahead, (**being**) **surrounded** by her maids.
→ surrounded는 '둘러싸인 채'의 의미로 〈동시동작〉을 나타내는 분사구문이다. surrounded 앞에 being이 생략되었다.

**15행** These were royal entertainers whose job was **to amuse** the king and queen.
→ to amuse는 '즐겁게 하는 것'의 의미로, 문장의 보어로 쓰인 명사적 용법의 to부정사이다.

**17행** More interestingly, you can see **the artist himself** on the left side of the painting.
→ himself는 the artist를 강조하는 재귀대명사이다.

**25행** [Focusing on the different objects of the painting] *makes the painting more interesting.*
→ [ ]는 동명사구로 문장의 주어이며, 동사는 makes이다. 동명사구 주어는 단수 취급한다.
→ 「make+목적어+형용사」는 '~을 …하게 만들다'의 의미이며, 이때 more interesting은 형용사의 비교급으로 동사 makes의 목적격 보어이다.

## READING 2 A Hidden Painting

**Mini Quiz**

1 a portrait of a rural Dutch woman 2 around two and a half years before *Patch of Grass*

**Reading Comprehension**

1 d 2 b 3 c 4 to practice color and light techniques

**해석** 빈센트 반 고흐는 역사상 가장 많이 사랑받는 예술가 중 하나이다. 흥미롭게도, 새로운 기술이 또 하나의 그의 작품을 찾는 데 공헌했다. 그렇다면 그것은 어디에서 발견되었을까? 사실 그것은 반 고흐의 다른 그림 아래에 숨겨져 있었다.

그 발견에 관한 이야기는 반 고흐의 「풀밭」이라는 그림에서 시작되었는데, 그것은 1887년에 그려졌다. 처음에 연구자들은 그 그림에서 흐릿한 머리 윤곽을 발견했다. 그것이 무엇인지 알아내기 위해, 그들은 새로운 엑스레이 기술을 이용했다.

그 엑스레이 기술은 숨겨진 그림의 윤곽뿐만 아니라 색도 보여줄 수 있고, 이미지를 컬러 사진과 같이 드러내기 때문에 특별하다. 연구자들이 그림의 깊은 층을 정밀하게 촬영했을 때, 마침내 네덜란드 시골 여성의 초상화가 나타났다.

그 여성의 그림은 연구자들이 반 고흐의 작품을 이해하는 것을 도왔다. 그 초상화는 「풀밭」보다 약 2년 반 전에 그려졌다. 그 당시 네덜란드에 거주하는 동안, 반 고흐는 색과 빛의 기법을 연습하기 위해 많은 모델들을 그렸다. 연구자들은 그가 가난했기 때문에, 캔버스를 재사용하기 위해 그 여성 위에 잔디를 덧그렸다고 생각한다. 이 발견은 그의 화풍과 색상 선정이 어떻게 발전했는지 보여준다. 그것은 또한 대가조차도 연습이 필요하다는 것을 입증한다!

**어휘** hidden [형] 숨겨진, 숨은 beloved [형] (대단히) 사랑하는 contribute to ~에 기여하다 artwork [명] 미술품 beneath [전] ~ 아래에 discovery [명] 발견 (discover [동] 발견하다) begin with ~으로 시작하다 researcher [명] 연구원 unclear [형] 불분명한 outline [명] 개요; *윤곽 find out 알아내다 technique [명] 기술, 기법 reveal [동] 드러내다 scan [동] 살피다; *정밀 촬영하다 deep [형] 깊은 layer [명] 막[층] rural [형] 시골의, 지방의 emerge [동] 나오다[모습을 드러내다] reuse [동] 재사용하다 drawing [명] 그림 choice [명] 선택 develop [동] 성장[발달]하다 prove [동] 입증하다 master [명] 주인; *대가 practice [명] 연습 [문제] artistic [형] 예술의, 예술적인 underneath [전] ~의 밑에 analyze [동] 분석하다

**구문**

[9행] The X-ray technique is special because it can show the color **as well as** the outline of hidden paintings, *revealing* the image like a color photo.

→ 「B as well as A」는 'A뿐만 아니라 B도'의 의미이다.

→ revealing 이하는 〈연속동작〉을 나타내는 분사구문이며, '~이고' 혹은 '그리고'로 해석한다.

[17행] [Living in the Netherlands at that time], Van Gogh painted many models **to practice** color and light techniques.

→ [ ]는 〈때〉를 나타내는 분사구문으로, 여기서는 '~하는 동안'으로 해석한다.

→ to practice는 '연습하기 위해'의 의미로, 〈목적〉을 나타내는 부사적 용법의 to부정사이다.

[18행] The researchers **believe** [**that**, being poor, he painted grass over the woman *to reuse* the canvas].

→ that은 명사절을 이끄는 접속사로, [ ]는 동사 believe의 목적어 역할을 한다.

→ to reuse는 '재사용하기 위해'의 의미로, 〈목적〉을 나타내는 부사적 용법의 to부정사이다.

[20행] This discovery **shows** [how his drawing style and color choice developed].

→ [ ]는 「의문사+주어+동사」 어순의 간접의문문으로, 동사 shows의 목적어 역할을 한다.

● VOCABULARY INSIDE

*Check Up* 1 royal 2 beneath 3 portrait 4 surrounded 5 amused 6 outline 7 artworks 8 staring

## UNIT 15 | Places

pp. 91-96

### READING 1 The Chocolate Hills

**[V] Mini Quiz**

1 his giant teardrops became the hills 2 amazing

▶ **Reading Comprehension**

1 c 2 b 3 d 4 turns brown in the dry season

▶ **Grammar Inside LEVEL 2**

[Check Up] Unless you eat

해석

각각이 언덕만큼 큰 키세스 초콜릿이 천 개가 있다고 상상해 보라. 만약 그 말이 듣기 좋다면, 당신은 필리핀을 방문해야 한다! '초콜릿 언덕'은 필리핀의 보홀섬에 위치해 있다. 그 언덕들은 꽤 작아 대부분 그 높이가 30미터에서 50미터에 이른다. 적어도 1,300개가 모두 서로의 곁에 서 있는 채로 있다. 언덕들의 풀이 건기에 갈색으로 변하면 그것들이 마치 초콜릿처럼 보여서 그러한 이름을 갖게 되었다.

언덕들이 어떻게 형성되었는지에 대한 많은 전설이 있다. 한 유명한 이야기는 다투는 두 거인들이 서로에게 바위와 흙을 던지며 며칠을 보냈다는 것이다. 싸움이 끝났을 때, 그들은 엉망인 것들을 치우지 않은 채 떠났고 그것들이 언덕이 되었다. 또 다른 이야기는 인간인 여자와 사랑에 빠진 거인, Arogo에 관해 말한다. 자신의 진정한 사랑이 슬프게 죽었을 때, 그의 거대한 눈물은 언덕이 되었다.

전설들은 접어두고, 과학자들은 그 언덕이 융기되기 전에 한때 바다에 있는 산호초였다고 믿는다. 그러고 나서 바람과 빗물이 수천 년에 걸쳐 언덕을 매끄럽게 만들었다. 그러나, 아무도 초콜릿 언덕이 어떻게 만들어졌는지 확실히 알지 못하므로 이것은 그저 이론일 뿐이다. 하지만 바로 그것이 이 자연 현상을 훨씬 더 놀랍게 만든다!

어휘

hill [명] 언덕 the Philippines 필리핀 be located on ~에 위치해 있다 quite [부] 꽤, 상당히 mostly [부] 주로, 일반적으로 high [형] 높은; *높이가 ~인 at least 적어도 next to ~의 옆에 each other 서로 dry season 건기(乾期) legend [명] 전설 throw [동] 던지다 dirt [명] 먼지, 흙 mess [명] 엉망인 상태 fall in love with ~와 사랑에 빠지다 sadly [부] 슬프게도 teardrop [명] 눈물 aside [부] 옆에; *제쳐두고[접어두고] once [부] 한 번; *언젠가[한때] coral reef 산호초 smooth [동] 매끈하게 하다 theory [명] 이론, 학설 for certain 확실히 natural [형] 자연적인 phenomenon [명] 현상 amazing [형] 놀라운 [문제] jewel [명] 보석 mysterious [형] 불가사의한 form [동] 형성하다

구문

[7행] There are at least 1,300, [all standing next to each other].

→ [ ]는 〈동시동작〉을 나타내는 분사구문이며, '~한 채'로 해석한다.

**10행** One famous story is [**that** two fighting giants *spent days throwing* rocks and dirt at each other].

→ that은 명사절을 이끄는 접속사로, [ ]는 문장의 보어 역할을 한다.

→ 「spend+시간+v-ing」는 '~하는 데 (시간을) 보내다'의 의미이다.

**13행** Another story tells of **a giant, Arogo**[, who fell in love with a human woman].

→ a giant와 Arogo는 동격 관계이다.

→ [ ]는 선행사 a giant, Arogo를 부연 설명하는 계속적 용법의 주격 관계대명사절이다.

**18행** ..., as nobody **knows** for certain [how the chocolate hills were made].

→ [ ]는 「의문사+주어+동사」 어순의 간접의문문으로, 동사 knows의 목적어 역할을 한다.

**19행** But that just **makes this natural phenomenon** *even* **more amazing**!

→ 「make+목적어+형용사」는 '~을 …하게 만들다'의 의미이며, 이때 more amazing은 형용사의 비교급으로 makes의 목적격 보어이다.

→ even은 '훨씬, 더욱'의 의미로, 비교급을 수식하는 부사이다. much, a lot, far 등으로 바꿔 쓸 수 있다.

## READING 2　Biosphere 2

**Ⓥ Mini Quiz**
1 the Earth　2 Biospherians

▶ **Reading Comprehension**
1 d　2 b, c　3 c　4 the growth of plants and animals, human relationships

▶ **Grammar Inside LEVEL 2**
Check Up　am to finish

**해석**　지구 환경이 우주선상에서 재현될 수 있을까? 그 답을 찾기 위해, 과학자들은 미국 소노란 사막에 미래 '온실'을 만들었다. 그것은 지구의 생태계를 재현하기 위해 1991년에 지어졌다. 과학자들은 그것을 바이오스피어 2라고 불렀는데, 이는 지구가 바이오스피어 1이기 때문이었다.

바다, 열대 우림, 사막과 같은 많은 인공 서식지가 그 구조물 내부에 만들어졌다. 그것들은 가능한 한 비슷하게 지구의 생태계를 모방하기로 되어 있었다. 그 서식지에는 3천 종 이상의 동식물들이 있었다. 또한 여덟 명의 '바이오스피어인'을 위한 업무 및 여가 공간이 있었다. 그들은 자신들의 식량을 재배하고 환경과 관련된 실험을 해야 했다. 어떠한 외부 접촉도 허용되지 않았다.

불행하게도, 그들의 임무는 단기간에 실패했다. 동식물은 차례대로 죽었고, 음식과 산소 둘 다 부족했다. 이후에, 바이오스피어인들은 서로 싸웠다. 부실한 관리 또한 그들의 실험을 더 악화시켰다.

하지만 오늘날, 과학자들은 그 실험이 가치 있었다고 생각한다. 그들은 동식물 성장에 관한 많은 것들을 배울 수 있었다. 그들은 밀폐된 공간에서의 인간관계에 관해서도 배웠다. 오늘날, 바이오스피어 2는 사람들이 우리의 행성에 관해 더 많은 것을 이해하도록 돕는 교육 장소이다.

**어휘**　environment 圐 환경 (environmental 圐 환경의)　recreate 屠 되살리다[재현하다]　spaceship 圐 우주선　create 屠 창조하다　futuristic 圐 미래의, 미래를 상상하는　greenhouse 圐 온실　ecosystem 圐 생태계　artificial 圐 인공[인조]의　habitat 圐 서식지　rainforest 圐 (열대) 우림　structure 圐 구조(물)　mimic 屠 모방하다　closely 剾 가깝게　contain 屠 ~이 들어 있다　leisure 圐 여가　experiment 圐 실험　contact 圐

접촉 allow [동] 허락하다; 용납하다 mission [명] 임무 fail [동] 실패하다 die off 차례대로[하나하나] 죽다 shortage [명] 부족 oxygen [명] 산소 management [명] 경영[관리] worthwhile [형] 가치 있는 growth [명] 성장 relationship [명] 관계 closed [형] 닫힌; *폐쇄된 educational [형] 교육의, 교육적인 planet [명] 행성
[문제] astronaut [명] 우주 비행사 a lack of ~의 부족

구문

[4행] Scientists called it Biosphere 2, **as** the Earth was Biosphere 1.
→ as는 〈이유〉를 나타내는 접속사이며, '~ 때문에'라고 해석한다.

[6행] They **were meant to mimic** the Earth's ecosystem *as closely as possible*.
→ 「be meant to-v」는 '~하기로 되어 있다, ~할 예정이다'의 의미이다.
→ 「as+부사+as possible」은 '가능한 한 ~하게'의 의미이다.

[17행] They **were able to learn** many things about the growth of plants and animals.
→ 「be able to-v」는 '~할 수 있다'는 의미로, 「can+동사원형」으로 바꿀 수 있다.

[19행] Today, Biosphere 2 is **an educational place** [that *helps people understand* more about our planet].
→ [ ]는 선행사 an educational place를 수식하는 주격 관계대명사절이다.
→ 「help+목적어+동사원형[to-v]」은 '~가 …하도록 돕다'의 의미이며, 이때 동사원형 understand는 helps의 목적격 보어이다.
→ 이때의 more는 '더 많은 수[양]'이라는 의미의 대명사이다.

**● VOCABULARY INSIDE**

*Check Up* 1 allow 2 created 3 habitat 4 legends 5 phenomenon 6 mess 7 ecosystem 8 worthwhile

# UNIT 16 | Sports

pp. 97-102

## READING 1 The Veolia Desert Challenge

**Mini Quiz**
1 Israel 2 the full moon and the runners' headlamps

▶ **Reading Comprehension**
1 a 2 c 3 d 4 their own food and water, the extreme temperature changes

▶ **Grammar Inside LEVEL 3**
[Check Up] neither, nor

해석

보름달 아래 사막에서 달리는 것을 상상해 보라. 조용하며 바람이 없고, 모래는 달빛에 빛난다. 당신은 이스라엘의 사

해 지역에서 12월마다 이런 마법의 순간을 경험할 수 있다. 이 지역은 세계에서 가장 장관을 이루는 사막 풍경 중 한 곳이다. 일 년 내내 따뜻하고 건조하며, 숨이 멎는 듯한 계곡과 협곡으로 가득하다. 이러한 이유로, 이곳은 세계에서 가장 독특한 자전거와 달리기 경기 중의 하나인 베올리아 사막 챌린지를 주최하도록 선정되었다.

주요 경기는 'The Ride'로, 거리가 23, 46, 69킬로미터의 세 가지 코스로 이루어진 산악자전거 경주이다. 두 명의 주자로 이뤄진 팀이 강가 계곡을 거치고 소돔 산을 나란히 지나면서 경주한다. 사이클 선수들은 장관을 이루는 절벽, 소금 동굴, 그리고 흰색 소금 바위를 경험한다.

또 다른 명소는 'The Night Run'이다. 주자들은 밤의 사막을 통과하여 14 또는 24킬로미터를 달린다. 이 코스는 오직 보름달과 주자들의 헤드램프만이 불을 밝혀 준다. 주자들은 본인의 음식과 물을 휴대해야 한다. 그들은 또한 사막의 극심한 기온 변화를 견뎌야 한다. 주말 내내 이어지는 이 경기들은 사막의 더운 낮과 별이 빛나는 밤을 감상할 좋은 기회를 제공한다.

**어휘** desert 몡 사막  challenge 몡 도전  calm 몡 고요한, 차분한; *바람이 없는  glow 통 빛나다  experience 통 경험하다  magical 몡 마법의[마술의]  region 몡 지역  spectacular 몡 장관을 이루는  landscape 몡 풍경  breathtaking 몡 숨이 멎는 듯한  valley 몡 계곡, 골짜기  canyon 몡 협곡  host 통 주최하다  unique 몡 독특한  length 몡 길이  alongside 젠 ~의 옆에, 나란히  cyclist 몡 자전거 타는 사람  cliff 몡 절벽  attraction 몡 명소[명물]  light 통 불을 붙이다; *(~가 가는 길을) 비춰 주다  carry 통 들고 있다; *휴대하다  withstand 통 견뎌내다  extreme 몡 극도의[극심한]  temperature 몡 온도[기온]  offer 통 제의하다; *제공하다  appreciate 통 진가를 알아보다[인정하다]; *감상하다  starry 몡 별이 빛나는  [문제] prepare for ~을 준비하다  take part in ~에 참여하다 (= participate in)

**구문**  **4행** This area has **one of the most spectacular desert landscapes** in the world.
→ 「one of the+최상급+복수 명사」는 '가장 ~한 … 중 하나'의 의미이다.

**5행** **(Being) Warm and dry all year round**, it *is filled with* breathtaking valleys and canyons.
→ Warm … round는 앞에 Being이 생략된 분사구문으로, 'It is warm and dry …., and it is filled with …'로 바꿔 쓸 수 있다.
→ 「be filled with」는 '~으로 가득 차다'의 의미이다.

**9행** The main event is "**The Ride,**" **a mountain bike race with three courses of 23, 46, and 69 km in length**.
→ The Ride와 a mountain bike … in length는 동격 관계이다.

**17행** These weekend-long events offer **a great chance** [to appreciate both the hot days and starry nights of the desert].
→ [ ]는 a great chance를 수식하는 형용사적 용법의 to부정사구이다.

---

### READING 2 Five-a-Side Football

**⦿ Mini Quiz**
1 F  2 T

▶ **Reading Comprehension**
1 d  2 c  3 touch their eyeshades, push their opponents  4 c

---

**해석**  내 남동생은 시각 장애를 가지고 있다. 그 아이는 축구를 매우 좋아하지만, 축구하는 것은 그 아이에게 쉽지 않다. 내

가 축구를 할 때마다, 그 아이는 벤치에 앉아 있어야 한다. 하지만 나는 오늘 그 아이를 위한 굉장한 스포츠를 발견했다! 나는 텔레비전으로 패럴림픽을 보고 있었는데, 시각 장애인 운동선수들이 축구를 하고 있는 것을 보았다! 그것은 five-a-side football이라고 불린다.

패럴림픽에서 five-a-side football은 축구와 몇 가지 다른 규칙이 있다. 그것은 앞을 못 보거나 거의 잘 보이지 않는 선수들로 구성된 두 팀이 경기한다. 각 팀은 다섯 명의 선수들로 구성되는데 볼 수 있거나 시각 장애를 가진, 한 명의 골키퍼 및 시각 장애를 가진 네 명의 필드 선수로 구성된다. 네 명의 필드 선수들은 눈가리개를 착용한다. <u>이것은 그들이 볼 수 없는 것을 확실하게 한다.</u> 공에는 선수들이 (공을) 찾을 수 있도록 소리를 내는 장치가 장착되어 있다. 두 팀은 25분씩 전·후반 경기를 치르고, 중간에 10분의 휴식이 있다. 경기장은 보통의 축구 경기장보다 더 작고, 벽으로 둘러싸여 있다.

심판은 자신의 눈가리개를 만지거나 상대편을 미는 선수들에게 벌칙을 준다. 부상을 막기 위해서, 선수들은 태클을 시도할 때 다른 선수들에게 경고해야 한다. 그들은 "voy"라고 외치면서 이를 수행하는데, 이는 스페인어로 '내가 간다'에 해당하는 단어이다.

만약 우리가 이 스포츠에 대해 더 일찍 알았더라면, 내 동생은 리그에 들어갈 수 있었을 것이다. 그 대신에 나는 내 동생과 내 모든 친구들에게 이것을 가르칠 계획이다.

**어휘** athlete 명 운동 선수  blind 형 앞을 보지 못하는  nearly 부 거의  sighted 형 앞을 볼 수 있는  eyeshade 명 눈가리개  equip 동 장비를 갖추다  noise-making 형 소리를 내는  device 명 장치  compete 동 경쟁하다; *~와 겨루다  half 명 반; *(경기의) 전반, 후반  break 명 휴식 시간  halftime 명 하프타임, 중간 휴식  regular 형 보통의  field 명 들판; *경기장  surround 동 둘러싸다  referee 명 심판  penalize 동 벌칙을 주다  opponent 명 (게임·대회 등의) 상대  prevent 동 막다, 방지하다  injury 명 부상[상처]  warn 동 경고하다  attempt 동 시도하다  tackle 명 태클 동 공을 뺏다  plan on ~할 계획이다  [문제] guarantee 동 보장하다; *확실하게 하다

**구문**

**1행** He loves soccer, but **it**'s not easy **for him to play**.
→ it은 가주어이며, to play는 진주어, for him은 to play의 의미상의 주어이다.

**8행** Each team **consists of** five players: *a goalkeeper*[, who can be sighted or visually impaired], ... .
→ 「consist of」는 '~으로 구성되다'라는 의미이다.
→ [ ]는 a goalkeeper를 부연 설명하는 계속적 용법의 주격 관계대명사절로, 문장 중간에 삽입되었다.

**10행** The ball **is equipped with** *a noise-making device* [to help players find it].
→ 「be equipped with」는 '~을 갖추고 있다'의 의미이다.
→ [ ]는 a noise-making device를 수식하는 형용사적 용법의 to부정사구이다.

**12행** The playing field is **smaller than** a regular soccer field, ... .
→ 「비교급+than」은 '~보다 더 …한[하게]'의 의미이다.

**17행** They **do this** *by shouting* "voy," which is the Spanish word for "I go."
→ do this는 앞 문장의 warn others when they are attempting a tackle을 가리킨다.
→ 「by v-ing」는 '~함으로써'의 의미이다.

● **VOCABULARY INSIDE**

| *Check Up* | 1 landscape | 2 opponent | 3 athlete | 4 withstand |
| --- | --- | --- | --- | --- |
| | 5 injury | 6 hosted | 7 attempted | 8 extreme |

# Answer Key

# READING Inside
## Workbook

# LEVEL 2

# UNIT 01 | Origins

pp. 2-5

## VOCABULARY TEST 1

01 봅슬레이; 봅슬레이를 타다　02 숙달하다, 통달하다
03 발명하다　04 전통의　05 영리한; 기발한
06 포르투갈　07 호텔 경영자　08 (식물의) 뿌리; 기원
09 이민자[이주민]　10 달리다; 경영하다　11 좌절감을
느끼는　12 사탕수수　13 들판, 밭　14 붐비는, 복잡한
15 견디다, 참다　16 창의적인　17 여정, 여행
18 매다　19 썰매; 썰매를 타다　20 안도하는
21 악기　22 온천　23 해안[해변]　24 경주하다
25 벼룩　26 오케스트라, 관현악단　27 민요
28 뛰다, 뛰어다니다　29 미네랄, 무기물　30 승선한,
탑승한　31 fit　32 impress　33 track
34 Portuguese　35 adopt　36 attract
37 throughout　38 pedestrian　39 essential
40 halfpipe　41 (해답을) 찾아내다, 내놓다
42 앞뒤로　43 ~와 충돌하다　44 무료로　45 ~에서
뛰어내리다

## VOCABULARY TEST 2

A 1 ⓒ　2 ⓐ　3 ⓓ　4 ⓔ　5 ⓑ
B 1 frustrated　2 clever　3 adopted　4 fit
C 1 back and forth　　2 for free
　3 come up with　　4 jumped off

## GRAMMAR TEST

A 1 나는 여기서 너를 보게 되어 매우 기쁘다.
　2 데이비드는 학교에 가고 나서야 일요일이라는 것을
　　알게 되었다.
　3 설탕을 사기 위해서, 나는 상점에 갔다.
　4 그녀는 커서 유명한 가수가 되었다.
　5 그는 여름방학 동안에 여행하기 위해서 돈을 저축했다.
　6 그의 성공에 관한 소식을 듣고 모두가 놀랐다.
B 1 which　　2 which　　3 that
　4 who　　5 that　　6 who
C 1 discovering → to discover
　2 who → which[that]　3 which → who[that]
　4 finding → to find　5 get → to get
　6 who → which[that]

## WRITING TEST

A 1 came to enjoy the spa

2 was famous for its mineral spa
3 To make the sleds go faster
4 named João jumped off the ship
5 immigrants who came to work
B 1 who play
2 were excited and relieved to
3 the most popular
4 became known as
5 to solve the problem

# UNIT 02 | Numbers

pp. 6-9

## VOCABULARY TEST 1

01 특히　02 이집트의; 이집트인　03 되풀이하여, 여러
차례　04 해결하다; 정착하다　05 부드럽게[순조롭게]
06 조직화된, 체계적인　07 나타내다　08 부유한; 비옥한
09 영원　10 목적　11 고대의　12 기록하다
13 통치자, 지배자　14 농사　15 궁전, 왕실
16 건설하다　17 로맨틱한, 낭만적인　18 웅장한
19 영원한　20 곱셈　21 상징　22 방법　23 부(富),
재산　24 수반[포함]하다　25 잡고 있는; 개최하다
26 두 배로 되다[만들다]　27 정확히　28 가정하다
29 기둥; (세로) 단　30 포함하다　31 early
32 comfortable　33 practical　34 flow
35 meaning　36 shape　37 fortune　38 chart
39 finally　40 important　41 총 ~가 되다
42 ~의 맞은편에　43 ~와 비슷한　44 이러한 이유로

## VOCABULARY TEST 2

A 1 eternity　　2 ancient　　3 settle
　4 practical　　5 comfortable
B 1 everlasting　2 construct　　3 symbol
　4 recording　　5 meaning
C 1 sounds like　2 adds up to　3 similar to
　4 across from

## GRAMMAR TEST

A 1 to　2 him　3 for　4 to the man　5 to
　6 me
B 1 eating　　2 to lend　　3 swimming
　4 smoking　　5 to go　　6 to change
C 1 of → to　2 to → for　3 to work → working

4 to me → me       5 meeting → to meet

A 1 send 99 or 999 roses to women
  2 to construct their grand pyramids
  3 keep doubling this number
  4 hold important events on dates
  5 makes everything flow smoothly
B 1 brings you a comfortable life
  2 started settling
  3 by using
  4 sounds similar to


# UNIT 03 | Fiction    pp. 10-13

## VOCABULARY TEST 1

01 이야기, 소설   02 여행[여정]   03 재능 있는
04 논리, 논리학   05 감추다, 숨기다   06 줄어들다
07 보통의, 정상적인   08 살아남다   09 현지의
10 파괴하다   11 (입으로) 빨다; (기계 등이) 빨아들이다
12 환상, 공상   13 오징어   14 지휘관   15 애벌레
16 제안하다   17 균형 잡힌   18 총액; 양   19 (전체의)
부분; (전체에서 차지하는) 비율   20 명령하다; 명령
21 예상 밖의   22 붙잡다, 생포하다   23 전투
24 짧은   25 생물   26 사나운   27 찾아보다, 수색하다
28 하인   29 탐험; 탐험대   30 정부   31 classic
32 magical   33 mathematician   34 publish
35 court   36 attack   37 submarine
38 captive   39 explore   40 escape   41 ~을
물리치다   42 ~을 알아내다   43 ~에 근거하여
44 ~으로 가득 차다

## VOCABULARY TEST 2

A 1 ⓑ   2 ⓔ   3 ⓒ   4 ⓐ   5 ⓓ
B 1 balanced           2 survive
  3 publish            4 brief
C 1 was full of        2 found out
  3 (to) fight off      4 based on

## GRAMMAR TEST

A 1 turn off   2 must not   3 prepare

4 has to   5 finish   6 don't have to
B 1 They went to the restaurant which[that]
    Luna recommended.
  2 The man who[that/whom] my sister loves
    is from Spain.
  3 Have you seen the book which[that] I put
    on the table?
  4 The woman who[that/whom] we
    interviewed wasn't very nice.
C 1 너는 숙제를 제때 제출해야 한다.
  2 우리는 그 박물관에 들어가기 위해 긴 줄을 기다려야
    했다.
  3 너는 차를 가지고 올 필요가 없다. 브라이언이 그의
    것을 가지고 올 것이다.
  4 네가 내게 주었던 쿠키들은 맛있었다.
  5 그것은 내가 지금까지 들어본 것 중 가장 우스운
    이야기이다.
  6 나는 조시가 가장 좋아하는 그 가수를 좋아하지 않는다.

## WRITING TEST

A 1 may not know that
  2 must eat balanced amounts
  3 that they have been searching for
  4 It seems like the Nautilus
  5 must leave the court
B 1 to hunt the monster
  2 are saved by
  3 a submarine called
  4 orders Alice to leave
  5 a mushroom that can change


# UNIT 04 | Business    pp. 14-17

## VOCABULARY TEST 1

01 발달하다   02 산업   03 용어; 기간   04 근로자
05 양   06 개인적인   07 가정교사   08 장점
09 통화   10 찢어진 곳   11 옛날식의, 구식의
12 힘든; 튼튼한   13 지폐   14 극도로   15 전세계적인
전염병   16 상당히   17 증가하다   18 그럼에도
불구하고   19 이득; (회사에서 받는) 혜택   20 경력
21 측면   22 옮기다; 바뀌다   23 종이를 쓰지 않는
24 지불   25 찬성하다; 선호하다   26 점점 더
27 메모; 지폐   28 특징, 특성   29 투명한   30 일정

31 economy　　32 temporary　　33 convenient
34 negative　　35 demand　　36 decade
37 security　　38 fake　　39 affect　　40 add
41 ~에 의존하다　　42 ~을 가리키다　　43 적어도
44 ~으로 만들어지다　　45 더 이상 ~ 아닌

## VOCABULARY TEST 2

A 1 affect　　　　　　2 payment
　 3 switch　　　　　　4 demand
B 1 ⓒ　　2 ⓑ　　3 ⓓ
C 1 rely on　　　　　　2 no longer
　 3 is made of　　　　4 at least

## GRAMMAR TEST

A 1 boys　　　　2 hot　　　　3 earlier, faster
　 4 good　　　　5 cannot　　6 must
B 1 이 수프는 지금 식었음에 틀림없다.
　 2 그는 존일 리가 없는데, 왜냐하면 존은 휴가 중이기
　　 때문이다.
　 3 맥스의 얼굴이 빨개졌다. 그는 긴장했음에 틀림없다!
　 4 너는 막 점심을 먹었잖니. 너는 배고플 리가 없어.
　 5 나는 그것에 대해 더 생각할수록, 그것이 진실이라고 더
　　 믿게 된다.
　 6 그 행성은 지구보다 네 배 더 크다.
C 1 must be　　2 cannot be[can't be]
　 3 the most popular foods
　 4 three times thicker　5 the more　6 longer

## WRITING TEST

A 1 This allows them to find
　 2 difficult for workers to develop
　 3 must be a demand for them
　 4 tougher than old-fashioned paper ones
　 5 see polymers as the future
B 1 make, difficult to　　2 times as long as
　 3 less affected by
　 4 gig economies can't[cannot] be

---

# UNIT 05 | Society　　　　pp. 18-21

## VOCABULARY TEST 1

01 구할[이용할] 수 있는　　02 달라붙다　　03 널리, 폭넓게
04 좋은; 아주 가는　　05 인공의　　06 배구　　07 보통의,
평범한　　08 붙잡다　　09 급여, 봉급　　10 효과적인
11 ~의 가치가 있는　　12 직물, 천; 재료　　13 직물, 천
14 수분, 습기　　15 조직, 단체　　16 정확한
17 갈라지다; 깨뜨리다　　18 지중해　　19 드문, 희귀한
20 강우량　　21 시민　　22 모으다[수집하다], 모이다
23 화려한　　24 거리　　25 왕족(들)　　26 관련성[연관성]
27 초상화　　28 의식하다[알다]　　29 과정　　30 귀중한;
값비싼　　31 wool　　32 shortage　　33 afford
34 harvest　　35 shell　　36 emperor　　37 tiny
38 desperate　　39 robe　　40 collector　　41 ~을
세우다[설치하다]　　42 A가 B하는 것을 금지하다
43 ~으로 (시간을) 거슬러 올라가다　　44 A와 B 사이에

## VOCABULARY TEST 2

A 1 ⓓ　　2 ⓑ　　3 ⓐ　　4 ⓔ　　5 ⓒ
B 1 costs　　　　2 afford　　　　3 harvested
　 4 exact　　　　5 clings
C 1 between, and　　2 set up　　3 ban, from
　 4 date back to

## GRAMMAR TEST

A 1 spacious, we can have a meeting
　 2 salty, a baby can't eat
　 3 boring, kids to enjoy
　 4 enough, everyone to fit in
B 1 My bicycle will be repaired by the
　　 mechanic.
　 2 This musical was loved by many people.
　 3 The play had to be performed by the
　　 college students.
　 4 Your kids can be taken care of by the
　　 resort staff.
C 1 steal → stolen
　 2 send → be sent
　 3 drinking → drink
　 4 carrying → carry
　 5 cancel → canceled
　 6 enough smart → smart enough

## WRITING TEST

A 1 the drops grow big enough
2 Building a fog collector costs
3 was purple considered the color
4 got purple dye from
5 had to be cracked open

B 1 that capture fog
2 is effective in capturing
3 were banned from wearing
4 purple dye was rare
5 were created

# UNIT 06 | Animals    pp. 22-25

## VOCABULARY TEST 1

01 비극적인   02 살아남다   03 유연한   04 끔찍한
05 갤런(액량 단위)   06 세포   07 혈액   08 독특한
09 결국   10 단일체, 단위   11 형성시키다; 모이다
[이루다]   12 정반대로   13 땀을 흘리다   14 구하다,
구조하다   15 돌봄[보살핌]   16 보호하다   17 공동체
[사회]   18 사냥꾼   19 낮, 주간   20 영향을 미치다
21 사냥하다   22 유지하다   23 고아원   24 목표;
표적, 목표물   25 줄어들다   26 원천   27 거대한; (수량
등이) 엄청난   28 지방으로 된, 지방이 많은   29 저장하다
30 강화하다   31 flow   32 practice
33 consume   34 exhausted   35 release
36 efficient   37 weak   38 conservation
39 overheat   40 temperature   41 A가 B하는
것을 막다   42 24시간 내내[밤낮으로]   43 한 번에
44 ~ 때문에

## VOCABULARY TEST 2

A 1 ⓔ   2 ⓑ   3 ⓒ

B 1 community   2 maintain   3 protection
4 release   5 traumatic

C 1 at a time   2 due to
3 prevented, from   4 around-the-clock

## GRAMMAR TEST

A 1 walk[walking]    2 play[playing]
3 is covered    4 cry[crying]

5 sing[singing]    6 is made

B 1 of   2 to   3 with   4 in

C 1 with
2 play[playing]
3 approach[approaching]
4 with
5 sleep[sleeping]

## WRITING TEST

A 1 Hunting adult elephants affects
2 As they grow older
3 Camels have been known to go
4 them from overheating and sweating
5 allow blood to flow

B 1 was given    2 Unless, is stopped
3 are left as    4 are filled with
5 which is stored as

# UNIT 07 | Social Media   pp. 26-29

## VOCABULARY TEST 1

01 사회자, 진행자   02 심리학자   03 영향   04 중요한
5 일상적인   6 접근   7 유명 인사   8 협력   9 경쟁
10 시작[개시]하다   11 ~에 이르다[닿다]   12 유익
[유용]하다; 혜택, 이득   13 이익, 이윤   14 기부, 기증
15 실제의   16 연결하다   17 제한, 한계   18 활동적인
19 외로움   20 끊임없이   21 우편; (인터넷) 게시글
22 아마도   23 사례[고려]하다   24 구입[구매];
구입[구매]하다   25 부정적으로   26 영향을 미치다
27 정서적인   28 (자금 등을) 모으다   29 회복시키다;
복원하다   30 사용; 사용량   31 recently   32 trend
33 communicate   34 depression   35 require
36 product   37 customer   38 donate
39 effective   40 effort   41 둔화되다   42 ~에
주의를 기울이다   43 잠시 휴식을 취하다   44 단 몇 ~

## VOCABULARY TEST 2

A 1 require   2 emotional   3 access
4 customer

B 1 communicate    2 celebrity
3 considered    4 daily   5 profit

C 1 Pay attention to   2 a matter of

3 took a break     4 slowed down

## GRAMMAR TEST

A 1 which    2 in which    3 in
   4 whom    5 at which    6 to which
B 1 완료   2 경험   3 결과   4 계속   5 경험   6 계속
C 1 with whom     2 eaten
   3 in which[where]    4 has gone
   5 for which

## WRITING TEST

A 1 makes cause marketing even more
    effective
   2 have companies make donations
   3 a new campaign in which they asked
   4 we have invited psychologist
   5 The social media trend hasn't slowed
    down
B 1 have made, an important part
   2 have found, can cause
   3 the idea on which
   4 help the world, buying

# UNIT 08 | Psychology    pp. 30-33

## VOCABULARY TEST 1

01 놀랍게도    02 붙이다, 첨부하다    03 호흡하다, 숨을
쉬다    04 상태, 질환    05 어지러운    06 감정 이입, 공감
07 존재하다    08 극도로, 극히    09 기절    10 얼어붙은
11 심장 박동    12 (비행기 여행) 시차증    13 지속하다
[되다]    14 내리다[낮추다]    15 측정하다[재다]
16 정신[심리]의, 정신[심리]적인    17 반응하다
18 알리다; 보고하다    19 세심한; 감성 있는; 민감한
20 심각한    21 땀투성이의, 땀에 젖은    22 증후군
23 온도계, 체온계    24 문제    25 자원봉사자; 지원자
26 거닐다[돌아다니다]    27 휴식    28 영향을 주다
29 떨어지다    30 벌거벗은    31 scene
32 researcher    33 dip    34 wonder    35 case
36 emotional    37 worsen    38 condition
39 normal    40 symptom    41 특히    42 갑자기
43 ~을 제외하고; ~ 이외에도    44 동시에

## VOCABULARY TEST 2

A 1 symptom    2 measure    3 exist
   4 react    5 wonder
B 1 wandered   2 thermometer   3 lower
   4 worsen
C 1 in particular     2 Apart from
   3 All of a sudden    4 at the same time

## GRAMMAR TEST

A 1 They want to know when to start the
    game.
   2 I did not know whom[who] to thank for this
    gift.
   3 Can you tell me how to fix this bicycle?
   4 We have to decide where to go for our
    summer vacation.
B 1 while    2 When    3 after
   4 when
C 1 when    2 Before    3 Until
   4 how

## WRITING TEST

A 1 imagined anything so beautiful could exist
   2 Watching someone feeling cold
   3 dipping their hands into icy water
   4 allows us to understand and share
B 1 what to do    2 had trouble breathing
   3 so strong that    4 while he was watching
   5 lets us experience how

# UNIT 09 | Winter    pp. 34-37

## VOCABULARY TEST 1

01 다양한    02 유래하다    03 (외국에 파견되는) 선교사
04 종교의    05 원주민    06 확신시키다; 설득하다
07 신성한    08 움켜쥠    09 가장자리, 모서리
10 드러내다    11 줄어들다[오그라지다]    12 미끄러지다
13 맨 아래; 바닥    14 적    15 출판(물)    16 영향
17 특징으로 하다; (영화 · 잡지 등에서) 특집으로 다루다
18 기념행사    19 관습    20 이주하다    21 유럽의
22 순록    23 힘든; 거친    24 북극    25 계속되다;

지속하다   **26** 발달시키다; 진화하다   **27** 최근에
**28** ~처럼 보이다   **29** 대표하다; 나타내다   **30** 전시하다
**31** tradition   **32** historian   **33** Germany
**34** pray   **35** century   **36** survivor
**37** decorate   **38** adaptation   **39** reflect
**40** sensitive   **41** 세우다   **42** ~에 대처하다
**43** ~에 영향을 주다[미치다]   **44** 베어 넘기다

**A** 1 ⓔ   2 ⓒ   3 ⓓ   4 ⓑ   5 ⓐ
**B** 1 exposed   2 reflected   3 sensitive
   4 edge   5 migrate
**C** 1 cope with   2 had, impact on
   3 chopped down   4 put up

**A** 1 good   2 most   3 faster
   4 less   5 funny   6 longest
**B** 1 to stop   2 use   3 to come
   4 drink   5 neat   6 to go
**C** 1 richest   2 easier   3 well
   4 leave   5 to tell   6 happy

**A** 1 the toughest environment on the planet
   2 the reindeer's eyes more sensitive to light
   3 made Christmas trees an official part
   4 convinced the people to worship
   5 has kept the tradition alive
**B** 1 allows, to run
   2 as low as
   3 had trees decorated
   4 to pray to their god

# UNIT 10 | People   pp. 38-41

**01** 업적, 성취   **02** 존경하다; 감탄하다   **03** 기념일
**04** 발표하다   **05** 운동 선수   **06** 장벽   **07** 찬란히;
뛰어나게   **08** 복잡한   **09** 작곡가   **10** 기술자
**11** 심지어   **12** 고향   **13** ~을 제외하고   **14** 영감을

주다   **15** 기구; 악기   **16** 일생   **17** 힘센; 장대한
**18** 움직임; (사람들이 조직적으로 벌이는) 운동
**19** 비폭력적인   **20** 이야기를 나누다   **21** 부분[일부];
부품   **22** 열정   **23** 인기   **24** 생산하다; 만들어내다
**25** 철로   **26** 은퇴하다; 영구결번으로 하다   **27** 권리,
권한   **28** 돌진하다   **29** 기술적인   **30** 귀중한
**31** victory   **32** behavior   **33** lead
**34** overwhelming   **35** insult   **36** threat
**37** impress   **38** dramatic   **39** effect
**40** talented   **41** 반격하다   **42** ~으로 유명하다
**43** ~와 사랑에 빠지다   **44** ~을 위해 싸우다

**A** 1 ⓔ   2 ⓐ   3 ⓑ   4 ⓒ   5 ⓓ
**B** 1 threats   2 complex   3 talented
   4 retired   5 barrier
**C** 1 fight back   2 fight for
   3 fall in love with   4 is famous for

**A** 1 had better   2 used to   3 would like to
   4 used to   5 had better
**B** 1 Although I was tired last night, I went to
   the gym.
   2 Although Jake is small, he is very strong.
   3 Although the heater was on, it was cold in
   the room.
   4 Although I got up late, I arrived at school
   on time.
**C** 1 그들은 방과 후에 영화를 보러 가곤 했다.
   2 너는 저 차가운 강에서 수영하지 않는 게 낫겠다.
   3 나는 신혼여행으로 뉴질랜드에 가고 싶다.
   4 그는 잘생기지 않았음에도 불구하고, 많은 소녀들이
   그를 좋아했다.
   5 비록 약을 먹었지만, 나는 여전히 배가 아프다.
   6 만약 그녀가 부유해지더라도, 그녀는 절대 변하지 않을
   것이다.

**A** 1 used to chat with
   2 was built right through his hometown
   3 was insulted and received hate mail
   4 impressed whites as well as blacks
   5 spent hours studying train schedules

B 1 was named
  2 making, overwhelming
  3 one of his greatest     4 tried to fight for
  5 helped, win

# UNIT 11 | Machines
pp. 42-45

## VOCABULARY TEST 1

01 비정상적인     02 항공기에 의한     03 힘든, 어려운
04 계산하다     05 포획하다; 정확히 포착하다[담아내다]
06 시민     07 지연시키다     08 드론, 무인 항공기
09 감정 이입, 공감     10 평가하다     11 나타내는; 표정이
있는     12 얼굴의     13 특징으로 삼다
14 확인하다[알아보다]     15 상호 작용     16 일치하다
17 보다[관찰하다]     18 제대로, 적절히     19 대답하다
20 반응     21 지방, 지역     22 훈련받은, 숙달된
23 대답; 반응     24 거친     25 급증하다; (하늘 높이) 날아
오르다     26 애쓰다, 힘겹게 나아가다     27 치료사
28 치료     29 사회의, 사회적인     30 풍경; 지표, 지형
31 fossil     32 surface     33 endure
34 meaningful     35 rub     36 isolated
37 notice     38 communicate     39 diagnose
40 owner     41 결과적으로     42 좁히다[줄이다]
43 A뿐만 아니라 B도     44 ~을 이용하다     45 ~ 덕택에

## VOCABULARY TEST 2

A 1 ⓒ     2 ⓓ     3 ⓑ     4 ⓐ     5 ⓔ
B 1 ⓔ     2 ⓑ     3 ⓐ
C 1 not only, but also     2 took advantage of
  3 As a result     4 narrow down

## GRAMMAR TEST

A 1 singing     2 written     3 exciting
  4 named     5 broken
B 1 some     2 each other     3 others
  4 the other
C 1 made     2 shocked
  3 standing     4 walking
  5 each other[one another]

## WRITING TEST

A 1 spending time with a smiling robot
  2 with autism struggle to communicate
  3 make it difficult to work
  4 can do this without enduring
B 1 flying robots
  2 can become isolated
  3 a website called
  4 for archaeologists to research
  5 the emotion matching

# UNIT 12 | Health
pp. 46-49

## VOCABULARY TEST 1

01 연결[결합]하는     02 조직     03 붙이다     04 팔뚝
05 신호     06 구조     07 팽팽해지다[팽팽하게 하다]
08 필요, 욕구     09 열량, 칼로리     10 정서적인     11 뇌
12 깡충깡충 뛰다; 거르다     13 작동하다     14 상황
15 휴식을 취하다; 긴장을 풀다     16 구체적인; 특정한
17 고르게     18 집게손가락(검지)     19 새끼손가락
20 넷째 손가락(약지)     21 나뉘다[나누다]     22 완전히
23 분리된     24 가능한     25 잘못된     26 이유
27 추가의[여분의]     28 욕구     29 똑바르게 하다
30 복잡한     31 muscle     32 palm     33 nerve
34 thumb     35 bend     36 physical     37 empty
38 independently     39 consume
40 difference     41 한동안     42 ~으로 불리다
43 A를 B로 생각하다     44 ~와 같은

## VOCABULARY TEST 2

A 1 ⓔ     2 ⓑ     3 ⓓ     4 ⓒ     5 ⓐ
B 1 ⓒ     2 ⓑ     3 ⓐ
C 1 for a while     2 is referred to as
  3 think of, as     4 such as

## GRAMMAR TEST

A 1 for     2 beside     3 in     4 between     5 by
B 1 was put off by the chairman
  2 were taken care of by volunteers
  3 is looked up to by a lot of students
  4 was laughed at by his classmates

C **1** 탁자 위의 음식을 마음껏 드세요.
  **2** 우리끼리 이야기인데, 나는 제이크를 좋아하지 않아.
  **3** 어린 여자아이가 혼자서 그 보고서를 썼다.
  **4** 맥스는 부유한 가정에서 키워졌다.
  **5** 나는 어렸을 때, 아이돌보미에게 보살핌을 받았다.

## WRITING TEST

A **1** move any body parts by themselves
  **2** connect these muscles to each finger bone
  **3** the brain sends a signal to a nerve
  **4** Most people think of hunger as
  **5** is caused by an emotional need
B **1** allows, to do amazing things
  **2** connected to the muscle
  **3** is referred to as
  **4** tells you to consume them

# UNIT 13 | Maps

## VOCABULARY TEST 1

**01** 표시하다  **02** 지역  **03** 거리  **04** 연결하다
**05** 중간점  **06** 수직의  **07** 과정  **08** 늘이다; 뻗어 있다  **09** 반도  **10** 상당한  **11** 회복되다; 되찾다
**12** 소유권  **13** 전체의  **14** 부여하다  **15** 다수
**16** 세포; 칸  **17** 귀중한  **18** 확인하다; 찾다  **19** 부분
**20** 지역  **21** 제거하다  **22** 10년  **23** 경쟁
**24** 정치적인  **25** 가치  **26** 접근하다  **27** 건설하다; 구성하다  **28** 광물  **29** 귀중한  **30** 비율
**31** random  **32** imagine  **33** invisible
**34** source  **35** separate  **36** tension  **37** rule
**38** defeat  **39** establish  **40** treaty
**41** A를 B로 나누다  **42** 일련의  **43** 그 대신[답례로]
**44** 얼마간의; 다수의

## VOCABULARY TEST 2

A **1** repeat  **2** separate  **3** gain
  **4** remain  **5** remove
B **1** ⓒ  **2** ⓑ  **3** ⓒ
C **1** a number of  **2** divided, into
  **3** a chain of  **4** in exchange

## GRAMMAR TEST

A **1** Opening the curtains
  **2** Finishing the appetizer
  **3** Preparing dinner
B **1** losing  **2** laughing  **3** not having
  **4** going  **5** learning  **6** not passing
C **1** 나는 숙제를 끝낸 후에 TV를 보았다.
  **2** 우리는 내일 회의에 가지 않는 것에 관해 이야기를 나누었다.
  **3** 마크는 다음 주에 집에 가는 것을 기대한다.
  **4** 공연을 보는 동안, 그들은 사진을 많이 찍었다.
  **5** 해변을 따라 걸으면서, 그 아이들은 아름다운 조개껍데기들을 주웠다.
  **6** 집에 도착했을 때, 조시는 문이 열려 있는 것을 발견했다.

## WRITING TEST

A **1** Start by marking a number of points
  **2** an upright line that passes
  **3** helped him locate the areas
  **4** The treaty gave Japan control
  **5** Growing competition between the two countries
B **1** After removing the pump
  **2** dividing a region can be
  **3** Defeating Japan
  **4** Both it and, remained

# UNIT 14 | Paintings
pp. 54-57

## VOCABULARY TEST 1

**01** 앞에  **02** ~ 외에  **03** 하녀[시녀]  **04** 주의 깊게, 신중히  **05** 선택  **06** 복잡한  **07** 성장[발달]하다
**08** 그림  **09** 나오다[모습을 드러내다]  **10** 연예인; 광대
**11** 숨겨진, 숨은  **12** 발견  **13** 흥미롭게도  **14** 막[층]
**15** 더 낮은 쪽의  **16** 주인; 대가  **17** 개요; 윤곽
**18** 물체; 대상  **19** 연습  **20** 입증하다  **21** (거울 등에 비친) 상[모습]  **22** 연구원  **23** 재사용하다
**24** 드러내다  **25** 왕실의  **26** 시골의, 지방의
**27** 살피다; 정밀 촬영하다  **28** 똑바로  **29** 기술, 기법
**30** ~의 밑에  **31** deep  **32** portrait  **33** stare
**34** surround  **35** amuse  **36** detail

Reading Inside Level 2 | **51**

37 artwork    38 face    39 unclear
40 beloved    41 ~에 집중하다, 초점을 맞추다    42 그
당시에    43 ~에 기여하다    44 ~으로 시작하다

## VOCABULARY TEST 2

A 1 outline    2 portrait    3 surround
  4 reveal
B 1 ⓒ    2 ⓐ    3 ⓔ
C 1 contributed to    2 focus on
  3 at that time    4 begin with

## GRAMMAR TEST

A 1 Calling my name
  2 Climbing up the mountain
  3 Feeling tired
B 1 I have a friend whose brother used to like
    my sister.
  2 She used to drive a red car whose window
    was broken.
  3 I know a man whose mother has worked
    in this hotel.
  4 Look at the child whose dog is jumping up
    and down.
C 1 가난했기 때문에, 그는 새 바지를 구입할 여유가 되지
    않았다.
  2 해변에 누워서, 나는 노을을 바라보았다.
  3 우리는 이름이 나와 같은 한 소년에 대해 이야기했다.

## WRITING TEST

A 1 One of his most famous portraits
  2 is more complex than it seems
  3 painting on a canvas
  4 proves that even masters need practice
B 1 Living in    2 what it was    3 as well as
  4 whose job was to
  5 the painting more interesting

# UNIT 15 | Places                    pp. 58-61

## VOCABULARY TEST 1

01 허락하다; 용납하다    02 접촉    03 미래의, 미래를

상상하는    04 놀라운    05 옆에; 제쳐두고[접어두고]
06 자연적인    07 꽤, 상당히    08 모방하다    09 산소
10 산호초    11 슬프게도    12 매끄럽게 하다
13 생태계    14 실험    15 실패하다    16 눈물
17 던지다    18 주로, 일반적으로    19 서식지    20 여가
21 경영[관리]    22 먼지, 흙    23 형성하다    24 높은;
높이가 ~인    25 (열대) 우림    26 되살리다[재현하다]
27 부족    28 우주선    29 가치 있는    30 관계
31 legend    32 educational    33 mission
34 mess    35 phenomenon    36 environment
37 artificial    38 create    39 hill    40 theory
41 ~의 옆에    42 서로    43 ~에 위치해 있다
44 차례대로[하나하나] 죽다

## VOCABULARY TEST 2

A 1 ⓔ    2 ⓓ    3 ⓑ    4 ⓐ    5 ⓒ
B 1 throw    2 artificial
  3 mess    4 educational
C 1 is located on    2 died off
  3 each other    4 next to

## GRAMMAR TEST

A 1 Unless    2 If    3 If    4 Unless
  5 Unless
B 1 예정, 나는 방과 후에 우리 선생님을 만날 것이다.
  2 운명, 그녀는 결국 그와 결혼할 운명이었다.
  3 의무, 너는 영어 성적을 향상하기 위해 열심히 공부해야
    한다.
  4 의도, 네가 잭한테 친구가 되고자 한다면, 그에게
    친절해라.
  5 가능, 그 집에서 아무도 볼 수 없었다.
C 1 unless    2 If    3 buy
  4 don't get

## WRITING TEST

A 1 spent days throwing rocks and dirt
  2 how the chocolate hills were made
  3 makes, even more amazing
  4 No outside contact was allowed
  5 helps people understand more about our
    planet
B 1 are located on
  2 were meant to mimic
  3 were to grow

**4** made their experiment worse

**5** standing next to each other

# UNIT 16 | Sports

pp. 62-65

## VOCABULARY TEST 1

**01** ~의 옆에, 나란히    **02** 절벽    **03** 진가를 알아보다
[인정하다]; 감상하다    **04** 운동 선수    **05** 시도하다
**06** 명소[명물]    **07** 앞을 보지 못하는    **08** 숨이 멎는 듯한
**09** 협곡    **10** 도전    **11** 경험하다    **12** 부상[상처]
**13** 풍경    **14** 길이    **15** 거의    **16** 제의하다; 제공하다
**17** (게임 · 대회 등의) 상대    **18** 사막    **19** 방지하다, 막다
**20** 심판    **21** 지역    **22** 보통의    **23** 들판; 경기장
**24** 장관을 이루는    **25** 별이 빛나는    **26** 태클; 공을 뺏다
**27** 들고 있다; 휴대하다    **28** 계곡, 골짜기    **29** 눈가리개
**30** 마법의[마술의]    **31** glow    **32** unique
**33** host    **34** extreme    **35** guarantee
**36** withstand    **37** compete    **38** device
**39** penalize    **40** warn    **41** ~할 계획이다
**42** ~으로 구성되다    **43** ~을 갖추고 있다    **44** ~에
참여하다

## VOCABULARY TEST 2

**A 1** ⓓ    **2** ⓑ    **3** ⓐ    **4** ⓒ
**B 1** challenge          **2** compete
  **3** attempt            **4** breathtaking
**C 1** consists of        **2** take part in
  **3** is equipped with   **4** plan on

## GRAMMAR TEST

**A 1** and          **2** but also       **3** or
  **4** nor
**B 1** weren't, could play
  **2** weren't, could go
  **3** hadn't lost, could have called
  **4** hadn't told, wouldn't have been
  **5** had gotten[got] up, wouldn't have missed
**C 1** and          **2** either         **3** not only
  **4** would fit    **5** had known

## WRITING TEST

**A 1** one of the most spectacular desert
    landscapes
  **2** have to withstand the temperature
    changes
  **3** The ball is equipped with
  **4** It was chosen to host
  **5** for my brother to play
**B 1** is filled with
  **2** is smaller than
  **3** who[that] push their opponents
  **4** had known, could have joined
  **5** plan on teaching

# READING Inside

## Answer Key

A 4-level curriculum
integration reading course

· **A thematic reading program that integrates with school curriculum**
중등 교육과정이 지향하는 문이과 통합 및 타교과 연계 반영한 독해서

· **Informative content with well-designed comprehension questions**
정보성 있는 지문과 질 높은 다양한 유형의 문항 그리고 서술형 평가도 대비

· **Grammar points directly related to the *Grammar Inside* series**
베스트셀러 Grammar Inside와 직접적으로 연계된 문법 항목 및 문항 제공

· **Exercises with useful, essential, and academic vocabulary**
중등 필수 어휘 학습 코너 제공

· **A workbook for more vocabulary, grammar, and reading exercises**
풍부한 양의 어휘, 문법, 그리고 쓰기 추가 문제 등을 수록한 워크북

| Level | Grade | Words Limit |
|---|---|---|
| Reading Inside Starter | Low-Intermediate | 140-160 |
| Reading Inside Level 1 | Intermediate | 160-180 |
| **Reading Inside Level 2** | **Intermediate** | **180-200** |
| Reading Inside Level 3 | Low-Advanced | 200-220 |

# NE능률 교재 MAP

아래 교재 MAP을 참고하여 본인의 현재 혹은 목표 수준에 따라 교재를 선택하세요.
NE능률 교재들과 함께 영어실력을 쑥쑥~ 올려보세요!
MP3 등 교재 부가 학습 서비스 및 자세한 교재 정보는 www.nebooks.co.kr 에서 확인하세요.

| 초1-2 | 초3 | 초3-4 | 초4-5 | 초5-6 |
|---|---|---|---|---|
| 초등영어 리딩이 된다 Start 1 | 리딩버디 1 | 리딩버디 2 | 리딩버디 3 | 초등영어 리딩이 된다 Jump 1 |
| 초등영어 리딩이 된다 Start 2 | | 초등영어 리딩이 된다 Basic 1 | 주니어 리딩튜터 스타터 1 | 초등영어 리딩이 된다 Jump 2 |
| 초등영어 리딩이 된다 Start 3 | | 초등영어 리딩이 된다 Basic 2 | | 초등영어 리딩이 된다 Jump 3 |
| 초등영어 리딩이 된다 Start 4 | | 초등영어 리딩이 된다 Basic 3 | | 초등영어 리딩이 된다 Jump 4 |
| | | 초등영어 리딩이 된다 Basic 4 | | 주니어 리딩튜터 스타터 2 |

| 초6-예비중 | 중1 | 중1-2 | 중2-3 | 중3 |
|---|---|---|---|---|
| 주니어 리딩튜터 1 | 1316 Reading 1 | 1316 Reading 2 | 1316 Reading 3 | 리딩튜터 입문 |
| Junior Reading Expert 1 | 주니어 리딩튜터 2 | 주니어 리딩튜터 3 | 주니어 리딩튜터 4 | 정말 기특한 구문독해 완성 |
| Reading Forward Basic 1 | Junior Reading Expert 2 | 정말 기특한 구문독해 입문 | 정말 기특한 구문독해 기본 | Reading Forward Advanced 1 |
| | Reading Forward Basic 2 | Junior Reading Expert 3 | Junior Reading Expert 4 | 열중 16강 독해+문법 3 |
| | 열중 16강 독해+문법 1 | Reading Forward Intermediate 1 | Reading Forward Intermediate 2 | Reading Inside 3 |
| | Reading Inside Starter | 열중 16강 독해+문법 2 | Reading Inside 2 | |
| | | Reading Inside 1 | | |

| 중3-예비고 | 고1 | 고1-2 | 고2-3, 수능 실전 | 고3 이상, 수능 고난도 |
|---|---|---|---|---|
| Reading Expert 1 | 빠바 기초세우기 | 빠바 구문독해 | 빠바 유형독해 | Reading Expert 5 |
| 리딩튜터 기본 | 리딩튜터 실력 | 리딩튜터 수능 PLUS | 빠바 종합실전편 | 능률 고급영문독해 |
| Reading Forward Advanced 2 | Reading Expert 2 | Reading Expert 3 | Reading Expert 4 | |
| | TEPS BY STEP G+R Basic | | TEPS BY STEP G+R 1 | |

| 수능 이상/<br>토플 80-89 ·<br>텝스 600-699점 | 수능 이상/<br>토플 90-99 ·<br>텝스 700-799점 | 수능 이상/<br>토플 100 ·<br>텝스 800점 이상 | | |
|---|---|---|---|---|
| ADVANCED Reading Expert 1 | ADVANCED Reading Expert 2 | RADIX TOEFL Black Label Reading 2 | | |
| TEPS BY STEP G+R 2 | RADIX TOEFL Black Label Reading 1 | TEPS BY STEP G+R 3 | | |
| RADIX TOEFL Blue Label Reading 1, 2 | | | | |

# workbook

# READING Inside

# LEVEL 2

A 4-level curriculum
integration reading course

NE _ Neungyule

# Workbook

# READING
# Inside

# LEVEL 2

# UNIT 01 | Origins

## VOCABULARY TEST 1

반 / 이름:

**[01-30] 다음 단어의 뜻을 쓰시오.**

01 bobsled _____

02 master _____

03 invent _____

04 traditional _____

05 clever _____

06 Portugal _____

07 hotelier _____

08 root _____

09 immigrant _____

10 run _____

11 frustrated _____

12 sugarcane _____

13 field _____

14 crowded _____

15 endure _____

16 creative _____

17 journey _____

18 fasten _____

19 sled _____

20 relieved _____

21 musical instrument _____

22 spa _____

23 shore _____

24 race _____

25 flea _____

26 orchestra _____

27 folk song _____

28 hop _____

29 mineral _____

30 on board _____

**[31-40] 다음 뜻을 지닌 단어를 쓰시오.**

31 맞다, 적합하다 _____

32 깊은 인상을 주다 _____

33 길; 경주로, 트랙 _____

34 포르투갈의; 포르투갈인 _____

35 취하다[차용하다] _____

36 (어디로) 끌어들이다 _____

37 도처에 _____

38 보행자 _____

39 필수적인, 극히 중요한 _____

40 하프파이프 _____

**[41-45] 다음 숙어의 뜻을 쓰시오.**

41 come up with _____

42 back and forth _____

43 crash into _____

44 for free _____

45 jump off _____

# VOCABULARY TEST 2

**A** 다음 단어의 영영풀이를 바르게 연결하시오.

1 immigrant •    • ⓐ to make or think of something for the first time

2 invent •    • ⓑ a natural, nonliving substance in the earth

3 impress •    • ⓒ someone who comes to another country to live

4 fasten •    • ⓓ to make someone feel respect or admiration

5 mineral •    • ⓔ to close something tight by using a tie, a button, or a zip


**B** 다음 빈칸에 들어갈 말을 보기 에서 찾아 쓰시오.

| 보기 | fit | adopted | clever | frustrated |

1 He got _____ after seeing his math grade.

2 My puppy is so _____ that he can understand what I say.

3 Our school _____ my recycling idea as a school-wide project.

4 This shirt is so small that it doesn't _____.


**C** 우리말과 같은 뜻이 되도록 빈칸에 들어갈 말을 보기 에서 찾아 알맞은 형태로 쓰시오.

| 보기 | jump off | for free | back and forth | come up with |

1 그 짜증이 난 말은 앞뒤로 이리저리 뛰었다.

▶ The irritated horse ran _____.

2 그 식당에서는 노인들에게 무료로 식사를 제공한다.

▶ The restaurant offers meals to the elderly _____.

3 창의적인 아이디어를 생각해내기 위해 당신의 상상력을 이용해라.

▶ Use your imagination to _____ a creative idea.

4 학생들은 바위에서 뛰어내려 호수로 다이빙했다.

▶ Students _____ the rock and dove into the lake.

Reading Inside Level 2 | **3**

**A** 밑줄 친 부분에 유의하여 다음 문장을 우리말로 해석하시오.

1 I'm so happy to see you here.

2 David went to school only to find that it was Sunday.

3 To buy some sugar, I went to the store.

4 She grew up to be a famous singer.

5 He saved money to travel during the summer vacation.

6 Everybody was surprised to hear the news of his success.

**B** ( ) 안에 들어갈 알맞은 관계대명사를 고르시오.

1 I want a pet (who, which) has short hair.

2 I saw a bus (who, which) had broken windows.

3 He likes the girl (that, which) lives next door.

4 The man (who, whom) is yelling will be stopped by a policeman.

5 Look at the birds (who, that) are in the sky.

6 I will introduce my friend (who, which) is my classmate.

**C** 어법상 어색한 곳을 찾아 바르게 고쳐 쓰시오.

1 He was angry discovering that his brother broke his toy.

2 He wanted to have a bag who had many pockets.

3 I met great painters which worked in Europe.

4 Jennifer woke up finding that she was late for school.

5 I came here early get a good seat.

6 She has a cat who can jump high.

**A**  우리말과 일치하도록 (  ) 안에 주어진 말을 알맞게 배열하시오.

1 많은 손님들이 여름 동안에 온천을 즐기기 위해 왔다.

(enjoy, came, the spa, to)

▶ Many guests _____ during the summer.

2 생모리츠는 그곳의 미네랄 온천으로 유명했다.

(its, was famous for, mineral spa)

▶ St. Moritz _____.

3 썰매를 더 빨리 가게 하려고, 그 팀들은 앞뒤로 '흔들었다'.

(the sleds, go, make, to, faster)

▶ _____, the teams "bobbed" back and forth.

4 João라는 이름의 남자는 배에서 뛰어내렸다.

(João, the ship, named, jumped off)

▶ A man _____.

5 그들은 사탕수수밭에 일하기 위해서 온 이주민들이었다.

(who, immigrants, to, came, work)

▶ They were _____ in the sugarcane fields.

**B**  우리말과 일치하도록 (  ) 안의 말을 이용하여 문장을 완성하시오.

1 우쿨렐레를 연주하는 아이들로 구성된 오케스트라가 있다. (play)

▶ There is a full orchestra of children _____ _____ ukuleles.

2 그 포르투갈인들은 신났고 마침내 도착하게 되어 안도했다. (excited, relieved)

▶ The Portuguese _____ _____ _____ _____ _____ finally arrive.

3 우쿨렐레가 하와이에서 가장 인기 있는 악기이다. (popular)

▶ The ukulele is _____ _____ _____ instrument in Hawaii.

4 그 운동은 봅슬레이로 알려졌다. (become, known)

▶ The sport _____ _____ _____ bobsled.

5 이 문제를 해결하기 위해, Badrutt는 하프파이프 트랙을 지었다. (solve, the problem)

▶ Badrutt built a halfpipe track _____ _____ _____ _____.

## VOCABULARY TEST 1

반 / 이름:

**[01-30] 다음 단어의 뜻을 쓰시오.**

01 especially _____

02 Egyptian _____

03 repeatedly _____

04 settle _____

05 smoothly _____

06 organized _____

07 indicate _____

08 rich _____

09 eternity _____

10 purpose _____

11 ancient _____

12 record _____

13 ruler _____

14 farming _____

15 palace _____

16 construct _____

17 romantic _____

18 grand _____

19 everlasting _____

20 multiplication _____

21 symbol _____

22 method _____

23 wealth _____

24 involve _____

25 hold _____

26 double _____

27 exactly _____

28 suppose _____

29 column _____

30 include _____

**[31-40] 다음 뜻을 지닌 단어를 쓰시오.**

31 초기의 _____

32 편한 _____

33 실용적인 _____

34 흐름; 흐르다 _____

35 뜻[의미] _____

36 모양, 형태 _____

37 운; 재산 _____

38 도표 _____

39 마침내 _____

40 중요한 _____

**[41-44] 다음 숙어의 뜻을 쓰시오.**

41 add up to _____

42 across from _____

43 similar to _____

44 for this reason _____

**A** 단어의 첫 철자를 참조하여 다음 정의에 해당하는 단어를 쓰시오.

1 the whole of time                                          e_____

2 having existed for a long time                             a_____

3 to start to live in a particular place                     s_____

4 connected with real situations and events                 p_____

5 not having physical or mental pain, worries, or difficulties   c_____


**B** 다음 빈칸에 들어갈 말을 보기에서 찾아 쓰시오.

> 보기  construct       meaning       symbol       everlasting       recording

1 The man wanted to show her his _____ love.

2 The CEO plans to _____ the biggest factory in the world.

3 This _____ represents the king's greatness at that time.

4 Many journalists are _____ the president's speech.

5 What is the _____ of the Chinese letters?


**C** 우리말과 같은 뜻이 되도록 빈칸에 들어갈 말을 보기에서 찾아 알맞은 형태로 쓰시오.

> 보기  similar to       add up to       sound like       across from

1 그것은 멜로디처럼 들린다.
   ▶ It _____ a melody.

2 식사비는 총 300달러가 된다.
   ▶ The price for the meals _____ $300.

3 그의 신발의 모양과 색깔은 내 것과 비슷하다.
   ▶ His shoes are _____ mine in shape and color.

4 나의 담임 선생님은 우리 집 바로 맞은편에 사신다.
   ▶ My homeroom teacher lives just _____ my house.

**A** 다음 ( ) 안에서 알맞은 것을 고르시오.

1 Pete sent a box of chocolate (to, of) me.

2 The teacher asked (him, of him) some questions.

3 The man is making cotton candy (for, to) the kid.

4 Julie showed her ticket (the man, to the man).

5 My sister used to teach math (to, of) me.

6 My dad bought (me, for me) the computer.

**B** ( ) 안에 주어진 단어를 알맞은 형태로 고쳐 쓰시오.

1 Try to avoid _____ sweets after a meal. (eat)

2 I didn't promise _____ $100 to him. (lend)

3 How many hours do you practice _____ a day? (swim)

4 My father quit _____ to get healthy. (smoke)

5 Everyone agreed _____ to Paris for the summer vacation. (go)

6 If you decide _____ your mind, call me. (change)

**C** 어법상 어색한 곳을 찾아 바르게 고쳐 쓰시오.

1 Can you lend those books of me?

2 Finally, Harry will buy a delicious lunch to us.

3 We don't mind to work on the weekends.

4 My grandmother told to me a funny story.

5 I didn't expect meeting you again like this.

**A** 우리말과 일치하도록 (  ) 안에 주어진 말을 알맞게 배열하시오.

1 중국 남성들은 여성에게 종종 99송이나 999송이의 장미를 보낸다.

(to, send, 99 or 999 roses, women)

▶ Chinese men often _____.

2 그들은 그들의 웅장한 피라미드를 건설하기 위해 수학을 사용했다.

(grand, pyramids, to, their, construct)

▶ They used math _____.

3 1부터 시작해서 이 숫자를 계속 두 배로 만들어라.

(this, keep, number, doubling)

▶ Start from 1 and _____.

4 사람들은 숫자 8을 포함하는 날짜에 중요한 행사를 개최한다.

(important, on, events, hold, dates)

▶ People _____ that include the number eight.

5 사람들은 숫자 6이 모든 일이 순조롭게 흘러가도록 해준다고 말한다.

(everything, smoothly, flow, makes)

▶ People say the number six _____.

**B** 우리말과 일치하도록 (  ) 안의 말을 이용하여 문장을 완성하시오.

1 숫자 6은 당신에게 편안한 삶을 가져다준다. (bring, comfortable)

▶ The number six _____ _____ _____ _____ _____.

2 초기 이집트인들은 비옥한 나일 계곡에 정착하기 시작했다. (start, settle)

▶ Early Egyptians _____ _____ in the rich Nile valley.

3 그들은 곱셈법을 이용함으로써 이 과업들을 수행했다. (use)

▶ They did these tasks _____ _____ a multiplication method.

4 '6'에 해당하는 단어는 '행운'과 '도로'를 뜻하는 단어와 비슷한 소리가 난다. (sound, similar)

▶ The word for "six" _____ _____ _____ the words for "luck" and "road."

# VOCABULARY TEST 1

반 / 이름:

**[01-30] 다음 단어의 뜻을 쓰시오.**

01 tale _____

02 journey _____

03 gifted _____

04 logic _____

05 hide _____

06 shrink _____

07 normal _____

08 survive _____

09 local _____

10 destroy _____

11 suck _____

12 fantasy _____

13 squid _____

14 commander _____

15 caterpillar _____

16 suggest _____

17 balanced _____

18 amount _____

19 proportion _____

20 order _____

21 unexpected _____

22 capture _____

23 battle _____

24 brief _____

25 creature _____

26 fierce _____

27 search _____

28 servant _____

29 expedition _____

30 government _____

**[31-40] 다음 뜻을 지닌 단어를 쓰시오.**

31 명작의, 걸작의 _____

32 마법의 _____

33 수학자 _____

34 출판하다 _____

35 법정, 법원 _____

36 공격하다 _____

37 잠수함 _____

38 포로 _____

39 탐험하다 _____

40 탈출하다 _____

**[41-44] 다음 숙어의 뜻을 쓰시오.**

41 fight off _____

42 find out _____

43 based on _____

44 be full of _____

# VOCABULARY TEST 2

반 / 이름:

**A** 다음 단어의 영영풀이를 바르게 연결하시오.

1 journey •       • ⓐ to recommend something to someone

2 include •       • ⓑ a trip from one place to another

3 capture •       • ⓒ to catch someone or something, especially by force

4 suggest •       • ⓓ to look for something or someone carefully

5 search •       • ⓔ to contain something or have it as part of a whole

**B** 다음 빈칸에 들어갈 말을 보기에서 찾아 쓰시오.

> 보기  publish      brief      balanced      survive

1 You need to eat a more _____ diet.

2 The plant cannot _____ in freezing temperatures.

3 We _____ more than 300,000 books every year.

4 He lived in the town for only a _____ period of time.

**C** 우리말과 같은 뜻이 되도록 빈칸에 들어갈 말을 보기에서 찾아 알맞은 형태로 쓰시오.

> 보기  based on      find out      fight off      be full of

1 그 파티는 즐거움으로 가득했다.
   ▶ The party _____ joy.

2 나는 마침내 무엇이 잘못됐는지 알아냈다.
   ▶ I finally _____ what was wrong.

3 백신은 질병을 물리치는 데 도움이 될 수 있다.
   ▶ Vaccines can help _____ disease.

4 이 이야기는 소설이지만, 사실에 근거를 두고 있다.
   ▶ This story is fiction, but it is _____ fact.

**A** 다음 ( ) 안에서 알맞은 것을 고르시오.

1 He must (turn off, turns off) the lights to save energy.

2 You (don't must, must not) make a sound in the library.

3 You must (prepare, to prepare) for the final exam.

4 Lisa (has to, have to) go to bed early tonight.

5 Do I have to (finish, finishing) the project by tomorrow?

6 The play is free. You (must not, don't have to) buy a ticket.

**B** 다음 두 문장을 관계대명사를 이용하여 한 문장으로 쓰시오.

1 They went to the restaurant. + Luna recommended the place.

▶ _____

2 The man is from Spain. + My sister loves him.

▶ _____

3 Have you seen the book? + I put it on the table.

▶ _____

4 The woman wasn't very nice. + We interviewed her.

▶ _____

**C** 다음을 우리말로 해석하시오.

1 You must hand in your homework on time.

2 We had to wait in a long line to get into the museum.

3 You don't have to bring your car. Brian will bring his.

4 The cookies you gave me were delicious.

5 It is the funniest story that I've ever heard.

6 I don't like the singer Josh likes the most.

**A** 우리말과 일치하도록 ( ) 안에 주어진 말을 알맞게 배열하시오.

1 사람들은 캐럴이 재능 있는 수학자였다는 것을 잘 모를 것이다.

   (not, may, that, know)

   ▶ People _____ Carroll was a gifted mathematician.

2 앨리스가 적절한 비율에 도달하기 위해서는 균형 잡힌 양을 먹어야 한다.

   (amounts, must, balanced, eat)

   ▶ Alice _____ to reach the right proportions.

3 탐험대는 자신들이 찾고 있던 그 사나운 생물을 발견한다.

   (searching for, they, have been, that)

   ▶ The expedition finds the fierce creature _____.

4 노틸러스호가 파괴될 것 같다.

   (the Nautilus, seems, it, like)

   ▶ _____ will be destroyed.

5 키가 1마일이 넘는 사람은 법정에서 떠나야 한다.

   (leave, must, the court)

   ▶ People more than a mile high _____.


**B** 우리말과 일치하도록 ( ) 안의 말을 이용하여 문장을 완성하시오.

1 미국 정부는 그 괴물을 사냥하기 위해 탐험대를 보낸다. (hunt, the monster)

   ▶ The US government sends an expedition _____ _____ _____ _____.

2 그들은 현지인들에 의해 구조된다. (save)

   ▶ They _____ _____ _____ local people.

3 배를 공격해 오던 그 괴물은 사실 노틸러스라는 잠수함이다. (a submarine, call)

   ▶ The monster that has been attacking ships is actually _____ _____ _____ the Nautilus.

4 여왕은 '규정 제42조'에 근거하여 앨리스에게 떠날 것을 명령한다. (order, leave)

   ▶ The queen _____ _____ _____ _____ based on "Rule 42."

5 그녀는 그녀의 크기를 변화시킬 수 있는 버섯을 먹어야 한다. (a mushroom, that, change)

   ▶ She should eat _____ _____ _____ _____ _____ her size.

# UNIT 04 | Business

반 / 이름:

**[01-30] 다음 단어의 뜻을 쓰시오.**

01 develop _____

02 industry _____

03 term _____

04 employee _____

05 amount _____

06 private _____

07 tutor _____

08 advantage _____

09 currency _____

10 rip _____

11 old-fashioned _____

12 tough _____

13 banknote _____

14 extremely _____

15 pandemic _____

16 significantly _____

17 increase _____

18 nevertheless _____

19 benefit _____

20 career _____

21 aspect _____

22 shift _____

23 paperless _____

24 payment _____

25 favor _____

26 increasingly _____

27 note _____

28 feature _____

29 transparent _____

30 schedule _____

**[31-40] 다음 뜻을 지닌 단어를 쓰시오.**

31 경제 _____

32 임시의 _____

33 편리한 _____

34 부정적인 _____

35 수요 _____

36 10년 _____

37 보안 _____

38 가짜의 _____

39 영향을 미치다 _____

40 첨가하다 _____

**[41-45] 다음 숙어의 뜻을 쓰시오.**

41 rely on _____

42 refer to _____

43 at least _____

44 be made of _____

45 no longer _____

**A** 단어의 첫 철자를 참조하여 다음 정의에 해당하는 단어를 쓰시오.

1 to influence or make a difference to something      a_____

2 the act of paying for something      p_____

3 to make a change from one thing to another      s_____

4 people's need for products or services      d_____

**B** 다음 밑줄 친 단어와 의미가 유사한 단어를 고르시오.

1 I learned that salt was once traded as <u>currency</u>.

    ⓐ spice       ⓑ fuel       ⓒ money       ⓓ medicine       ⓔ food

2 Mia thinks her parents <u>favor</u> her little sister.

    ⓐ admire       ⓑ prefer       ⓒ trust       ⓓ rely on       ⓔ protect

3 It takes around 10 years to become a <u>skilled</u> artisan.

    ⓐ poor       ⓑ happy       ⓒ active       ⓓ expert       ⓔ terrible

**C** 우리말과 같은 뜻이 되도록 빈칸에 들어갈 말을 보기에서 찾아 알맞은 형태로 쓰시오.

| 보기    no longer      rely on      at least      be made of |
| --- |

1 그 마을의 사람들은 물 공급을 그 우물에 의존한다.

   ▶ People in the village _____ the well for their water supply.

2 그는 더 이상 사람들이 자신에 대해 어떻게 생각하는지 신경 쓰지 않는다.

   ▶ He _____ cares about what people think about him.

3 그 꽃병을 조심해라! 그것은 유리로 만들어졌다.

   ▶ Be careful with that vase! It _____ glass.

4 너는 적어도 하루에 두 번은 이를 닦아야 한다.

   ▶ You need to brush your teeth _____ twice a day.

**A**  다음 (  ) 안에서 알맞은 것을 고르시오.

1  Jack is one of the strongest (boy, boys) in his school.

2  This coffee is two times as (hot, hotter) as that black tea.

3  The (early, earlier) you get up, the (fast, faster) you can leave home.

4  Your previous room was twice as (good, best) as your current one.

5  This diary (must, cannot) be Emily's. She doesn't keep one.

6  She is on time every day. She (must, can't) be a diligent student.


**B**  밑줄 친 부분에 유의하여 우리말로 해석하시오.

1  This soup <u>must</u> be cold now.

2  He <u>can't</u> be John, because John is on vacation.

3  Max's face has turned red. He <u>must</u> be nervous!

4  You have just had lunch. You <u>cannot</u> be hungry.

5  <u>The more</u> I think about it, <u>the more</u> I believe it's the truth.

6  The planet is <u>four times as large as</u> Earth.


**C**  밑줄 친 부분을 어법에 맞게 고쳐 쓰시오.

1  He <u>must being</u> interested in online games.

2  The rumor about Jenny <u>be cannot</u> true.

3  Pizza is one of <u>the much popular foods</u> in the world.

4  This book is <u>three time thicker</u> than that one.

5  The older she gets, <u>the most</u> she resembles her mother.

6  This bridge is two times <u>as long</u> than the previous one.

**A** 우리말과 일치하도록 ( ) 안에 주어진 말을 알맞게 배열하시오.

1 이는 그들이 숙련된 근로자를 빨리 찾을 수 있게 해준다.

(them, this, to, allows, find)

▶ _____ skilled workers quickly.

2 근로자들이 장기적인 경력을 쌓기 어렵다.

(workers, to, difficult, for, develop)

▶ It's _____ long-term careers.

3 그것들에 대한 수요가 틀림없이 있다.

(a demand, must, them, be, for)

▶ There _____.

4 폴리머 지폐는 구식의 종이 지폐보다 더 튼튼하다.

(tougher, old-fashioned, than, paper ones)

▶ Polymer banknotes are _____.

5 많은 은행들이 폴리머를 돈의 미래라고 본다.

(the future, polymers, as, see)

▶ Many banks _____ of money.

**B** 우리말과 일치하도록 ( ) 안의 말을 이용하여 문장을 완성하시오.

1 이것들은 위조 지폐를 만드는 것을 매우 어렵게 한다. (make, difficult)

▶ These _____ it extremely _____ _____ produce fake money.

2 그것들은 종이 화폐보다 적어도 2.5배는 더 오래간다. (time, as, long)

▶ They last at least 2.5 _____ _____ _____ _____ paper currency.

3 그것들은 찢김의 영향을 덜 받는다. (affect)

▶ They are _____ _____ _____ rips.

4 gig 경제가 그저 지나가는 유행일 리가 없다는 것은 분명하다. (gig economies)

▶ It's clear that _____ _____ _____ _____ just a passing trend.

# UNIT 05 | Society

**[01-30] 다음 단어의 뜻을 쓰시오.**

01 available _____

02 cling _____

03 widely _____

04 fine _____

05 artificial _____

06 volleyball _____

07 ordinary _____

08 capture _____

09 salary _____

10 effective _____

11 worth _____

12 material _____

13 fabric _____

14 moisture _____

15 organization _____

16 exact _____

17 crack _____

18 Mediterranean Sea _____

19 rare _____

20 rainfall _____

21 citizen _____

22 gather _____

23 fancy _____

24 distance _____

25 royalty _____

26 connection _____

27 portrait _____

28 notice _____

29 process _____

30 valuable _____

**[31-40] 다음 뜻을 지닌 단어를 쓰시오.**

31 털, 모직 _____

32 부족 _____

33 (~하거나 살) 여유가 되다 _____

34 수확하다, 거둬들이다 _____

35 껍데기[껍질] _____

36 황제 _____

37 아주 작은 _____

38 자포자기한; 간절히 원하는 _____

39 예복 _____

40 수집가; 수집기 _____

**[41-44] 다음 숙어의 뜻을 쓰시오.**

41 set up _____

42 ban A from B _____

43 date back to _____

44 between A and B _____

**A** 다음 단어의 영영풀이를 바르게 연결하시오.

1 afford •        • ⓐ a lack of something that you need or want

2 gather •        • ⓑ to come together in one place

3 shortage •     • ⓒ having a certain value in money

4 rare •          • ⓓ to have enough money to pay for or do something

5 worth •        • ⓔ not commonly found or happening very often

**B** 다음 빈칸에 들어갈 말을 보기에서 찾아 쓰시오.

> 보기   clings        harvested        afford        costs        exact

1 It _____ a lot of money to throw a good birthday party.

2 We can _____ to go abroad for a trip.

3 How many oranges are _____ per year?

4 A(n) _____ amount of rainfall cannot be estimated.

5 The shirt is so wet that it _____ to me.

**C** 우리말과 같은 뜻이 되도록 빈칸에 들어갈 말을 보기에서 찾아 알맞은 형태로 쓰시오.

> 보기   ban A from B        date back to        set up        between A and B

1 보스턴과 뉴욕 사이의 거리는 400킬로미터이다.
   ▶ The distance _____ Boston _____ New York is 400 km.

2 우리는 산 초입에 텐트를 세웠다.
   ▶ We _____ the tents at the foot of the mountain.

3 그들은 건물 내에서 아이들이 자전거를 타는 것을 금지한다.
   ▶ They _____ kids _____ riding bicycles inside the building.

4 몇몇 겨울 축제들은 메소포타미아 시대로 거슬러 올라간다.
   ▶ Some winter festivals _____ the Mesopotamians.

**A** 두 문장의 의미가 같도록 빈칸에 알맞은 말을 쓰시오.

1 This room is spacious enough for us to have a meeting.

   ▶ This room is so _____ that _____ there.

2 The soup is too salty for a baby to eat.

   ▶ The soup is so _____ that _____ it.

3 The book was so boring that kids couldn't enjoy it.

   ▶ The book was too _____ for _____ .

4 The car was so big that everyone could fit in it.

   ▶ The car was big _____ for _____ .

**B** 다음 문장을 보기와 같이 수동태 문장으로 고쳐 쓰시오.

> 보기   The CEO delayed the meeting. ▶ <u>The meeting was delayed by the CEO.</u>

1 The mechanic will repair my bicycle.

   ▶ _____

2 Many people loved this musical.

   ▶ _____

3 The college students had to perform the play.

   ▶ _____

4 The resort staff can take care of your kids.

   ▶ _____

**C** 어법상 어색한 곳을 찾아 바르게 고쳐 쓰시오.

1 Her car was steal by a stranger yesterday.

2 This package will send to Cathy tomorrow.

3 The coffee was too bitter for me to drinking.

4 Daniel is too weak to carrying boxes for her.

5 The service will be cancel due to a lack of interest.

6 He was enough smart to answer all the difficult questions.

**A** 우리말과 일치하도록 ( ) 안에 주어진 말을 알맞게 배열하시오.

1 물방울이 충분히 커지면, 그것들은 아래에 있는 물탱크에 떨어진다.

(big, the drops, grow, enough)

▶ When _____ , they drip into water tanks below.

2 안개 수집기를 세우는 비용은 15달러 미만이다.

(costs, a fog collector, building)

▶ _____ less than $15.

3 보라색은 왜 왕족의 색깔로 여겨졌는가?

(the color, considered, purple, was)

▶ Why _____ of royalty?

4 염료 제조업자들은 보라색 염료를 작은 바다 우렁이에서 얻었다.

(purple dye, from, got)

▶ Dye makers _____ a small sea snail.

5 우렁이들의 껍데기는 깨뜨려져 열어 놓아야 했다.

(had, open, to be, cracked)

▶ The snails' shells _____ .

**B** 우리말과 일치하도록 ( ) 안의 말을 이용하여 문장을 완성하시오.

1 단체들은 안개를 잡는 특별한 그물을 개발했다. (that, capture)

▶ The organizations developed special nets _____ _____ _____ .

2 이 물질은 물방울을 채집하는 데 효과적이다. (effective, capture)

▶ This material _____ _____ _____ _____ water drops.

3 로마의 시민들은 황제에 의해 보라색 옷을 입는 것을 금지당했다. (ban, wear)

▶ Roman citizens _____ _____ _____ _____ purple clothing by their emperors.

4 그것은 보라색 염료가 희귀했기 때문이었다. (rare, purple dye)

▶ It was because _____ _____ _____ _____ .

5 19세기 중반에, 최초의 인공 염료가 만들어졌다. (create)

▶ In the mid-19th century, the first artificial dyes _____ _____ .

## VOCABULARY TEST 1

반 / 이름:

**[01-30] 다음 단어의 뜻을 쓰시오.**

01 tragic _____

02 survive _____

03 flexible _____

04 horrible _____

05 gallon _____

06 cell _____

07 blood _____

08 unique _____

09 eventually _____

10 unit _____

11 form _____

12 conversely _____

13 sweat _____

14 rescue _____

15 care _____

16 protect _____

17 community _____

18 hunter _____

19 daytime _____

20 affect _____

21 hunt _____

22 maintain _____

23 orphanage _____

24 target _____

25 shrink _____

26 source _____

27 massive _____

28 fatty _____

29 store _____

30 reinforce _____

**[31-40] 다음 뜻을 지닌 단어를 쓰시오.**

31 흐르다 _____

32 실행; 관행 _____

33 소비하다; 섭취하다 _____

34 탈진한 _____

35 풀어 주다 _____

36 효율적인 _____

37 약한, 힘이 없는 _____

38 보호, 보존 _____

39 과열되다 _____

40 온도 _____

**[41-44] 다음 숙어의 뜻을 쓰시오.**

41 prevent A from B

42 around-the-clock _____

43 at a time _____

44 due to _____

**A** 다음 밑줄 친 단어와 의미가 반대인 단어를 고르시오.

1 The manual says it's <u>illegal</u> to copy this program.

ⓐ practical ⓑ wide ⓒ equal ⓓ traditional ⓔ legal

2 The pants do not <u>shrink</u> in the wash.

ⓐ clean ⓑ expand ⓒ pour ⓓ connect ⓔ cure

3 A <u>massive</u> stone blocked the road, so we stopped driving.

ⓐ unique ⓑ heavy ⓒ tiny ⓓ average ⓔ huge

**B** 다음 빈칸에 들어갈 말을 보기에서 찾아 쓰시오.

| 보기 | protection | community | traumatic | release | maintain |

1 This is a popular bazaar in this _____.

2 The prime minister needs to _____ his popularity for the next election.

3 The little orphans in the war need special care and _____.

4 The organization decided to _____ the turtles into the sea.

5 I haven't slept well since I suffered a _____ experience.

**C** 우리말과 같은 뜻이 되도록 빈칸에 들어갈 말을 보기에서 찾아 알맞은 형태로 쓰시오.

| 보기 | due to | around-the-clock | prevent A from B | at a time |

1 그 상자들을 한 번에 옮길 수 있니?

▶ Can you carry the boxes _____?

2 그 기차는 폭설 때문에 취소되었다.

▶ The train was canceled _____ heavy snow.

3 궂은 날씨는 그들이 떠나는 것을 막았다.

▶ Bad weather _____ them _____ leaving.

4 그들은 정시에 그 프로젝트를 끝내기 위해 24시간 내내 일했다.

▶ They worked _____ to finish the project on time.

**A** ( ) 안에 주어진 단어를 알맞은 형태로 고쳐 쓰시오.

1 I saw her _____ down the street yesterday. (walk)

2 We heard a guy _____ the drums in the music room. (play)

3 Look! Your forehead _____ with sweat. (cover)

4 Did you see Karen _____ in her class? (cry)

5 I often hear the kids _____ songs at night. (sing)

6 Mars _____ of silicon, oxygen, iron, and magnesium. (make)

**B** 다음 빈칸에 들어갈 전치사를 보기 에서 찾아 쓰시오.

| 보기 | in | with | of | to | from |
|------|-----|------|-----|-----|------|

1 His room is full _____ a lot of books.

2 Her brave story is known _____ lots of people in the world.

3 My parents were satisfied _____ my grades.

4 No one was interested _____ working out.

**C** 밑줄 친 부분을 어법에 맞게 고쳐 쓰시오.

1 The worker is pleased of his salary increase.

2 I heard her to play the violin at the concert.

3 I saw someone approaches me.

4 The closet is filled from thick winter clothes.

5 I noticed some of the students to sleep in the middle of the class.

**A** 우리말과 일치하도록 ( ) 안에 주어진 말을 알맞게 배열하시오.

1 성체 코끼리를 사냥하는 것은 그들의 공동체 전체에 영향을 미친다.

(affects, hunting, elephants, adult)

▶ _____ their whole community.

2 점차 자라면서, 그들은 자신들만의 사회적 단위를 형성한다. (grow, as, they, older)

▶ _____, they form their own social units.

3 낙타는 몇 달 동안 물 없이 지내는 것으로 알려져 왔다.

(have, camels, go, known, been, to)

▶ _____ for months without water.

4 그것은 그들이 과열되고 땀을 흘리는 것을 방지한다. (overheating, from, and, them, sweating)

▶ It prevents _____.

5 그것들은 체내 수분이 떨어질 때 혈액이 더 쉽게 흐르도록 한다. (flow, allow, to, blood)

▶ They _____ more easily when water levels in the body drop.

**B** 우리말과 일치하도록 ( ) 안의 말을 이용하여 문장을 완성하시오.

1 그 아기 코끼리는 웬디라는 이름이 주어졌다. (give)

▶ The baby elephant _____ _____ the name Wendi.

2 그 끔찍한 관행이 멈춰지지 않는다면, 이러한 비극적인 상황은 계속될 것이다. (unless, stop)

▶ _____ the horrible practice _____ _____, this tragic situation will

continue.

3 어미 코끼리가 죽임을 당하면, 어린 새끼들은 고아로 남겨진다. (leave)

▶ When a mother elephant is killed, her young children _____ _____

_____ orphans.

4 많은 사람들은 낙타의 혹이 물로 가득 차 있다고 추측하지만, 그것은 사실이 아니다. (fill)

▶ Many people assume that the humps of a camel _____ _____ _____

water, but it's not true.

5 그들의 혹은 지방 조직으로 이루어져 있는데, 지방 조직은 에너지원으로 저장된다. (store)

▶ Their humps are made of fatty tissue, _____ _____ _____ _____ a

source of energy.

# VOCABULARY TEST 1

반 / 이름:

**[01-30] 다음 단어의 뜻을 쓰시오.**

01 host _____

02 psychologist _____

03 effect _____

04 important _____

05 daily _____

06 access _____

07 celebrity _____

08 cooperation _____

09 competition _____

10 launch _____

11 reach _____

12 benefit _____

13 profit _____

14 donation _____

15 real _____

16 connect _____

17 limit _____

18 active _____

19 loneliness _____

20 constantly _____

21 post _____

22 probably _____

23 consider _____

24 purchase _____

25 negatively _____

26 affect _____

27 emotional _____

28 raise _____

29 restore _____

30 usage _____

**[31-40] 다음 뜻을 지닌 단어를 쓰시오.**

31 최근에 _____

32 트렌드, 추세 _____

33 의사소통 하다 _____

34 우울증 _____

35 요구하다[필요로 하다] _____

36 상품, 제품 _____

37 고객, 소비자 _____

38 기부[기증]하다 _____

39 효과적인 _____

40 수고; 노력 _____

**[41-44] 다음 숙어의 뜻을 쓰시오.**

41 slow down _____

42 pay attention to _____

43 take a break _____

44 a matter of _____

# VOCABULARY TEST 2

**A** 단어의 첫 철자를 참조하여 다음 정의에 해당하는 단어를 쓰시오.

1 to need something        r_____

2 relating to someone's mind and feelings        e_____

3 a way that lets you use or get something        a_____

4 someone who pays for a product or service        c_____


**B** 다음 빈칸에 들어갈 말을 보기에서 찾아 쓰시오.

| 보기 profit     considered     celebrity     communicate     daily |
| --- |

1 We need to learn how to _____ effectively.

2 She became a _____ after winning a gold medal at the Olympics.

3 I never _____ changing my job because I loved it.

4 You should add exercise to your _____ routine.

5 She made a huge _____ through her online shopping mall.


**C** 우리말과 같은 뜻이 되도록 빈칸에 들어갈 말을 보기에서 찾아 알맞은 형태로 쓰시오.

| 보기 pay attention to     a matter of     slow down     take a break |
| --- |

1 선생님이 말씀하시는 것에 주의를 기울여라.

▶ _____ what your teacher says.

2 기차는 단 몇 분 뒤에 도착할 것이다.

▶ The train will arrive in _____ minutes.

3 그들은 일을 멈추고 잠시 휴식을 취했다.

▶ They stopped working and _____ for a while.

4 작년에 그 회사의 성장이 약간 둔화되었다.

▶ The company's growth _____ a little last year.

**A** 다음 ( ) 안에서 알맞은 것을 고르시오.

1 It is a club to (that, which) many celebrities belong.

2 It is the park (which, in which) the children like to bike.

3 The chair that I am sitting (in, to) isn't comfortable.

4 The people with (who, whom) I live are very nice.

5 The hotel (at which, at that) we stayed had friendly staff.

6 She went to the school (to, to which) her mother went.

**B** 밑줄 친 부분의 의미로 적절한 것을 보기에서 골라 쓰시오.

| 보기 | 완료 | 경험 | 계속 | 결과 |

1 I have just finished cleaning my room. _____

2 We haven't met each other before. _____

3 They have all gone to attend the festival. _____

4 I have been in New York for two years. _____

5 Have you ever been to Jeju Island? _____

6 My sister has had a toothache for years. _____

**C** 밑줄 친 부분을 어법에 맞게 고쳐 쓰시오.

1 Jason is the man with who I traveled around Europe.

2 I have already ate all of the cookies in the box.

3 The jungle in they lived was full of unusual plants.

4 He gone to Russia, so he doesn't live with me now.

5 What is the name of the company for that your father works?

**A** 우리말과 일치하도록 (   ) 안에 주어진 말을 알맞게 배열하시오.

1 소셜 미디어가 코즈 마케팅을 훨씬 더 효과적으로 만든다.

(even more, makes, cause marketing, effective)

▶ Social media _____.

2 소비자들은 단지 소셜 네트워킹 사이트에 정보를 공유하는 것만으로 기업들이 기부하도록 할 수 있다.

(make, donations, companies, have)

▶ Customers can _____ just by sharing information on social networking sites.

3 그들은 고객들에게 자금을 요청하는 새로운 캠페인에 착수했다.

(campaign, a, new, which, asked, they, in)

▶ They launched _____ customers for money.

4 오늘 우리는 심리학자 레베카 스탠포드를 이 쇼에 초대했습니다.

(have, we, invited, psychologist)

▶ Today, _____ Rebecca Stanford to the show.

5 소셜 미디어 트렌드가 둔화되진 않았죠, 그렇죠?

(hasn't, down, the social media trend, slowed)

▶ _____, has it?

**B** 우리말과 일치하도록 (   ) 안의 말을 이용하여 문장을 완성하시오.

1 사람들은 그것을 일상생활의 중요한 부분으로 만들었어요. (have, make, important)

▶ People _____ _____ it _____ _____ _____ of their daily life.

2 연구들은 소셜 미디어가 정서적인 문제를 일으킬 수 있다는 것을 알아냈어요. (have, find, cause)

▶ Studies _____ _____ that social media _____ _____ emotional problems.

3 이것이 코즈 마케팅이 기초를 둔 아이디어이다. (the idea, on)

▶ This is _____ _____ _____ _____ cause marketing is based.

4 물건을 구입함으로써 세상을 도울 수 있다면 당신은 어떻게 느낄까? (help, world, buy)

▶ How would you feel if you could _____ _____ _____ by _____ a product?

## VOCABULARY TEST 1

반 / 이름:

**[01-30] 다음 단어의 뜻을 쓰시오.**

01 amazingly _____

02 attach _____

03 breathe _____

04 condition _____

05 dizzy _____

06 empathy _____

07 exist _____

08 extremely _____

09 fainting _____

10 frozen _____

11 heartbeat _____

12 jet lag _____

13 last _____

14 lower _____

15 measure _____

16 psychological _____

17 react _____

18 report _____

19 sensitive _____

20 serious _____

21 sweaty _____

22 syndrome _____

23 thermometer _____

24 trouble _____

25 volunteer _____

26 wander _____

27 rest _____

28 influence _____

29 drop _____

30 naked _____

**[31-40] 다음 뜻을 지닌 단어를 쓰시오.**

31 장면 _____

32 연구원 _____

33 (액체에) 살짝 담그다 _____

34 궁금해하다 _____

35 경우; 사례 _____

36 감정의 _____

37 악화시키다 _____

38 상태, 질환 _____

39 평범한; 정상적인 _____

40 증상 _____

**[41-44] 다음 숙어의 뜻을 쓰시오.**

41 in particular _____

42 all of a sudden _____

43 apart from _____

44 at the same time _____

**A** 단어의 첫 철자를 참조하여 다음 정의에 해당하는 단어를 쓰시오.

1 a sign that someone has an illness         s_____

2 to find the size, amount, or degree of something     m_____

3 to be present in the real world             e_____

4 to respond to something that happens       r_____

5 to have a desire to know something         w_____

**B** 다음 빈칸에 들어갈 말을 보기에서 찾아 쓰시오.

| 보기 | worsen | wandered | lower | thermometer |

1 We _____ around the park, waiting for David.

2 The _____ records a temperature of 35℃.

3 Can you _____ the price of this bag?

4 His cold seems to _____ at night.

**C** 우리말과 같은 뜻이 되도록 빈칸에 들어갈 말을 보기에서 찾아 쓰시오.

| 보기 | apart from | at the same time | all of a sudden | in particular |

1 그는 특별히 누구에게도 화가 난 것은 아니었다.

▶ He wasn't angry at anyone _____.

2 두 명의 누나 이외에도, 그는 남동생이 있다.

▶ _____ two sisters, he has a brother.

3 갑자기, 양 떼가 우리 앞에 나타났다.

▶ _____, a herd of sheep appeared in front of us.

4 너와 나는 나이가 같고, 우리는 동시에 태어났다.

▶ You and I are the same age and we were born _____.

**A** 다음 문장을 보기와 같이 고쳐 쓰시오.

> 보기  I don't know what I should wear for the party.
> ▶ <u>I don't know what to wear for the party.</u>

1 They want to know when they should start the game.

▶ _____

2 I did not know whom I should thank for this gift.

▶ _____

3 Can you tell me how I should fix this bicycle?

▶ _____

4 We have to decide where we should go for our summer vacation.

▶ _____


**B** 다음 ( ) 안에서 알맞은 것을 고르시오.

1 I was shopping at a mall (while, after) he was watching a movie.

2 (After, When) it was raining, we stayed inside.

3 We will have lunch (after, while) the movie is over.

4 She started to cry (when, until) she heard the sad story.


**C** 우리말과 일치하도록 빈칸에 알맞은 말을 쓰시오.

1 언제 그 회의를 시작할지 알려드리겠습니다.

▶ I will inform you _____ to start the meeting.

2 자러 가기 전에, 나는 컴퓨터 게임을 했다.

▶ _____ I went to bed, I played a computer game.

3 네가 숙제를 끝낼 때까지, 너는 나갈 수 없다.

▶ _____ you finish your homework, you can't go out.

4 내가 그 문제를 어떻게 풀어야 할지 가르쳐 주세요.

▶ Let me know _____ to solve the problem.

**A** 우리말과 일치하도록 (  ) 안에 주어진 말을 알맞게 배열하시오.

1 나는 그렇게 아름다운 것이 존재할 거라고는 상상도 못 했다.

(anything, could, imagined, so beautiful, exist)

▶ I never _____.

2 누군가가 추워하는 것을 보는 것이 그 자신의 체온을 낮췄다.

(someone, cold, watching, feeling)

▶ _____ had lowered his own body temperature.

3 사람들은 얼음물에 손을 담그고 있었다.

(their hands, icy water, dipping, into)

▶ People were _____.

4 감정 이입은 우리가 다른 사람들의 감정을 이해하고 공유하게 한다.

(us, to, and, share, understand, allows)

▶ Empathy _____ others' emotions.


**B** 우리말과 일치하도록 (  ) 안의 말을 이용하여 문장을 완성하시오.

1 나는 무엇을 해야 할지 몰랐다. (what, do)

▶ I didn't know _____ _____ _____.

2 갑자기, 나는 숨을 쉬기가 힘들었다. (trouble, breathe)

▶ All of a sudden, I _____ _____ _____.

3 그 감정은 너무 강렬해서 그는 자신이 문제를 겪고 있다고 생각했다. (so, strong)

▶ The feeling was _____ _____ _____ he thought he was having problems.

4 그는 영화를 보는 동안 추위를 느꼈다. (while, watch)

▶ He felt cold _____ _____ _____ _____ a film.

5 이것은 우리가 그들이 어떻게 느끼는지를 경험하도록 한다. (let, experience)

▶ This _____ _____ _____ _____ they feel.

## VOCABULARY TEST 1

반 / 이름:

**[01-30] 다음 단어의 뜻을 쓰시오.**

01 various _____

02 originate _____

03 missionary _____

04 religious _____

05 native _____

06 convince _____

07 holy _____

08 grip _____

09 edge _____

10 expose _____

11 shrink _____

12 slip _____

13 bottom _____

14 enemy _____

15 publication _____

16 influence _____

17 feature _____

18 celebration _____

19 custom _____

20 migrate _____

21 European _____

22 reindeer _____

23 tough _____

24 the Arctic _____

25 last _____

26 evolve _____

27 recently _____

28 appear _____

29 represent _____

30 display _____

**[31-40] 다음 뜻을 지닌 단어를 쓰시오.**

31 전통 _____

32 역사학자 _____

33 독일 _____

34 기도하다 _____

35 세기, 100년 _____

36 생존자 _____

37 장식하다[꾸미다] _____

38 적응 _____

39 반사하다 _____

40 세심한; 민감한 _____

**[41-44] 다음 숙어의 뜻을 쓰시오.**

41 put up _____

42 cope with _____

43 have an impact on _____

44 chop down _____

**A** 다음 단어의 영영풀이를 바르게 연결하시오.

1 represent •          • ⓐ something that people do that is traditional or usual

2 religious  •          • ⓑ to develop new features over generations

3 condition •          • ⓒ relating to the belief in the existence of a god or gods

4 evolve     •          • ⓓ the physical state of something

5 custom    •          • ⓔ to serve as a sign or symbol of something

**B** 다음 빈칸에 들어갈 말을 보기에서 찾아 쓰시오.

| 보기 sensitive     exposed     migrate     reflected     edge |

1 He took off his shirt and _____ his injury.

2 The girl saw herself _____ in the window of the subway.

3 Young people are very _____ about what they look like.

4 Don't go to the _____ of the cliff. You might fall off.

5 Every year, thousands of people _____ to this area to find work.

**C** 우리말과 같은 뜻이 되도록 빈칸에 들어갈 말을 보기에서 찾아 알맞은 형태로 쓰시오.

| 보기 chop down     have an impact on     cope with     put up |

1 스트레스에 대처하는 좋은 방법을 공유해 주실 수 있나요?
  ▶ Can you share good ways to _____ stress?

2 그 책은 내 인생에 큰 영향을 주었다.
  ▶ The book _____ a huge _____ my life.

3 그들은 정원에 있는 몇몇 나무들을 베어냈다.
  ▶ They _____ some trees in the garden.

4 우리는 해변에 작은 텐트를 세웠다.
  ▶ We _____ a small tent on the beach.

**A** 다음 ( ) 안에서 알맞은 것을 고르시오.

1 His car is as (good, better) as mine.

2 This is the (much, most) expensive dish in this café.

3 Jack runs much (faster, fastest) than David.

4 This musical is (little, less) interesting than that one.

5 The comedy I saw was as (funny, funnier) as I had expected.

6 Lauren has the (most long, longest) hair in her class.

**B** ( ) 안에 주어진 단어를 알맞은 형태로 쓰시오.

1 The police officer told the man _____. (stop)

2 Jacob let me _____ his laptop whenever I wanted to. (use)

3 Chris asked me _____ over to his house. (come)

4 My mom made me _____ more milk for my health. (drink)

5 My sister always keeps her room _____. (neatly)

6 My mom allowed me _____ to the amusement park with my friends. (go)

**C** 밑줄 친 부분을 어법에 맞게 고쳐 쓰시오.

1 Daniel is one of the <u>rich</u> men in this town.

2 History is much <u>easy</u> than math for me.

3 Mark plays soccer as <u>better</u> as Kevin does.

4 Don't make me <u>to leave</u> this house.

5 My dad wanted me <u>telling</u> the truth.

6 Buying a present will make your mom <u>to be happy</u>.

**A** 우리말과 일치하도록 ( ) 안에 주어진 말을 알맞게 배열하시오.

1 순록은 지구상에서 가장 척박한 환경에서 산다.

(on the planet, the toughest, environment)

▶ Reindeer live in _____.

2 이것은 순록의 눈을 빛에 더 민감하게 만든다.

(more, light, to, the reindeer's eyes, sensitive)

▶ This makes _____.

3 그들은 크리스마스트리를 그들의 휴일 기념행사의 공식적인 부분으로 만들었다.

(Christmas trees, official, made, an, part)

▶ They _____ of their holiday celebrations.

4 그는 사람들이 근처의 상록수를 그들의 신성한 나무로 숭배하도록 설득했다.

(the people, convinced, worship, to)

▶ He _____ a nearby evergreen as their holy tree.

5 미디어 출판물의 영향은 그 후 계속 그 전통이 살아있도록 해 왔다.

(the tradition, kept, alive, has)

▶ The influence of media publications _____ ever since.

**B** 우리말과 일치하도록 ( ) 안의 말을 이용하여 문장을 완성하시오.

1 이것은 순록이 눈 위를 달리게 해준다. (allow)

▶ This _____ reindeer _____ _____ on the snow.

2 그곳의 기온은 섭씨 영하 40도만큼이나 낮다. (low)

▶ The temperatures there are _____ _____ _____ -40℃.

3 조지 3세의 독일인 부인은 윈저 성에 나무들이 장식되도록 했다. (have, decorate)

▶ The German wife of King George III _____ _____ _____ at Windsor Castle.

4 그는 몇몇 원주민들이 그들의 신에게 기도하기 위해 떡갈나무에 모여 있는 것을 지켜보았다.

(pray, their god)

▶ He watched some natives gathering at an oak tree _____ _____ _____ _____ _____.

# UNIT 10 | People

반 / 이름:

**[01-30] 다음 단어의 뜻을 쓰시오.**

01 achievement _____

02 admire _____

03 anniversary _____

04 announce _____

05 athlete _____

06 barrier _____

07 brilliantly _____

08 complex _____

09 composer _____

10 engineer _____

11 even _____

12 hometown _____

13 except _____

14 inspire _____

15 instrument _____

16 lifetime _____

17 mighty _____

18 movement _____

19 nonviolent _____

20 chat _____

21 part _____

22 passion _____

23 popularity _____

24 produce _____

25 railway _____

26 retire _____

27 right _____

28 rush _____

29 technical _____

30 valuable _____

**[31-40] 다음 뜻을 지닌 단어를 쓰시오.**

31 승리 _____

32 행동 _____

33 이끌다 _____

34 압도적인 _____

35 모욕하다 _____

36 협박, 위협 _____

37 깊은 인상을 주다 _____

38 극적인 _____

39 영향, 효과 _____

40 재능이 있는 _____

**[41-44] 다음 숙어의 뜻을 쓰시오.**

41 fight back _____

42 be famous for _____

43 fall in love with _____

44 fight for _____

# VOCABULARY TEST 2

**A** 다음 단어의 영영풀이를 바르게 연결하시오.

1 last •        • ⓐ a very strong feeling about something

2 passion •      • ⓑ to respect someone or something

3 admire •      • ⓒ the state of being liked by a lot of people

4 popularity •    • ⓓ to say or do something offensive and aggressive

5 insult •       • ⓔ to continue existing or happening in time

**B** 다음 빈칸에 들어갈 말을 [보기]에서 찾아 쓰시오.

> [보기]  threats      complex      retired      barrier      talented

1 The people in this area are afraid of terrorist _____.

2 His lecture was so _____ that we couldn't understand it.

3 Any _____ young musicians can enter this audition.

4 I heard that you've recently _____ from your company.

5 They came from different countries, so there is a language _____ between them.

**C** 우리말과 같은 뜻이 되도록 빈칸에 들어갈 말을 [보기]에서 찾아 알맞은 형태로 쓰시오.

> [보기]  fight back      be famous for      fall in love with      fight for

1 내가 그를 때렸지만, 그는 반격하지 않았다.

   ▶ I hit him, but he didn't _____.

2 그 선수들은 우승을 놓고 싸울 것이다.

   ▶ The players will _____ the championship.

3 나는 잘생긴 남자와 사랑에 빠지고 싶다.

   ▶ I want to _____ a handsome guy.

4 그녀는 이 동네에서 그녀의 수제 쿠키로 유명하다.

   ▶ She _____ her homemade cookies in this neighborhood.

**A** 다음 빈칸에 들어갈 말을 보기에서 찾아 쓰시오. (중복 가능)

보기    used to         would like to         had better

1 You _____ take a taxi, or you will be late.

2 He _____ walk around when he had something on his mind.

3 I _____ finish this project today, but I don't have to.

4 There _____ be a pizza shop here, but it disappeared.

5 You _____ not talk about the rumor anymore.

**B** 접속사 Although를 이용하여 짝지어진 두 문장을 한 문장으로 쓰시오.

1 I was tired last night. I went to the gym.

▶ _____

2 Jake is small. He is very strong.

▶ _____

3 The heater was on. It was cold in the room.

▶ _____

4 I got up late. I arrived at school on time.

▶ _____

**C** 밑줄 친 부분에 유의하여 다음 문장을 우리말로 해석하시오.

1 They <u>used to</u> go to the movies after school.

2 You <u>had better</u> not swim in that cold river.

3 I <u>would like to</u> go to New Zealand for my honeymoon.

4 <u>Though</u> he was not handsome, a lot of girls liked him.

5 <u>Even though</u> I took the medicine, I still have a stomachache.

6 <u>Even if</u> she becomes rich, she will never change.

**A** 우리말과 일치하도록 (  ) 안에 주어진 말을 알맞게 배열하시오.

1 그는 기차에 대해 기관사들과 이야기하곤 했다.

(to, used, with, chat)

▶ He _____ the engineers about trains.

2 새로운 철로가 그의 고향을 바로 통과하여 지어졌다.

(right through, was, his hometown, built)

▶ A new railway line _____.

3 그는 모욕을 당했고 혐오 메일을 받았다.

(and, received, insulted, was, hate mail)

▶ He _____.

4 그의 행동은 흑인뿐만 아니라 백인에게도 깊은 인상을 주었다.

(as, blacks, as, whites, well, impressed)

▶ His behavior _____.

5 기차로 여행할 때마다, 그는 열차 시간표를 살피는 데 몇 시간을 보냈다.

(hours, train schedules, spent, studying)

▶ Whenever he traveled by train, he _____.

**B** 우리말과 일치하도록 (  ) 안의 말을 이용하여 문장을 완성하시오.

1 그는 내셔널 리그의 최우수 선수(MVP)에 지명되었다. (name)

▶ He _____ _____ the National League's Most Valuable Player (MVP).

2 기차 한 대가 압도적인 소리를 내며 그를 지나쳐 돌진했다. (make, overwhelming)

▶ A train rushed past him, _____ a(n) _____ sound.

3 이것은 그의 가장 멋진 작품 중 하나가 되었다. (one, great)

▶ This became _____ _____ _____ _____ works.

4 그는 흑인 인권을 위해 싸우려고 애썼다. (try, fight)

▶ He _____ _____ _____ _____ the rights of African Americans.

5 그는 그 경기에서 다저스팀이 우승하도록 도왔다. (win, help)

▶ He _____ the Dodgers _____.

## VOCABULARY TEST 1

반 / 이름:

[01-30] 다음 단어의 뜻을 쓰시오.

01 abnormal _____

02 aerial _____

03 tough _____

04 calculate _____

05 capture _____

06 citizen _____

07 delay _____

08 drone _____

09 empathy _____

10 evaluate _____

11 expressive _____

12 facial _____

13 feature _____

14 identify _____

15 interaction _____

16 match _____

17 observe _____

18 properly _____

19 reply _____

20 reaction _____

21 region _____

22 trained _____

23 response _____

24 rough _____

25 soar _____

26 struggle _____

27 therapist _____

28 treatment _____

29 social _____

30 landscape _____

[31-40] 다음 뜻을 지닌 단어를 쓰시오.

31 화석 _____

32 표면[표층] _____

33 견디다[참다] _____

34 의미 있는 _____

35 문지르다[비비다] _____

36 고립된 _____

37 의식하다; 알아채다 _____

38 의사소통을 하다 _____

39 진단하다 _____

40 주인, 소유주 _____

[41-45] 다음 숙어의 뜻을 쓰시오.

41 as a result _____

42 narrow down _____

43 not only A but also B _____

44 take advantage of _____

45 thanks to _____

**A** 다음 단어의 영영풀이를 바르게 연결하시오.

1 feature •              • ⓐ in an acceptable or suitable way

2 diagnose •           • ⓑ to watch something closely

3 observe •            • ⓒ to have a particular thing as an important aspect

4 research •           • ⓓ to identify an illness or problem by examining it

5 properly •           • ⓔ a detailed study of something done in order to find new knowledge about it

**B** 다음 밑줄 친 단어와 의미가 유사한 단어를 고르시오.

1 We will <u>identify</u> new information by doing experiments.

  ⓐ know        ⓑ experience     ⓒ question     ⓓ realize     ⓔ find

2 I had to <u>endure</u> a severe stomachache all morning.

  ⓐ gain        ⓑ bear        ⓒ protect     ⓓ attack     ⓔ produce

3 I was seeking an opportunity to <u>communicate</u> with you.

  ⓐ talk        ⓑ play        ⓒ open      ⓓ cover     ⓔ compete

**C** 우리말과 같은 뜻이 되도록 빈칸에 들어갈 말을 〈보기〉에서 찾아 알맞은 형태로 쓰시오.

| 보기 | narrow down    as a result    take advantage of    not only A but also B |
|---|---|

1 그는 돈을 훔쳤을 뿐만 아니라 차도 가져갔다.

  ▶ He _____ stole the money, _____ took the car.

2 나는 중국어 실력을 늘리기 위해 여가 시간을 이용했다.

  ▶ I _____ the spare time to improve my Chinese.

3 결과적으로, 그는 자신이 실패했다는 것을 받아들여야 했다.

  ▶ _____, he had to admit that he failed.

4 너는 선택의 폭을 줄이는 것이 낫겠다.

  ▶ You'd better _____ your choices.

**A** 다음 ( ) 안에서 알맞은 것을 고르시오.

1 The kid (singing, sung) with them is my son.

2 Have you ever read a book (writing, written) in English?

3 This zoo is an (exciting, excited) place for little kids.

4 Diana has a pet pig (naming, named) Mr. Rollo.

5 I can't drive with a (breaking, broken) leg.

**B** 다음 빈칸에 들어갈 말을 보기에서 찾아 쓰시오. (단, 한 번씩만 쓸 것)

> 보기   each other      the other      some      others

1 Would you like _____ donuts?

2 Sarah and Don understand _____.

3 Some people go by bus and _____ walk.

4 I have two dogs. One is a Chihuahua, and _____ is a poodle.

**C** 밑줄 친 부분을 어법에 맞게 고쳐 쓰시오.

1 I brought a box making of wood.

2 Mom seemed shocking by the sad news.

3 Look at the children stood next to the tree.

4 The people walked on the sidewalk had to step aside.

5 A: How did you meet another?
  B: We met in a café.

**A** 우리말과 일치하도록 (   ) 안에 주어진 말을 알맞게 배열하시오.

1 그는 웃고 있는 로봇과 함께 시간을 보내고 있다.

(time, a, with, spending, robot, smiling)

▶ He is _____.

2 자폐가 있는 아이들은 힘겹게 의사소통하는 데 어려움을 겪는다.

(struggle, with, to, autism, communicate)

▶ Children _____.

3 높은 온도는 이 지역에서 일하는 것을 어렵게 만든다.

(it, difficult, make, work, to)

▶ High temperatures _____ in the area.

4 그들은 이것을 힘든 환경을 견디지 않고 할 수 있다.

(do, this, without, can, enduring)

▶ They _____ the tough conditions.

**B** 우리말과 일치하도록 (   ) 안의 말을 이용하여 문장을 완성하시오.

1 이 비행 로봇은 건물 위로 날아오를 수 있다. (fly)

▶ These _____ _____ can soar above buildings.

2 그들 중 일부는 고립될 수 있다. (isolate, become)

▶ Some of them _____ _____ _____.

3 고고학자들은 Fossil Finder라고 불리는 웹 사이트를 이용했다. (call, a website)

▶ Archaeologists used _____ _____ _____ Fossil Finder.

4 이것은 고고학자들이 광범위한 지역을 조사할 수 있는 방법이 되고 있다. (archaeologists, research, to)

▶ It has become a way _____ _____ _____ _____ wide regions.

5 아이들은 로봇의 표정과 일치하는 감정을 선택하라고 요구된다. (match, the emotion)

▶ Children are asked to choose _____ _____ _____ the robot's facial expression.

# UNIT 12 | Health

반 / 이름:

[01-30] 다음 단어의 뜻을 쓰시오.

01 connective _____

02 tissue _____

03 attach _____

04 forearm _____

05 signal _____

06 structure _____

07 tighten _____

08 need _____

09 calorie _____

10 emotional _____

11 brain _____

12 skip _____

13 function _____

14 situation _____

15 relax _____

16 specific _____

17 evenly _____

18 index finger _____

19 little finger _____

20 ring finger _____

21 divide _____

22 completely _____

23 separate _____

24 possible _____

25 wrong _____

26 reason _____

27 extra _____

28 desire _____

29 straighten _____

30 complex _____

[31-40] 다음 뜻을 지닌 단어를 쓰시오.

31 근육 _____

32 손바닥 _____

33 신경 _____

34 엄지손가락 _____

35 굽히다 _____

36 신체적인 _____

37 비어 있는 _____

38 독립하여 _____

39 소비하다; 먹다 _____

40 차이(점) _____

[41-44] 다음 숙어의 뜻을 쓰시오.

41 for a while _____

42 be referred to as _____

43 think of A as B _____

44 such as _____

# VOCABULARY TEST 2

## A 다음 단어의 영영풀이를 바르게 연결하시오.

1 bend •          • ⓐ to work in the correct way

2 empty •          • ⓑ to have nothing inside

3 bone •          • ⓒ a type of body tissue that produces movement

4 muscle •          • ⓓ the hard parts that form the frame of the body

5 function •          • ⓔ to fold or curve

## B 다음 밑줄 친 단어와 의미가 반대인 단어를 고르시오.

1 Some children were not in good <u>physical</u> condition.

ⓐ medical          ⓑ financial          ⓒ mental          ⓓ nutritional          ⓔ healthy

2 You have to <u>connect</u> these two parts to set up the tent.

ⓐ link          ⓑ separate          ⓒ fasten          ⓓ control          ⓔ push

3 The human body is like a <u>complex</u> machine.

ⓐ simple          ⓑ another          ⓒ final          ⓓ common          ⓔ similar

## C 우리말과 같은 뜻이 되도록 빈칸에 들어갈 말을 보기 에서 찾아 알맞은 형태로 쓰시오.

| 보기 | such as | be referred to as | think of A as B | for a while |

1 나는 한동안 그 문제에 대해 생각했다.

▶ I thought about the problem _____.

2 그 섬은 '태평양의 낙원'으로 불린다.

▶ The island _____ the "Paradise of the Pacific."

3 우리는 그를 가족 중 한 사람이라고 생각한다.

▶ We _____ him _____ a part of our family.

4 차, 커피, 핫 초콜릿과 같은 뜨거운 음료가 제공될 것이다.

▶ Hot drinks _____ tea, coffee, and hot chocolate will be served.

# GRAMMAR TEST

**A** 다음 빈칸에 들어갈 말을 보기에서 찾아 쓰시오. (단, 한 번씩만 쓸 것)

> 보기    beside        by        between        for        in

1 He wanted to succeed _____ himself.

2 She got angry, so she was _____ herself.

3 This book is _____ itself worth reading.

4 Let's keep this information _____ ourselves and not tell anyone.

5 I don't want to exercise _____ myself. It is quite lonely.

**B** 다음 문장을 수동태로 바꾸어 쓰시오.

1 The chairman put off the meeting.

  ▶ The meeting _____.

2 Volunteers took care of the cats.

  ▶ The cats _____.

3 A lot of students look up to Mr. Smith.

  ▶ Mr. Smith _____.

4 His classmates laughed at his idea.

  ▶ His idea _____.

**C** 밑줄 친 부분에 유의하여 다음 문장을 우리말로 해석하시오.

1 Help yourself to the food on the table.

2 Between ourselves, I don't like Jake.

3 The little girl wrote the report by herself.

4 Max was brought up in a rich family.

5 I was looked after by a babysitter when I was young.

**A** 우리말과 일치하도록 ( ) 안에 주어진 말을 알맞게 배열하시오.

1 힘줄은 스스로는 어떤 신체 일부도 움직이게 할 수 없다.

(themselves, any body parts, move, by)

▶ Tendons can't _____.

2 힘줄은 이 근육들을 각각의 손가락뼈에 연결한다.

(these muscles, connect, each finger bone, to)

▶ The tendons _____.

3 우리가 손가락을 사용하고 싶을 때, 뇌는 신경에 신호를 보낸다.

(sends, the brain, to, a nerve, a signal)

▶ When we want to use our fingers, _____.

4 대부분의 사람들은 배고픔을 음식에 대한 몸의 신체적 필요로 생각한다.

(as, think of, most people, hunger)

▶ _____ the body's physical need for food.

5 쾌락성 허기는 정서적 필요에 의해 일어난다.

(caused, an emotional need, is, by)

▶ Hedonic hunger _____.


**B** 우리말과 일치하도록 ( ) 안의 말을 이용하여 문장을 완성하시오.

1 이 구조는 우리의 손가락이 놀라운 일들을 하게 한다. (allow, do, amazing)

▶ This structure _____ our fingers _____ _____ _____ _____.

2 근육에 연결된 힘줄은 특정 손가락뼈를 당긴다. (connect, the muscle)

▶ The tendons _____ _____ _____ _____ pull on specific finger bones.

3 그것은 항상성 허기라고 불린다. (refer to)

▶ It _____ _____ _____ _____ homeostatic hunger.

4 당신의 뇌는 당신에게 그것들을 먹으라고 말한다. (tell, consume)

▶ Your brain _____ _____ _____ _____ _____.

# UNIT 13 | Maps

반 / 이름:

**[01-30] 다음 단어의 뜻을 쓰시오.**

01 mark _____

02 region _____

03 distance _____

04 connect _____

05 midpoint _____

06 upright _____

07 process _____

08 stretch _____

09 peninsula _____

10 significant _____

11 recover _____

12 ownership _____

13 entire _____

14 grant _____

15 multitude _____

16 cell _____

17 valuable _____

18 identify _____

19 section _____

20 area _____

21 remove _____

22 decade _____

23 competition _____

24 political _____

25 value _____

26 access _____

27 construct _____

28 mineral _____

29 precious _____

30 rate _____

**[31-40] 다음 뜻을 지닌 단어를 쓰시오.**

31 무작위의 _____

32 상상하다 _____

33 보이지 않는 _____

34 근원 _____

35 별개의 _____

36 긴장 _____

37 규칙; 통치 _____

38 패배시키다[이기다] _____

39 설립[수립]하다 _____

40 조약 _____

**[41-44] 다음 숙어의 뜻을 쓰시오.**

41 divide A into B _____

42 a chain of _____

43 in exchange _____

44 a number of _____

**A** 단어의 첫 철자를 참조하여 다음 정의에 해당하는 단어를 쓰시오.

1 to do something again and again                                    r_____

2 not joined or related, different from something else              s_____

3 to get or achieve something as a result of effort                 g_____

4 to continue to be in a particular situation                       r_____

5 to take something away from a place                               r_____

**B** 다음 밑줄 친 단어와 의미가 반대인 단어를 고르시오.

1 You can find a lot of <u>valuable</u> information in this book.

    ⓐ practical    ⓑ helpful    ⓒ useless    ⓓ basic    ⓔ false

2 They tasted the samples in <u>random</u> order.

    ⓐ reverse    ⓑ planned    ⓒ different    ⓓ correct    ⓔ perfect

3 He could earn a <u>significant</u> amount of money in two years.

    ⓐ large    ⓑ certain    ⓒ small    ⓓ similar    ⓔ limited

**C** 우리말과 같은 뜻이 되도록 빈칸에 들어갈 말을 보기에서 찾아 알맞은 형태로 쓰시오.

| 보기 in exchange    a chain of    a number of    divide A into B |
| --- |

1 난 오늘 할 일이 많이 있다.

    ▶ I have _____ things to do.

2 제시카는 피자를 여덟 조각으로 나누었다.

    ▶ Jessica _____ the pizza _____ eight pieces.

3 하와이 섬들은 일련의 화산들이다.

    ▶ The Hawaiian Islands are _____ volcanoes.

4 나는 그녀의 개를 산책시켰고, 그녀는 대신 나에게 케이크 한 조각을 주었다.

    ▶ I walked her dog, and she gave me a piece of cake _____.

**A** 다음 문장을 분사구문으로 바꾸어 쓰시오.

1 When I opened the curtains, I saw the beautiful sunrise.

  ▶ _____ _____ _____, I saw the beautiful sunrise.

2 After we finished the appetizer, we started to eat the main dish.

  ▶ _____ _____ _____, we started to eat the main dish.

3 While she prepared dinner, she spoke on the phone.

  ▶ _____ _____, she spoke on the phone.

**B** ( ) 안에 주어진 단어를 알맞은 형태로 쓰시오.

1 We are afraid of _____ the game. (lose)

2 I cannot tell the joke without _____. (laugh)

3 She doesn't care about _____ a lot of friends. (not, have)

4 They are excited about _____ to the festival. (go)

5 Are you interested in _____ new languages? (learn)

6 Jamie is disappointed about _____ the test. (not, pass)

**C** 다음 문장을 우리말로 해석하시오.

1 I watched TV after finishing my homework.

2 We talked about not going to the meeting tomorrow.

3 Mark looks forward to going home next week.

4 Watching the show, they took a lot of pictures.

5 Walking along the beach, the children picked up beautiful shells.

6 Arriving home, Josh found the door open.

**A** 우리말과 일치하도록 ( ) 안에 주어진 말을 알맞게 배열하시오.

1 종이에 여러 개의 점을 표시하는 것으로 시작하라.

(a number of, marking, start by, points)

▶ _____ on paper.

2 이 중심점을 통과하는 수직선을 그려라.

(that, upright, line, an, passes)

▶ Draw _____ through this midpoint.

3 그 다이어그램은 그가 물이 오염된 지역을 찾는 것을 도왔다.

(him, locate, helped, the areas)

▶ The diagram _____ with polluted water.

4 그 조약은 일본에 남부의 섬 네 개에 대한 통제권을 주었다.

(gave, the treaty, control, Japan)

▶ _____ of the four southern islands.

5 두 나라 사이의 심화되는 경쟁은 러일전쟁으로 이어졌다.

(between, competition, the two countries, growing)

▶ _____ led to the Russo-Japanese War.

**B** 우리말과 일치하도록 ( ) 안의 말을 이용하여 문장을 완성하시오.

1 소호에서 그 펌프를 제거한 후, 사망률은 급락했다. (after, remove)

▶ _____ _____ _____ _____ in Soho, death rates quickly dropped.

2 지역을 신중하게 나누는 행위는 꽤 강력할 수 있다. (divide, a region)

▶ The practice of carefully _____ _____ _____ _____ _____ quite powerful.

3 제2차 세계대전에서 일본을 이겼을 때, 러시아는 다시 한번 열도 전체의 소유권을 되찾았다. (defeat)

▶ _____ _____ in World War II, Russia once again recovered the ownership of the entire island chain.

4 그것과 쿠릴 열도 모두는 제2차 세계 대전이 끝날 때까지 일본의 통치하에 있었다. (both, remain)

▶ _____ _____ _____ the Kuril Islands _____ under Japanese rule until the end of World War II.

## VOCABULARY TEST 1

반 / 이름:

**[01-30] 다음 단어의 뜻을 쓰시오.**

01 ahead _____

02 besides _____

03 maid _____

04 carefully _____

05 choice _____

06 complex _____

07 develop _____

08 drawing _____

09 emerge _____

10 entertainer _____

11 hidden _____

12 discovery _____

13 interestingly _____

14 layer _____

15 lower _____

16 master _____

17 outline _____

18 object _____

19 practice _____

20 prove _____

21 reflection _____

22 researcher _____

23 reuse _____

24 reveal _____

25 royal _____

26 rural _____

27 scan _____

28 straight _____

29 technique _____

30 underneath _____

**[31-40] 다음 뜻을 지닌 단어를 쓰시오.**

31 깊은 _____

32 초상화 _____

33 응시하다 _____

34 둘러싸다 _____

35 즐겁게 하다 _____

36 세부 사항 _____

37 미술품 _____

38 ~을 마주보다; 직면하다 _____

39 불분명한 _____

40 대단히 사랑하는 _____

**[41-44] 다음 숙어의 뜻을 쓰시오.**

41 focus on _____

42 at that time _____

43 contribute to _____

44 begin with _____

**A** 단어의 첫 철자를 참조하여 다음 정의에 해당하는 단어를 쓰시오.

1 the outer shape of something       o_____

2 a painting or photograph of a person       p_____

3 to be all around something       s_____

4 to cause something to be seen       r_____

**B** 다음 밑줄 친 단어와 의미가 유사한 단어를 고르시오.

1 A strange man <u>emerged</u> from nowhere.

   ⓐ escaped      ⓑ removed      ⓒ appeared      ⓓ destroyed      ⓔ disappeared

2 I think she knows how to <u>amuse</u> little kids.

   ⓐ entertain      ⓑ teach      ⓒ blame      ⓓ frighten      ⓔ admire

3 Mark doesn't like it when people <u>stare</u> at him.

   ⓐ help      ⓑ call      ⓒ wake      ⓓ yell      ⓔ gaze

**C** 우리말과 같은 뜻이 되도록 빈칸에 들어갈 말을 보기에서 찾아 알맞은 형태로 쓰시오.

| 보기 | focus on | begin with | at that time | contribute to |
|---|---|---|---|---|

1 대런은 그 문제를 해결하는 데 기여한 유일한 남자였다.

   ▶ Darren was the only man who _____ solving the problem.

2 나는 바깥의 소음 때문에 내 일에 집중할 수가 없었다.

   ▶ I could not _____ my work because of the noise outside.

3 그 당시에 나는 작은 마을에 살았다.

   ▶ I lived in a small town _____.

4 작고 쉬운 것으로 시작하자.

   ▶ Let's _____ something small and easy.

**A** 다음 문장을 분사구문으로 바꾸어 쓰시오.

1 As she called my name, she entered my room.

▶ _____ _____ _____, she entered my room.

2 As I climbed up the mountain, I saw a bear catching fish in the distance.

▶ _____ _____ _____ _____, I saw a bear catching fish in the distance.

3 Because she feels tired, she lays down to get some rest.

▶ _____ _____, she lays down to get some rest.

**B** 다음 두 문장을 소유격 관계대명사 whose를 이용하여 한 문장으로 쓰시오.

1 I have a friend. Her brother used to like my sister.

▶ _____

2 She used to drive a red car. Its window was broken.

▶ _____

3 I know a man. His mother has worked in this hotel.

▶ _____

4 Look at the child. His dog is jumping up and down.

▶ _____

**C** 밑줄 친 부분에 유의하여 다음 문장을 우리말로 해석하시오.

1 <u>Being poor</u>, he couldn't afford new pants.

▶ _____

2 <u>Lying on the beach</u>, I watched the sunset.

▶ _____

3 We talked about a boy <u>whose name</u> is the same as mine.

▶ _____

**A** 우리말과 일치하도록 (   ) 안에 주어진 말을 알맞게 배열하시오.

1 그의 가장 유명한 초상화 중 하나는 마르가리타 공주의 것이었다.

(his, one, portraits, famous, of, most)

▶ _____ was of Princess Margarita.

2 그 그림은 보이는 것보다 더 복잡하다.

(more, than, seems, it, is, complex)

▶ The painting _____.

3 그는 캔버스에 그림을 그리면서, 공주 뒤에 서 있다.

(canvas, a, painting, on)

▶ He is standing behind the princess, _____.

4 그것은 대가조차도 연습이 필요하다는 것을 입증한다!

(that, need, proves, even masters, practice)

▶ It _____!


**B** 우리말과 일치하도록 (   ) 안의 말을 이용하여 문장을 완성하시오.

1 네덜란드에 거주하는 동안, 그는 많은 모델들을 그렸다. (live, in)

▶ _____ _____ the Netherlands, he painted many models.

2 그것이 무엇인지 알기 위해, 그들은 새로운 기술을 사용했다. (what)

▶ To find out _____ _____ _____, they used a new technique.

3 그것은 숨겨진 그림의 윤곽뿐만 아니라 색도 보여줄 수 있다. (well)

▶ It can show the color _____ _____ _____ the outline of hidden paintings.

4 이들은 왕과 왕비를 즐겁게 하는 것이 직업인 왕실의 광대들이었다. (whose, job)

▶ These were royal entertainers _____ _____ _____ _____ amuse the king and queen.

5 그림의 각기 다른 대상에 집중하는 것은 그 그림을 더욱 흥미롭게 만든다. (the painting, interesting)

▶ Focusing on the different objects of the painting makes _____ _____ _____ _____.

## VOCABULARY TEST 1

반 / 이름:

**[01-30] 다음 단어의 뜻을 쓰시오.**

01 allow _____

02 contact _____

03 futuristic _____

04 amazing _____

05 aside _____

06 natural _____

07 quite _____

08 mimic _____

09 oxygen _____

10 coral reef _____

11 sadly _____

12 smooth _____

13 ecosystem _____

14 experiment _____

15 fail _____

16 teardrop _____

17 throw _____

18 mostly _____

19 habitat _____

20 leisure _____

21 management _____

22 dirt _____

23 form _____

24 high _____

25 rainforest _____

26 recreate _____

27 shortage _____

28 spaceship _____

29 worthwhile _____

30 relationship _____

**[31-40] 다음 뜻을 지닌 단어를 쓰시오.**

31 전설 _____

32 교육의, 교육적인 _____

33 임무 _____

34 엉망인 상태 _____

35 현상 _____

36 환경 _____

37 인공[인조]의 _____

38 창조하다 _____

39 언덕 _____

40 이론, 학설 _____

**[41-44] 다음 숙어의 뜻을 쓰시오.**

41 next to _____

42 each other _____

43 be located on _____

44 die off _____

**A** 다음 단어의 영영풀이를 바르게 연결하시오.

1 habitat • • ⓐ something interesting that is known to exist or happen

2 worthwhile • • ⓑ to let someone have or do something

3 allow • • ⓒ to make something that didn't exist before

4 phenomenon • • ⓓ useful, important, and worth the time or effort

5 create • • ⓔ the type of place that a particular animal or plant usually lives in

**B** 다음 빈칸에 들어갈 말을 보기에서 찾아 쓰시오.

| 보기 | educational | throw | mess | artificial |

1 Please _____ the ball to me!

2 These _____ flowers look like they are real.

3 Look at this _____! You need to clean up your room.

4 The museum has a lot of historical materials that are _____ for children.

**C** 우리말과 같은 뜻이 되도록 빈칸에 들어갈 말을 보기에서 찾아 알맞은 형태로 쓰시오.

| 보기 | each other | die off | be located on | next to |

1 그 병원은 건물의 2층에 위치한다.

▶ The hospital _____ the second floor of the building.

2 왜 공룡이 차례로 멸종했는지에 대한 이론들이 몇 가지 있다.

▶ There are some theories about why dinosaurs _____.

3 고속도로에서 두 자동차가 서로 충돌했다.

▶ Two cars crashed into _____ on the highway.

4 가게 매니저 옆의 남자는 누구인가?

▶ Who is the man _____ the store manager?

**A** 다음 ( ) 안에서 알맞은 것을 고르시오.

1 (If, Unless) you help me, I will be very disappointed with you.

2 (If, Unless) it's clear tomorrow, we will go hiking.

3 (If, Unless) you see Eric, tell him to call me.

4 (If, Unless) you try your best, you'll never be a great dancer.

5 (If, Unless) you get up early tomorrow, you will miss the first train.

**B** 밑줄 친 부분의 의미로 알맞은 것을 보기에서 골라 쓰고 문장을 해석하시오.

| 보기 | 예정 | 의무 | 의도 | 운명 | 가능 |
| --- | --- | --- | --- | --- | --- |

1 I am to meet my teacher after school. _____

▶ _____

2 She was to marry him in the end. _____

▶ _____

3 You are to study hard to improve your English grade. _____

▶ _____

4 If you are to be a friend to Jack, be friendly to him. _____

▶ _____

5 No one was to be seen in the house. _____

▶ _____

**C** 밑줄 친 부분을 어법에 맞게 고쳐 쓰시오.

1 He'll show up soon if there is a traffic jam.

2 Unless you study harder, you'll pass the test.

3 Unless you don't buy a ticket, you cannot get in.

4 If you get enough sleep, you will be tired.

**A** 우리말과 일치하도록 ( ) 안에 주어진 말을 알맞게 배열하시오.

1 다투는 두 거인들이 서로에게 바위와 흙을 던지며 며칠을 보냈다.

(throwing, days, spent, rocks and dirt)

▶ Two fighting giants _____ at each other.

2 아무도 초콜릿 언덕이 어떻게 만들어졌는지 확실히 알지 못한다.

(were, how, the chocolate hills, made)

▶ Nobody knows for certain _____.

3 그것은 이 자연 현상을 훨씬 더 놀랍게 만든다. (makes, more, even, amazing)

▶ That _____ this natural phenomenon _____.

4 외부의 접촉은 허용되지 않았다. (outside, allowed, was, no, contact)

▶ _____.

5 그것은 사람들이 우리의 행성에 관해 더 많은 것을 이해하도록 돕는 교육 장소이다.

(people, more, understand, about, helps, our planet)

▶ It is an educational place that _____.

**B** 우리말과 일치하도록 ( ) 안의 말을 이용하여 문장을 완성하시오.

1 '초콜릿 언덕'은 필리핀의 보홀섬에 있다. (locate)

▶ The "Chocolate Hills" _____ _____ _____ Bohol Island in the Philippines.

2 그것들은 지구의 생태계를 모방하기로 되어 있었다. (mean, mimic)

▶ They _____ _____ _____ _____ the Earth's ecosystem.

3 그들은 자신들의 식량을 재배해야 했다. (be, grow)

▶ They _____ _____ _____ their own food.

4 부실한 관리가 그들의 실험을 더 악화시켰다. (make, experiment, worse)

▶ Poor management _____ _____ _____ _____.

5 적어도 1,300개가 모두 서로의 곁에 서 있는 채로 있다. (stand, next, each)

▶ There are at least 1,300, all _____ _____ _____ _____.

## VOCABULARY TEST 1

반 / 이름:

**[01-30] 다음 단어의 뜻을 쓰시오.**

01 alongside _____

02 cliff _____

03 appreciate _____

04 athlete _____

05 attempt _____

06 attraction _____

07 blind _____

08 breathtaking _____

09 canyon _____

10 challenge _____

11 experience _____

12 injury _____

13 landscape _____

14 length _____

15 nearly _____

16 offer _____

17 opponent _____

18 desert _____

19 prevent _____

20 referee _____

21 region _____

22 regular _____

23 field _____

24 spectacular _____

25 starry _____

26 tackle _____

27 carry _____

28 valley _____

29 eyeshade _____

30 magical _____

**[31-40] 다음 뜻을 지닌 단어를 쓰시오.**

31 빛나다 _____

32 독특한 _____

33 주최하다 _____

34 극도의[극심한] _____

35 보장하다; 확실하게 하다 _____

36 견뎌내다 _____

37 경쟁하다; ~와 겨루다 _____

38 장치 _____

39 벌칙을 주다 _____

40 경고하다 _____

**[41-44] 다음 숙어의 뜻을 쓰시오.**

41 plan on _____

42 consist of _____

43 be equipped with _____

44 take part in _____

**A** 다음 단어의 영영풀이를 바르게 연결하시오.

1 withstand •          • ⓐ damage to the body

2 extreme •          • ⓑ very great in degree

3 injury •          • ⓒ someone who you compete with in a game

4 opponent •          • ⓓ to deal with difficult situations

**B** 다음 빈칸에 들어갈 말을 보기에서 찾아 쓰시오.

| 보기 | attempt | compete | challenge | breathtaking |
|---|---|---|---|---|

1 The training was a great _____. I learned a lot from it.

2 Some people like to _____ with others in every sport.

3 I don't usually _____ to talk to strangers.

4 The tourists were amazed by the _____ ocean view.

**C** 우리말과 같은 뜻이 되도록 빈칸에 들어갈 말을 보기에서 찾아 알맞은 형태로 쓰시오.

| 보기 | plan on | take part in | consist of | be equipped with |
|---|---|---|---|---|

1 내 가족은 부모님, 여동생 두 명과 나로 구성되어 있다.

▶ My family _____ my parents, my two sisters, and me.

2 우리는 이 게임에 참여하기 위해 이곳에 왔다.

▶ We have come here to _____ this game.

3 이 새 자전거는 USB 포트와 강력한 모터가 갖춰져 있다.

▶ This new bike _____ a USB port and a powerful motor.

4 나는 올해 새로운 차를 살 계획이다.

▶ I _____ buying a new car this year.

**A** ( ) 안에서 알맞은 것을 고르시오.

1 Both Jenny (and, or) I live in the same town.

2 Not only Nancy (but, but also) Ronald enjoys playing tennis.

3 I think either a yellow (and, or) pink shirt will suit you well.

4 I neither want to go to the beach (or, nor) the mountains this weekend.

**B** 다음 문장을 가정법으로 바꿀 때, 빈칸에 알맞은 말을 쓰시오.

1 As he is busy, he can't play with us.
▶ If he ＿＿＿＿＿＿＿＿ busy, he ＿＿＿＿＿＿＿＿＿＿＿＿ with us.

2 As she is sick, she can't go hiking.
▶ If she ＿＿＿＿＿＿＿＿ sick, she ＿＿＿＿＿＿＿＿＿＿＿＿ hiking.

3 As I lost her phone number, I couldn't call her.
▶ If I ＿＿＿＿＿＿＿＿ her phone number, I ＿＿＿＿＿＿＿＿＿＿＿＿ her.

4 As you told a lie, your dad was angry.
▶ If you ＿＿＿＿＿＿＿＿ a lie, your dad ＿＿＿＿＿＿＿＿＿＿＿＿ angry.

5 As you didn't get up early, you missed the train.
▶ If you ＿＿＿＿＿＿＿＿ early, you ＿＿＿＿＿＿＿＿＿＿＿＿ the train.

**C** 밑줄 친 부분을 어법에 맞게 고쳐 쓰시오.

1 I like both chocolate <u>or</u> strawberry ice cream.

2 I will go to <u>neither</u> China or Japan this summer.

3 This music <u>not</u> calms you down but also helps you sleep better.

4 If I were slim, these skinny jeans <u>fit</u> me.

5 If he <u>has known</u> the truth, he would have forgiven you.

**A** 우리말과 일치하도록 ( ) 안에 주어진 말을 알맞게 배열하시오.

1 이 지역은 세계에서 가장 장관을 이루는 사막 풍경 중 한 곳이다.

(the most, desert landscapes, one, of, spectacular)

▶ This area has _____ in the world.

2 그들은 사막의 기온 변화를 견뎌야 한다.

(withstand, changes, the temperature, have, to)

▶ They _____ of the desert.

3 그 공에는 소리를 내는 장치가 장착되어 있다. (equipped, the ball, with, is)

▶ _____ a noise-making device.

4 그곳은 세계에서 가장 독특한 이벤트 중의 하나를 주최하도록 선정되었다.

(was, to, chosen, it, host)

▶ _____ one of the world's most unique events.

5 내 남동생이 축구를 하는 것은 쉽지 않다. (to, my brother, play, for)

▶ It's not easy _____ soccer.

**B** 우리말과 일치하도록 ( ) 안의 말을 이용하여 문장을 완성하시오.

1 이 사막은 숨이 멎는 듯한 계곡과 협곡으로 가득하다. (filled)

▶ This desert _____ _____ _____ breathtaking valleys and canyons.

2 그 경기장은 보통의 경기장보다 작다. (small)

▶ The playing field _____ _____ _____ a regular field.

3 심판은 그들의 상대편을 미는 선수들에게 벌칙을 준다. (push, opponents)

▶ Referees penalize players _____ _____ _____ _____.

4 만약 우리가 그것에 대해 더 일찍 알았더라면, 그는 리그에 들어갈 수 있었을 것이다. (know, join)

▶ If we _____ _____ about it earlier, he _____ _____ _____ a league.

5 나는 그에게 그것을 가르칠 계획이다. (plan on, teach)

▶ I _____ _____ _____ it to him.

# MEMO

# MEMO

# MEMO

# READING
# Inside

**workbook**

A 4-level curriculum
integration reading course

· **A thematic reading program that integrates with school curriculum**
중등 교육과정이 지향하는 문이과 통합 및 타교과 연계 반영한 독해서

· **Informative content with well-designed comprehension questions**
정보성 있는 지문과 질 높은 다양한 유형의 문항 그리고 서술형 평가도 대비

· **Grammar points directly related to the *Grammar Inside* series**
베스트셀러 Grammar Inside와 직접적으로 연계된 문법 항목 및 문항 제공

· **Exercises with useful, essential, and academic vocabulary**
중등 필수 어휘 학습 코너 제공

· **A workbook for more vocabulary, grammar, and reading exercises**
풍부한 양의 어휘, 문법, 그리고 쓰기 추가 문제 등을 수록한 워크북

| Level | Grade | Words Limit |
|---|---|---|
| Reading Inside Starter | Low-Intermediate | 140-160 |
| Reading Inside Level 1 | Intermediate | 160-180 |
| **Reading Inside Level 2** | **Intermediate** | **180-200** |
| Reading Inside Level 3 | Low-Advanced | 200-220 |